Teaching Social Justice

*Intercultural and Development Education Perspectives
on Education's Context, Content and Methods*

Edited by
Roland Tormey

Centre for Educational Disadvantage Research
Mary Immaculate College, Limerick
and
Ireland Aid

…written in rage and love, without which there is no hope.

Paulo Freire *Pedagogy of Hope*

For Christine

First published in 2003

by

Centre for Educational Disadvantage Research

Mary Immaculate College

South Circular Road

Limerick

and

Ireland Aid

Bishop's Square

Redmond's Hill

Dublin 2

ISBN: 1 900146 17 7

Design, layout and printing by SNAP Printing Limerick

ACKNOWLEDGEMENTS

There are quite a few people without whom this book would not exist. Anne Dolan and Ger Horgan both worked to organise the conference, without which there would be no book. Kitty Martin toiled above and beyond the call of duty to make both the conference and this book happen. Her work is what fuels the projects undertaken by the Centre for Educational Disadvantage Research. Without the financial support provided by the National Committee for Development Education, now Ireland Aid Development Education Unit, neither the conference nor the book would have become a reality. Huge support was also given by the group of development educators working at Mary Immaculate College, especially Peadar Cremin, Kathleen Horgan, and Paddy Fullam. Without them, this work would not have been started. To you all I say, 'long may you run!'

Tony Meade, whose eye for detail, punctuation and overly academic writing kept the show on the road, and whose tolerance for obscene deadlines was limitless, carried out proof reading. Christine Farget also proof read some chapters. The design, layout and printing of the book was done by Lu and rest of the crew at SNAP Printing in Limerick. There is no finer bunch of Human Rights printers in the west. Front cover photos by Carol Lee and Joan Duggan, used with permission from Ireland Aid and Joan Duggan.

Special thinks is owed to Christine Farget. For your tolerance, patience and support, thank you.

TABLE OF CONTENTS

INTRODUCTION

Roland Tormey

Nearly a billion people will enter the 21st century unable to read a book or sign their names and two thirds of them are women. And they will live, as now, in more desperate poverty and poorer health than those who can. They are the world's functional illiterates—and their numbers are growing.

The total includes more than 130 million school age children, 73 million of them girls, who are growing up in the developing world without access to basic education. Millions of others languish in substandard schools where little learning takes place... The Convention on the Rights of the Child is clear: Education is the foundation of a free and fulfilled life. It is the right of all children and the obligation of all governments. (UNICEF 1999)

One in 10 [Irish] children still leave primary school with significant literacy problems, a situation which has not improved in almost 20 years, according to a major Government survey to be released today. (*The Irish Times*, 21st January 2000)

Education is intimately bound up with social justice issues at local, national and global levels. When education enables people in Ireland to learn about the justice and development struggles of people in Third World countries, it facilitates them in supporting those struggles. When it opens eyes to the way the world is, and the way it could be, it promotes activism for justice. At the same time, when the right to education is denied or limited, education becomes a site of injustices and of justice struggles. When it ignores justice and injustice issues locally and globally, when it says, "that is not my subject", instead of asking whose subject it is, when it seeks to make people conform rather than facilitating them in learning how to challenge, then education plays a role in teaching people not to think about it, not to worry about it, and, in doing so, helps prevent justice struggles from taking place.

These ideas provide a lens with which to view educational practice in Ireland today: education is either part of the solution or part of the problem. We may even be both, but we can never be neither. As the Brazilian educator Paulo Freire once put it: "When we try to be neutral, like Pilate, we support the dominant ideology. Not being neutral, education must be either liberating or domesticating" (quoted in Sterling *et al.* 1995, p. 63).

This book grew out of a conference held in Mary Immaculate College, University of Limerick, in March 2002, which was hosted by the Centre for

Educational Disadvantage Research and supported by the Department of Foreign Affairs through the Development Education Unit, Ireland Aid (at the time the Development Education Unit was known as the National Committee for Development Education, [NCDE]). The conference aimed to bring a Development Education perspective or lens to bear on the Irish Education system, particularly the Irish higher education system.

Although development education has many definitions which emphasise different components of the whole, the broad definition used by Ireland Aid sees it as:

> ...an educational process aimed at increasing awareness and understanding of the rapidly changing, interdependent and unequal world in which we live.... It seeks to engage people in analysis, reflection and action for local and global citizenship and participation.... It is about supporting people in understanding and acting to transform the social, cultural, political and economic structures which affect their lives at personal, community, national and international levels (National Committee for Development Education 1996, p. 11)

As such, it contains a number of elements. It is education *as* personal development, facilitating the development of critical thinking skills, analytical skills, empathetic capacity and the ability to be an effective person who can take action to achieve desired development outcomes. It is education *for* local, national and global development, encouraging and supporting learners in developing a sense that they can play a role in working for (or against) social justice and development issues. It is education *about* development, focused on social justice, human rights, poverty and inequality and other development issues locally, nationally, and internationally.

Central to development education is the process through which it works. Development education sees the learner as an active participant in the learning process and seeks to provide opportunities for people to actively explore ideas and to develop thinking and action skills in a democratic context. Development educators avoid 'chalk-and-talk' or 'teacher-directed' learning:

> In Freirean critical classrooms, teachers reject the methods which make students passive and anti-intellectual. They do not lecture students into sleepy silence. They do not prepare students for a life of political alienation in society. Rather Freirean educators pose critical problems to students, treat them as complicated, substantial beings, and encourage curiosity and activism about knowledge and the world (Shor 1993, p. 25 – 26).

Development education is closely related to other brands of 'adjectival' education such as Peace Education, Human Rights Education, Multicultural Education and Intercultural Education. Indeed, these various approaches often share common methodological assumptions and cover much the same content, albeit with a different emphasis. Given the recent changes in the ethnic make up of Irish society (dealt with in chapter two), it is not surprising that many of the authors in this book approach the issue of social justice as much from an intercultural perspective as from a development education perspective. This is a reflection of the way in which development education changes as the world in which it operates changes.

In Ireland, development education is often associated with the work of overseas development agencies and is sometimes regarded primarily as being education about the Third World. Many well-known resources deal largely with global or Third World inequality rather than inequality at home. Indeed, the Development Education Unit of Ireland Aid operates under the Department of Foreign Affairs, rather than under the Department of Education and Science. This view of development education may also be a comfortable one for many educators: while we are happy to deal with what are perceived to be 'simple' injustices and inequalities in South Africa, Rwanda or Brazil, inequality, human rights or development issues at home may seem more complex, controversial or political. As a consequence, it is possible that many would happily deal with inequality issues in Brazil but never discuss poverty, patriarchy or racism in our own backyard, or never draw a connection between inequality in Nigeria and in Ireland. In the case of educational inequality, applying the concepts of development education at home may force teachers and educators into the uncomfortable job of looking at the ways in which their own practices and the practices of the institutions in which they work may play a role in actually producing inequality. As such, it may be a lot easier to teach about Third World development than it is to engage in a development education process.

It was no accident that this development education conference was hosted by the Centre for Educational Disadvantage Research. We wished to explore these connections, between the global and the local, between the things we teach and the way we teach them, and between development education processes and educational inequality. In this respect, the work of Freire, who was in many respects the father of development education, is instructive. For Freire, the people to work with in the first instance were the oppressed. His emphasis was not so much on those who would do well in school, attain a good grade and go on to be respected members of their society, but on those who were illiterate, disadvantaged and oppressed. His task was not simply to create a better (development) education for those who already take a full part in education, but to provide, first and foremost, a culturally responsive education for those who were not regarded as educational successes. He asked: "Who are better prepared than the oppressed to understand the terrible significance of an oppressive society?...Who can better understand the necessity of liberation?" (1970, p. 27).

Freire recognised that alongside the potential for education to be a tool for development and social change lay the reality of much existing education – an education which saw the poor underachieving and then blamed for it ("Of course he didn't do well. Education just isn't valued in the home!"). Freire regarded with some dismay an education system which failed to teach all learners in a manner that respected and reflected the diversity of their backgrounds, capacities and interests. The development education lens through which we view the world must, therefore, balance the rose-tinted optimism of education's potential with this darker vision of its current role in reproducing existing inequalities.

This is not to suggest that development education has nothing to offer to comparatively advantaged pupils: clearly, the process and content of development education is without a doubt relevant for students who get a Leaving Certificate or who take part in higher education. It would, however, be bitterly ironic if development education itself gave rise to the same patterns of inequality in educational attainment and participation as traditional teaching does. If we deal with inequality in the Third World without, at the same time, dealing with inequality in the local context, or without seeing the inequality in opportunity which is built into the structure of our education system, then clearly we are not living up to our aims.

CONTENT AND ORGANISATION OF THIS BOOK

The chapters in this book deal in various ways with these issues. The book is divided into five sections. Section one sets the scene. It identifies some of the social justice issues that constitute the global and local social contexts within which education takes place. Section two explores the ways in which a social justice lens can shed new and interesting light on tired and traditional subjects. The chapters in section two deal with a range of subject areas such as English, Foreign Languages, Maths, Sciences, Visual Arts and Philosophy. Section three focuses on attempts to integrate a social justice perspective in initial teacher education in Ireland, while section four looks at equality issues within the educational context and has a particular focus on higher education experience in Ireland. Section five explores some of the new thinking on development education currently happening in the Irish context.

Ken Wiwa's chapter recounts the story of the Ogoni and their peaceful struggle with the then Nigerian Government and the oil multinational, Shell, a struggle which ultimately led to the arrest, detention and execution of his father, the Nobel Prize nominee, Ken Saro-Wiwa. It also tells of his own journey to activism. It is an intimate and personal story, which identifies the connections between 'here' and 'there' and the need to act on and in our world to make it better: because "...without Justice, without due process, we cannot reclaim a proportionate and fair sense of history and tomorrow becomes pregnant with the orphans of yesterday", he writes. Chapter two accompanies this international account of social justice issues with a more local account, focusing on inequality, poverty and discrimination within the Irish context. Together, these two chapters set out the international and local context of development education, and tell us something about the shape of the world that we must act within and upon.

Leavy's chapter draws together the local and global elements of the development education perspective and applies this lens to mathematics education. She shows that maths is not a fixed subject or set of techniques that exists outside culture and morality, and uses this insight to highlight both global and local implications. On the global level, maths can show the diversity of ways of making sense of the world of numbers, can highlight that such diversity is normal, and, can highlight the contribution of different cultures to what we know as maths. At a local level, the embedding of maths in culture and practice can help us to understand a divergence between the mathematical culture of the school and that of the pupil, which may have an impact on pupil learning and which may explain some of the educational inequalities which are an outcome of our system of schooling. The similarities with Ó Conaill's chapter, which explores the political, economic and moral context within which science education takes place, are striking. Ó Conaill explores the relationship between science and colonial expansion, noting that the scientific and technological advancements that accompanied the colonial expansion led to the enrichment of the colonisers but "delivered increases in mortality rates and human bondage" (Harding 1998, p. 46) for the colonised. He suggests that science education cannot be true to its aims of recognising the contribution of the scientist to society if it does not identify clearly the two-faced nature of science: part of both human development and underdevelopment at one and the same time.

Donnelly moves us from the alleged objectivity of mathematics and science to the realm of the artistic and the literary. She explores the common assumption that there is a body of art that constitutes great art, against which other arts, artefacts and cultures can be measured – and found wanting. Inevitably, this canon is composed of the products of Dead White Males, but Donnelly also shows that the decision as to what went into the canon and what was excluded was tied to a sense that 'taste' was a matter for the wealthy and the colonial masters. Turning the Dead White Males upon themselves, she uses the aesthetic philosophy of Immanuel Kant to identify a more democratic approach to viewing art which seeks to release us from the hold of the ghosts of British eighteenth-century thought which still stalk the gallery, Channel Four and the art class. Such an approach opens a space for non-Western art and culture to be appreciated in its own right rather than being subjected to the jaundiced gaze of what is 'normal' or 'great' in the Western tradition.

O'Brien's starting point is also 'the canon', this time the Great Literary

Tradition. Like Donnelly, he seeks to turn the tradition upon itself, and, through wondering why a pulp fiction novel does not currently enjoy the status of James Joyce (who was, himself, once derided as an author of dirty books), he argues that by exploring the basis on which the canon is constructed, the edges become blurred and the canon becomes multiplied and fractured into a diversity of canons sitting alongside and overlapping each other. As such, a framework for a more inclusive understanding of literary traditions is unearthed.

Egger's chapter is also concerned with the relationship between literature and social justice. She focuses on the foreign language classroom as a place where people can learn about what Bhikhu Parekh (1986, p. 27) has referred to as the "inherent plurality of the world – the plurality of systems, beliefs, ways of life, cultures, modes of analysing familiar experiences, ways of looking at historical events and so on". As such, while German as a foreign language may or may not deal with Third World issues *per se*, it can always play a role in exploring how our images of other peoples are constructed and can, through this, create openness to difference. Egger provides a methodological background to such work and shows how it can be done in the language classroom in practice, using literature and poetry as a reference point. While Egger draws her examples from the teaching of German, it is clear that the learning from this could easily be applied to other languages such as French, Spanish or even Irish.

Irwin focuses on how we have been encouraged to misunderstand the non-Western world through the partial telling of our own history. Taking his lead from the way in which Islam is often portrayed in the West as anti-rational, he identifies that what we know as the Western philosophical tradition is only available to us today because it was protected and nurtured in Islamic countries. Indeed, he shows how the medieval Islamic philosopher Averroes played a key role in promoting the rationalist tradition that we think of as our own. The story of Averroes is one of the many gaps in our telling of our own history, he suggests, which allows us to misunderstand others through our misunderstanding of ourselves.

Section three focuses on teaching the teachers: development education in initial teacher education. Chapters nine, ten and eleven, by Dolan and Fullam, Gill, and Malone and Jeffers provide three accounts of practice in initial teacher education in Ireland. Dolan and Fullam's account of development education in Mary Immaculate College identifies the importance of a co-ordinated and integrated approach, while identifying some of the limitations built into the current system of initial teacher education. Gill describes a programme which has been developed by the NCDE with a number of Dublin-based initial teacher education colleges, while Malone and Jeffers provide a fascinating account of how development education is perceived and understood by post-primary teachers in training. Ehrenreich focuses on the methodology which is used to generate intercultural understanding among teachers in training, with a particular focus on the language learning context.

Chapters thirteen and fourteen together look at some of the innovations which have taken place in attempting to increase the social justice impact of higher education. Collins and McGuire argue that the current demographic profile of the country means that we have a window of opportunity which can be used to transform the culture of third-level from being a bastion of middle class education to being an open and supportive environment for all. It is unclear as to whether or not that opportunity will be taken before the window is closed once more. Brosnan, O'Keefe and Binchy have attempted to provide an opportunity for third-level teachers to procure and reflect on the feedback from students as to their needs and wants. They show similarities and discrepancies between the lecturer and student accounts of the education process and highlight how models for ensuring open and genuine feedback can play a role in ensuring that teachers are responsive to their students' needs.

Section five looks at some of the recent developments in development education thinking. Duke looks at the effects of development education in practice and reveals some disturbing findings. She argues that the underlying ideology of much development education work is that of charity rather than that of respect for human rights. As a consequence, young people's sense of an Us/Them divide between themselves and the people of the Third World is increased, not lessened. She notes that "many of the children and teachers I interviewed in the course of my research were unable to conceive of the people and countries of the South in any but eurocentric terms in which poverty dominated their lives and only Western intervention could help them". Her chapter should be read as a wake-up call to development education practitioners, at least some of whom may well be engaging in well-meaning but potentially dangerous practices.

Duke argues that a more critical 'post-development' perspective offers opportunities to develop an alternative to such counterproductive practices. This 'post-development' perspective, in different ways, forms the basis for the last two chapters. In my chapter, I explore the way in which the term 'critical thinking' has been understood in development education, arguing that if development education is to be truly critical we must engage in an "unflinching examination of our most cherished and comforting assumptions" (Dreyfus and Rabinow, 1986, p. 110), which means critiquing the practices and ideas of those bodies we traditionally think of as positive, such as development agencies and anti-poverty campaigning groups, as well as those who are traditionally painted as the bad guys (the World Bank, the WTO and so on). In the spirit of Freirean pedagogy, the last chapter offers, not answers, but critical questions. Dillon explores the terrain of post-development theory and suggests a range of questions which this approach raises for both development co-operation and development education.

CONCLUSION

The conference which gave rise to this volume was an exciting time for those of us involved in organising it. People and perspectives that had never before engaged in development education were there alongside some more familiar faces. As well as looking at the integration of development education perspectives into 'traditional' subjects like Geography and Social Studies, people discussed the interesting ways in which development education could be, and had to be, integrated into Science, Mathematics, Literature, Foreign Language and the Visual and Dramatic Arts. At the same time, the differences between the various perspectives present in the conference (and in this volume) gave rise to debate and discussion which, in itself, opened up new spaces of possibility.

Together, these chapters provide a rich and interwoven tapestry of ideas concerning development education and the related area of intercultural education. They provide opportunities to explore pathways that have not previously been adequately explored, such as maths and science education. Many of them link the content and methodology of development education to the social justice context within which that education takes place and as such, challenge development educators to be more consistent with their own origins and aims. Others challenge us to think through what exactly we understand by development education.

The moment we cease to question what we do is the moment we begin to lose our relevance to development, to education and to the world in which we live. This book explores some of the potential of development education to take sides and make a difference. There are still more riches to be tapped and more work to be done. *A luta continua!*

REFERENCES

Dreyfus, H.L. and Rabinow, P. (1986) 'What is Maturity? Habermas and Foucault on 'What is Enlightenment?" in Hoy, D.C. (ed.) *Foucault: A Critical Reader.* Oxford: Basil Blackwell

Freire, P. (1970) *Pedagogy of the Oppressed.* Harmondsworth: Penguin.

Harding, S. (1998) *Is Science Multicultural?* Bloomington and Indianapolis: Indiana University Press

The Irish Times 21st January 2000

National Committee for Development Education (1996) *1994-1996 Annual Report.* Dublin: NCDE

Parekh, B. (1986) 'The Concept of Multi-Cultural Education' in Mogdil, S., Verma, G., Mallick, K., and Mogdil, C. (eds.) *Multicultural Education, The Interminable Debate.* Lewes and Philadelphia: Falmer Press

UNICEF (1999) *The State of the World's Children*. Geneva: UNICEF

Shor, I. (1993) 'Education is Politics: Paulo Freire's Critical Pedagogy' in McLaren, P. and Leonard, P. (eds.) *Paulo Freire, A Critical Encounter*. London: Routledge.

Sterling, S., Bobbett, P. and Norris, A. (1995) *Unit 1: Introduction to Environmental and Development Education Study Guide*. London: Distance Learning Environmental and Development Education, South Bank University.

CHAPTER 1

OGONI: PAST IMPERFECT, FUTURE TENSE

Ken Wiwa

(The following is the text of the address given by Ken Wiwa at the NCDE Third-level Conference, 2002)

Although I have given many presentations before, I must admit that I have always been a reluctant speaker: I prefer writing to talking. Nevertheless, I was happy to accept this invitation because I have always felt an empathy for this country -for your politics, your history and, especially, your literature. I think many Nigerian artists and intellectuals have been greatly influenced by Irish culture, the history, the literature and the politics. I know that my father, for one, was a great follower of the writers of the Irish revival and, if Nigeria and Ireland enjoy a special relationship, that should not be surprising because Ireland, I believe, was the first country to be colonised by the British. Your country's experience and subsequent struggles have been an example and inspiration for many countries and individuals wrestling with the dilemmas of moving into a postcolonial future.

If I am a reluctant speaker, it is largely because of an anxiety that much of what I know about my people's struggle is inherited. My father did all the work, he defined my past, he wrote my history and I must confess to an Oedipal desire to escape that history and embrace my future. This is the essence of my presentation today as well as the motivation of my engagement with social justice issues as a journalist and as a writer.

I often describe myself as an accidental activist because it was only after many years of dedicated agnosticism about my community's struggle for social justice that I became involved in the Ogoni struggle for cultural survival.

On May 21, 1994, my father, Ken Saro-Wiwa, was arrested in Nigeria. I was working as a journalist in England while my father was fighting for the rights of the Ogoni at home. My world was turned upside down that night. Although I was born and brought up in Nigeria, my father had sent me to school in England so that I would receive a first class education and return to Nigeria with what Chinua Achebe, the Nigerian writer, once described as the boon of a prophetic vision.

As an apolitical 25-year-old in May, 1994, the only vision I had of Nigeria was that it was a country where the rule of law was arbitrarily exercised; where government preyed on the misery of millions of disenfranchised people living below the poverty line; and where a voracious and venal elite had taken the country hostage, stripping it of its wealth and draining our economy of public funds. As far as I could see, and was given to understand by my father, Nigeria was on the brink of disaster. Our leaders had so mismanaged our human and material resources that unborn generations of Nigerians would inherit billions of dollars of debt and I was reluctant to bear the burden of, or bear witness, to that legacy.

My father, on the other hand, had spent his whole life trying to save Nigeria from itself. 'A writer is his cause', he would say as he set the quest for social justice for our people as the leitmotif of his literary life. He always expected that his first son and namesake would play some role in our struggle but this was a vision of my future that I had studiously avoided, choosing to remain in England where I was struggling to find and define myself as a writer.

When my father was arrested in May 1994, Nigeria began to reclaim me, slowly at first, then with an inexorable logic that I now understand as destiny. Once I started to campaign to bring his arrest and our struggle for social justice to world attention, I began to find my sea legs as an activist and I came, in due course, to envisage myself as a chronicler of our struggle. So my education as a writer engaged in social justice issues began, and that education has continued beyond my father's execution in November 1995, beyond my first book five years later, and is still continuing through my writing as I look to engage with the issues for which my father and many others died.

Since my last book, *In the Shadow of a Saint*, my intellectual enquiry has gathered pace and I am starting to see a pattern in the mass of research and information I have been gathering. My tentative observation from all this research tells me this: that the struggle for social justice everywhere will redefine our world, it will redraw the map of the world, it will reconfigure a world that was assembled between the 14th and 20th centuries.

Before I explain what I mean by that, I want to recap my community's story to illustrate how I have arrived at this observation.

I am an Ogoni. That means I am one of an estimated five hundred thousand people who live on four hundred and four square miles of an oil rich and fertile plateau of the Niger River Delta in southern Nigeria. We have lived in this place for anything from four hundred years to since time began, depending on which of our histories, oral or written, you subscribe to.

The Ogoni - we say Ogoni rather than Ogoniland or the Ogoni people to emphasise the symbiotic relationship between land and people - the Ogoni were never involved in the slave trade, we were largely a community unto ourselves until the British arrived on the scene in the early twentieth century. Our eventual absorption into the British colony of Southern Nigeria was without consultation but by a decision made at the Treaty of Berlin in 1884, giving Queen Victoria the right to exploit the geographical space now known as Nigeria.

During the 19th century, the Niger Delta was a lucrative sphere of commerce for the British, especially its palm oil merchants. But it was the discovery in 1956 of another kind of oil, crude oil, that really changed the dynamics of the relationship between the British and the inhabitants of the Niger Delta.

Since 1958 an estimated nine hundred million barrels of oil has been pumped out of my community. But instead of benefiting from this resource, the presence of oil companies has proved to be a curse for the people and a blight on the land. A region that ought to be as rich as a small gulf state is underdeveloped. Pipe-borne water is virtually non-existent, the electricity supply is limp and functional, schools and health services are perennially under-funded. The patchy distribution of social services is a poor return for a community that has provided an estimated thirty billion dollars worth of oil to Nigeria's federal coffers.

To compound my people's misery, the activities of an unregulated, largely unaccountable oil industry has compromised our existence. The oil industry derives fantastic profits from Ogoni while paying scant attention to the impact of their operations on the social, economic, ecological and cultural needs of the community.

In 1990 the Ogoni took stock of the situation and concluded that we were getting a raw deal, both from the Nigerian government and the oil industry.

It was then that my father, Ken Saro-Wiwa, formed MOSOP (The Movement for the Survival of the Ogoni People). In his vision of what was to be a non-violent grassroots organisation, my father hoped that MOSOP would not only sensitise our people to what was happening to the land, the people and our culture, but would also mobilise the community to stand up for our rights. So successful was MOSOP's mobilisation of the community that on January 4, 1993, an estimated three hundred thousand Ogoni came out in support of the aims and ideals of MOSOP in a peaceful protest march. Shell was declared *persona non grata* and served a quit notice to stay away from Ogoni until the company paid back-rents and cleaned up its operations. Shell pulled out of Ogoni claiming that its workers had been attacked.

The then military government of Nigeria responded, not by trying to mediate between the community and the oil companies, but by trying to intimidate the community into silence. The military dictatorship's response was predictable: oil accounts for ninety per cent of Nigeria's foreign exchange revenues and the billions of dollars that accrue from oil is what attracts soldiers to politics in

Nigeria. Although Ogoni only accounts for a small proportion of the oil that comes from the Delta, the military government viewed the implications of a small community driving out a multinational as a threat to national security. So Nigeria's then military dictator, General Abacha, sent in soldiers to, and I quote, rid Ogoni of the MOSOP virus to enable oil production to resume.

Ogoni leaders and people experienced rising levels of harassment and intimidation. The commitment of some was allegedly bought off in time-honoured fashion, sowing a climate of confusion and mutual suspicion within the community, undermining the collective purpose of a community that had been united under MOSOP.

The brutal murder of four Ogoni chiefs during a riot in Ogoni on May 21, 1994, must be seen as a consequence of the military dictatorship's resolve to settle the Ogoni issue through a mixture of bribery and intimidation. The issue was further compounded by the authorities' wilful negligence in the investigation of those murders.

On the night of May 21, my father and scores of other MOSOP activists were arrested and held in connection with the murders of the four chiefs whom the government described as moderate and pro-government. The next day, the military administrator of the region held a press conference, parading a bag of bones purportedly the remains of the murdered chiefs. Lt.-Colonel Komo declared that he was satisfied that the investigations were complete and singled out what he described as MOSOP thugs and radicals to fit the crime.

My father and scores of MOSOP activists were hunted down and arrested. They were held for nine months without trial. When they were finally charged, they were brought before a military tribunal, the very same military that had openly declared war on the Ogoni. My father was accused of inciting his supporters to murder the four chiefs. Following nine months of a trial process that was roundly condemned by international jurists and observers, the presiding judge sentenced my father and eight other defendants to death. They were executed ten days after sentencing.

Some of you may already know much of the foregoing, but I am drawing attention to it because it is central to my life, to my work as a writer, and to my community's continuing struggle for social justice. Everything flows into and out of this sequence of events.

When I started writing *In the Shadow of A Saint*, I saw it as a chance to re-establish the salient facts of the struggle. I wanted to set the record straight because both Shell and the Nigerian military had spent millions on an advertising and public relations campaign to defend themselves against the charges of human rights abuses in Ogoni. The objective of the media offensive was to deflect public attention from scrutiny of their human rights record in Ogoni onto my father's character and MOSOP's credibility.

As my father's son, and as a writer now fully engaged and committed to our struggle for social justice, I saw it as my task to defend my father's reputation and remind the world of the crimes that had been committed - and were still being committed - against our people. In short, I saw myself as a literary advocate against the expensive and sophisticated propaganda offensive of a giant corporation.

At the time I began the book, in 1997, the global outrage against the activities of Shell in Nigeria had subsided somewhat. I realised that the task I faced as a writer was similar to the one my community faced. Let me explain.

With multinationals like Shell colonising more and more of our public space with their glowing logos and shiny commercials, it will be hard to find a compelling space to offer an alternative view, to convince the world that the Ogoni story has not run its course, to remind the world that thousands of Ogoni were extra-judicially murdered, were internally and externally displaced, suffered and continue to suffer emotional and physical abuse, that many in my community still bear the scars of the struggle and have not been adequately compensated. Those stories will now need to be told in a court of law and that is only right and proper because the quest for truth, which is the basis of the struggle for social justice, can, ultimately, be settled only in a properly constituted court of law.

Some of you will already be aware that we have filed a complaint against Shell in the district courts of New York. I was at home when we received news last week that we have won the legal arguments over the court's competence to hear the case in a New York assize.

The decision to take the case to a court in the State of New York was born out of our frustration and suspicion of the prevailing power dynamics in Nigeria. We felt that we would not receive fair hearing in a country that was, and is, run for, and on behalf of, the oil industry.

For me, the Ogoni story is a poignant illustration of what happens in countries like Nigeria where the national interest is aligned almost exclusively to the commercial dictates of business. The government of Nigeria was privatised well before the country became independent in 1960. Nigeria was carved out of the old borders of the British sphere of influence, in turn both the UAC (United African Company) and the Niger Trading Company eventually became known as Nigeria. And so a pre-colonial arrangement was morphed into a postcolonial construct. Nigeria remains, essentially, a country trapped in the corporations that own it. For instance, Shell's worldwide annual revenue of one hundred billion dollars dwarfs Nigeria's GDP of forty billion dollars. And since fourteen per cent of Shell's worldwide revenue comes from Nigeria, my country could, to all intents and purposes, be viewed as a division of Shell. The nation state, the will of the people, has been sold off and leased to giant corporations with the financial clout and muscle to influence and even dictate the country's political culture. The multinationals and their agents and clients who effectively rule the country are able to flout the laws of the land and ignore governments whose power and willingness to mediate between the people and the corporations is determined by the realities of these power dynamics.

While I was writing what I suppose is a memoir, I felt a nagging unease and then what I can only describe as a mounting sense of creative relish that my community's struggle against Shell had been, and was, being played out in the media.

Relish because such nuances are the spark of the creative impulse but unease because I knew that we - my father, my community and myself - were not entirely innocent against those charges. We had also used, if that's the right word, the media to get our voice heard.

Those who advocate their causes through the media run the risk of trial by media. I must add that my father had no choice but to use the media to advance our cause. Our political, economic and cultural power was limited by our minority status. In the circumstance, we were fortunate that in Ken Saro-Wiwa the Ogoni had a tireless and skilled writer. My father was very good at public relations - he understood the power of the word of information. In his formative years as a writer he had also been acutely aware of, and engaged in, the debates over language and cultural appropriation in postcolonial Africa. He agonised about the role of the writer and his audience. He tried to square the circle of writing in a colonial language for a polyglot audience that had been reared on the oral tradition. He never quite resolved that dilemma which is why he once said that his words became most potent once he abandoned writing and took his words on to the streets and formed MOSOP.

Of course, he never abandoned writing as such - many of the books and pamphlets he produced over a twenty-five year career contained the words that were subsequently used to inspire our people.

My father had an acute sense of history and saw himself as forging, in the Joycean tradition, the uncreated conscience of his people in the smithy of his soul.

I think it is ironic that he achieved his ambition, not so much through his writing but, through his actions and, ultimately, through his martyrdom. And the ultimate irony for me is that his martyrdom has invested his words with a sacred weight and it is a bold Ogoni man or woman who dares to question those words. But it is those very words that haunt me as his first son, as someone who now sees himself as his, Ken Saro-Wiwa's, literary executor.

I was acutely aware of this fine line between honouring the past while claiming the future when I wrote *In the Shadow of A Saint*. I now relish the fact that it is a very nuanced book that invites multiple readings and interpretations and even disquiet in friendly quarters. Where my father's writing was direct and unequivocal, I am less certain. As something of a pioneer, as an advocate in our quest for social justice, my father saw the struggle as black and white while I tend to see a few grey spots. I like to think that my father's life and death allowed me, afforded me, the opportunity to have this nuanced perspective, that he cleared a space for me to play with as a writer. I am, of course, eternally grateful for that but not everyone feels that way about my writing.

It is not that I am insensitive to criticism - in fact I welcome it - but once I began to think deeply about our struggle, I wrestled with a dilemma, a profound anxiety really about the value and potency of pursuing the cause of social justice through writing. I keep asking myself the same questions - will my choice end up in the same cul-de-sac of futility and frustration that my father ran into when he decided to abandon writing in 1990?

In trying to answer this question I have spent much of my intellectual energy probing this tension between words and action, trying to figure out the points of departure between oral and written traditions and trying to understand how these dilemmas play themselves out in life. And it was while I was re-examining my faith that I found myself questioning some of the assumptions I have long held about the quest for social justice.

I'd like to expand on this here but I have to admit that I am not quite ready to workshop the themes and ideas that will form the subtext of my next book. But what I will say is this: I have become acutely interested in the link between the stories we tell about ourselves, our creation myths, our history, how these stories impact and reflect on our identity, our legal, religious and social organisation. Our ethnicity.

Let me briefly expound on this. My father always trumpeted the idea that before the Europeans arrived on the scene the Ogoni had always lived in perfect harmony with the land and with each other. He knew that it was a myth; he, of course, understood the value of storytelling, of creating a mythic past to inspire the quest for social justice. However the truth - if there is such a thing - is that the Ogoni like all other nations have always been a community in flux, in a state of constant agitation, of change. Myths can work both ways; they can inspire and can also be a burden. I have no problem with using mythic utopian pasts to inspire a vision of the future, but my concern is that to define a community, or a nation, is to fix it in time and place and, ultimately, to arrest the evolutionary process that is necessary for the survival of any community. In other words a people, a nation, must move with the times. I think it is the message Gabriel Garcia Marquez is suggesting when he says communities that spend one hundred years in solitude rarely get a second chance on earth.

But the irony for me is that, in the quest for social justice, communities often resort to the past, retreat into solitude. This retreat, this nostalgia, is where we find ourselves, where we take stock to identify and define ourselves against the other encroaching on our territory.

The sense of Ogoni identity of community really only arose out of our conflict with the oil industry. In the process of challenging the oil companies we had to define what was being threatened, to describe an Ogoni utopia before our innocence, our solitude was exposed. It was this promise of the recovery of a paradise lost that exercised such a powerful hold on my community's imagination, rallying our people to the cause. But now, after all the sacrifices, with the heightened sensitivity to the injustices that are still very fresh in the collective memory, the nostalgia for paradise lost remains a potent attraction that could still inspire both positive and negative responses in the community.

The quest for justice is now more pertinent in my community, if only to ensure that the lessons of the past have been learned. The danger lies in delay - the longer economic, social and cultural justice is denied to peoples like the Ogoni, the longer that the human rights abuses go unpunished, so the longer we will all operate under the lies, myths and misconceptions that divide us.

Because without justice, without due process, we cannot reclaim a proportionate and fair sense of history and tomorrow becomes pregnant with the orphans of yesterday. In short, an imperfect past makes the future tense.

CHAPTER 2

EDUCATION AND SOCIAL JUSTICE IN IRELAND

Roland Tormey and *Neil Haran*

...let it not be said that, if I am a biology teacher, I must not "go off into other considerations" – that I must *only* teach biology, as if the phenomenon of life could be understood apart from its historico-social, cultural and political framework. As if life, just life, could be lived in the same way, in all of its dimensions, in a *favela* (slum) or *cortiço* ("beehive" – slum tenement building) as in a prosperous area of Sao Paulo's Gardens! If I am a biology teacher, obviously I must teach biology. But in doing so, I must not cut it off from the framework of the whole (Freire 1999, p. 78).

This chapter is concerned with the social justice context within which Irish education takes place – it is about the 'framework of the whole'. The classroom is not hermetically sealed: the people who come in each day, the teachers and the learners, bring something of the outside world with them into the classroom. When they leave, they bring something from that experience back out into the world again. For a teacher like Paulo Freire, what happens in the classroom is crucial to making sense of the shape of the outside world. School could be a place where the pupil never learned about the shape and nature of their social world, never learned a language of social justice, never learned to view their world critically and never learned how to challenge the world and change it: it could be a place where we "lecture students into sleepy silence" (Shor 1993, pp. 25 – 26). On the other hand, it could be a place where they learn about the shape of their world and about how their world could be made different. Of course, to teach people about the shape of their world, we need to first know something about it. That is the issue addressed in this chapter.

Here we look at the data on inequality and poverty in Ireland and identify the relationship between economic inequality and educational inequality. It is shown that Ireland is actually one of the most unequal countries in the industrialised world, and that, despite the recent economic progress, inequality continues to be one of the hallmarks of Irish society. It identifies that one form that this inequality takes is educational inequality. This chapter then looks at gender-based inequalities in Irish society. Although it is clear that Ireland has made significant progress in relation to gender equality over the last thirty years (something which cannot be said in relation to economic inequality) there are significant gender issues still to be addressed in Irish education. Racism and discrimination are also important issues in Irish society. They have become manifest as a result of recent immigration but, at the same time, discrimination is something to which the Irish Traveller community has long been subjected. Although individual racism is easily identified, there is evidence that institutional racism, although often not recognised, has a significant grip on Irish institutions, including the educational system.

ECONOMIC GROWTH AND INEQUALITY

In recent years the Irish economy has enjoyed one of its healthiest periods since the foundation of the state. Ireland experienced a period of sustained and unprecedented economic growth, placing it among the top twenty wealthiest and most developed nations in the world (United Nations Development Programme 2002). The *National Development Plan 2000 – 2006* (Ireland 1999, p. 25) identified that the country had at that time a substantial budget surplus. While the extent of budgetary surplus has declined since then, it is still envisaged that Ireland will continue to grow economically in the next few years. In the early years of the new century the country was experiencing almost full employment, while GNP per head represented eighty eight per cent of the EU average compared to seventy nine per cent in 1994.

The buoyancy of the Irish economy brought substantial changes to the quality of life experienced by Irish citizens. The Combat Poverty Agency (2001, p. 9) notes that practically all sections of Irish society are better off in absolute terms, a point reflected in the steady fall in the number of people experiencing consistent poverty in Ireland. The data on poverty from 2000 shows that six point two per cent of Irish households experienced consistent poverty compared to a figure of fifteen point one per cent in 1994.

During this period the reduction of poverty was also identified as a key aim of Government policy. The National Anti-Poverty Strategy, outlining how Government policy would tackle poverty in Irish society, was put in place in 1997 (Ireland 1997). The Government in 2001-2002 reviewed this strategy and its key targets. Under this plan, the Government aims to reduce consistent poverty to a maximum of two per cent (Department of Social, Community and Family Affairs 2002).

However, despite this strategy, it is quite apparent that certain sectors of society have benefited from the boom years more than others. A substantial proportion of Irish society still lives in relative poverty (which is to say they are precluded from having a standard of living considered the norm for Irish society generally). In fact, research indicates that the gap between rich and poor in Ireland is increasing. For instance, the Combat Poverty Agency (2001, p. 1), based on 1997 data, has highlighted that twenty two per cent of the population lives on less than fifty per cent of average national household income, representing an increase since 1994 in the number of people experiencing relative poverty in Ireland. The United Nations Development Programme has pointed out that the richest ten per cent of the Irish population is eleven times richer than the poorest ten per cent (*Irish Times*, 24th July, 2002). Indeed, "the richest ten per cent of the population received twenty five per cent of the budget giveaways during the five years of the [1997 –2002] Government, while the poorest twenty per cent received under five per cent" (*Irish Times*, 17th April, 2002).

It is worthwhile putting the Irish situation in an international context. Alongside the well-known Human Development Index, the United Nations Development Programme also uses a Human Poverty Index which is essentially a measure of 'quality of life' and is based on the extent to which people are poor or rich in longevity, knowledge and standard of living. When human poverty is measured, Ireland fares poorly as compared to other developed countries. In a list of seventeen developed countries, Ireland is listed in second-last place (United Nations Development Programme, 2002). The countries at the head of the list include Sweden, Norway, the Netherlands, Finland and Denmark. Ireland is in sixteenth place, between the UK in fifteenth place and the US in seventeenth. As Cantillon *et al.* have recently noted:

> Inequality is one of the hallmarks of Irish society. Our recent prosperity has not benefited all but has, in fact, marginalised and excluded a sizeable part of our population, including the long-term unemployed, single parents, Travellers, early-school leavers, small farmers and the elderly (2001, p. xxxv).

EDUCATIONAL DISADVANTAGE

In many ways, education in Ireland reflects the levels of inequality found in broader society. The term 'educational disadvantage' is widely used in Ireland by policy-makers, teachers and academics as a synonym for the lower attainment of poor or working class pupils in the education system as compared to other pupils. Sometimes it is measured in terms of a lack of educational qualifications (no Leaving Certificate, for example), while sometimes it is measured in comparative terms (lower attainment in assessment or in access to college, for example).

Towards the end of the 1990s, between eight hundred and one thousand pupils did not transfer from primary to post-primary school. A further three thousand did not stay on to sit their Junior Certificate, while over twelve thousand more did not sit their Leaving Certificate:

> In all, at the end of the 1990s, about 17,500 young people (almost a quarter of the cohort) left school annually without the Leaving Certificate. It is clear then that, if the Leaving Certificate is regarded as a necessary qualification for life..., the school system is currently failing almost a quarter of our young

people (Hyland 2002, p. 48).

The figures on early school leaving alone hide the true extent of educational disadvantage. As Power and Tormey (2000) have shown, even when working class pupils do make it to Leaving Certificate, they take few honours subjects and get lower grades than their middle class counterparts. As such, they argue that the "glaring social class differences in...educational outcomes confirm that early school leaving is not an adequate representation of educational disadvantage" (2000, p. 13).

In Ireland it is commonly assumed that educational disadvantage is an urban phenomenon. When we think of educational disadvantage, images of high-rise flats or suburban wastelands with high levels of unemployment, drug abuse, violence, or other social ills come readily to mind. However, one of the most striking things about educational disadvantage in Ireland is that it is predominantly a rural phenomenon. A 1995 study by Kellaghan *et al.* (1995, p. 46), examined the geographical distribution of the sixteen per cent most disadvantaged pupils (those who were poor and had low attainment on a standardised test) and discovered that over sixty per cent of them lived in small towns (towns with less than ten thousand people) or in the open countryside. In comparison, about twenty six per cent lived in Dublin with the remainder in other urban areas and large towns.

It is worth asking why this finding is so at odds with the commonly held assumption that educational disadvantage is an urban phenomenon. Jackson and Haase (1996, p. 61-66) suggest that, in Ireland, rural poverty is largely hidden for a range of reasons. One reason is that it carries with it a stigma that is not so evident in cities - a stigma that may cause rural dwellers to hide their poverty. A second is because the low population density causes the impression of a greater mixing of social classes in rural areas which, in turn, creates the impression that rural areas are classless. Therefore, it may well be that children from poor or working class homes are not as easily recognised in rural areas as in urban areas. Consequently, their comparatively poor performance may not be associated by educators with their background and, instead, be put down to a lack of ability rather than recognised as educational disadvantage.

Educational disadvantage is also likely to present itself differently in rural areas than in urban areas. While urban areas have some schools that are easily recognisable as drawing pupils from poor or working class communities and will have a high concentration of pupils from such communities, in rural areas greater social mixing may mean that educationally disadvantaged pupils are found in most schools but in far smaller concentrations. Although such rural schools are unlikely to be identified or designated as 'disadvantaged', the data suggests that many if not most rural teachers are teachers of pupils who are being disadvantaged.

GENDER INEQUALITIES AND EDUCATION IN IRELAND

In her book *Emerging Voices, Women in Contemporary Irish Society*, Pat O'Connor identifies that any "discussion of changes in the position of women in Irish society over the last thirty years tends to elicit two views: that it has changed completely, and that it has not changed at all" (1998, p. 1). If we look at the measures proposed by the United Nations Development Programme, the Gender-related Development Index (GDI) and Gender Empowerment Measure (GEM), it is clear that the situation of women in Ireland has improved over the period 1970 to the present – Ireland's GDI score has improved by thirty-two per cent since 1970 (O'Connor 1998, p. 35). Nonetheless it is clear that we have not become a society which treats its women as well as its men. This can be demonstrated in relation to a number of measures such as access to positions of power and earning capacity.

Of the thirty-three most senior politicians with executive powers in Ireland (Ministers, Ministers of State and the Attorney General), four are women (twelve per cent). In the Dáil as a whole, women account for twenty-two of the one hundred and sixty six seats (thirteen per cent) (IPA 2003, pp. 4-12). These low levels of access to senior decision making positions are mirrored in other areas of Irish public life, such as managerial positions in industry (United Nations Development Programme 2002, p. 226). According the Central Statistics Office, the average weekly earnings of an adult male industrial worker in 2001 was five hundred and twelve Euro, as compared to three hundred and forty-seven Euro for an adult female industrial worker (Central Statistics Office 2003). Overall, the United Nations Development Programme lists Ireland at the seventeenth most gender equal country in the world, behind countries like Australia, Belgium, Sweden, Norway, the UK and France, but ahead of countries like Spain, Luxembourg, Greece and Portugal.

O'Connor identifies that the concept of patriarchy is a useful one to apply to Ireland (1998, p. 7). She notes that, by seeing Irish society as one which is characterised by male control, frequently ignored realities of Irish life are revealed. It identifies that both public and private policies and practices may be accepted as normal while discriminating against women. It identifies that a blindness or an indifference to the differential effects of policies or practices on women and men is embedded in many of the institutions of our society such as government, the workplace and cultural institutions. As such, decisions taken by such bodies will often be to the benefit of men or the detriment of women, but nonetheless are understood as being 'in the national interest' (the decision not to invest more heavily in a national system of child care, because such investment would be deemed too costly for the taxpayer, for example). It identifies that such bias may take different forms in the public sphere of government and work when compared to the private sphere of home life (Walby 1990), and that the relationship between these two spheres is likely to be quite important, if often ignored. Crucially for education, it identifies that, for each of us, gender-based differences in our "temperament, character, interests, status, worth, gesture and expression" may have been learned over a long period of time growing up and living in a biased society, and may be deeply held by both men and women (Millett 1977, p. 31).

Gender roles and relationships have been the focus of much of the equality-focused research in Irish education (which is not to say that the subject matter is exhausted by any means). As Lynch points out (1999, p. 155), if we look at women as learners in the education system, women have reached, and indeed, surpassed the point of equality, being equally represented across almost all levels of education and surpassing men in performance in state examinations (including in subjects traditionally understood as male subjects).

Studies of other areas of educational life do point to important gender differences in the treatment of male and female pupils. As we noted above, Millett draws attention to the different ways in which women and men are socialised to have different attitudes and self-expectations. This area has been explored in Irish schools, at post-primary level by Lynch (1989) and at primary level by Lewis and Kellaghan (1993). Both identified that schools operated different patterns of expectations of male and female pupils. Lewis and Kellaghan found that young girls were encouraged by teachers to take care, whether that means taking care of their environment (watering plants, tidying) or taking care of younger children. Where possible, girls were not required to engage in heavy, physical work. On the other hand, their evidence suggested that in relation to non-school work related activities, boys were not encouraged by teachers to take care of others or of the environment. They were encouraged, however, to be physical, to lift and carry. Lynch's findings at post-primary level show developments from this pattern. She found that girls' schools placed more of an emphasis on promoting qualities like caring for others, sincerity, refinement and self-control than boys' schools. Boys' schools on the other hand placed a greater emphasis on physical prowess and sporting achievement. Lynch argues that in girls' schools there was an emphasis on achievement and competition, and on caring and community-orientation. The girls' schools studied by Lynch were more likely than the boys' schools to have religious societies and arts societies like debating, drama and arts and crafts. In boys' schools competition alone was emphasised. Lynch concludes that schools reflect the values of society in that they socialise women into accepting responsibility for both the private sphere of home and the public sphere of work.

Schools do this without exploring or highlighting that it may be difficult or impossible for a woman to be successful in both spheres as they both demand time and energy: this burden of two workloads and the potential for guilt which may be felt by a woman who 'fails' to achieve on both fronts is not questioned by the school. As Drudy and Lynch put it:

> The inherent conflicts between the two systems that these worlds represent (the worlds of caring and capital) are not really explored or examined in schools. It remains a private dilemma for individual women, not a public problem to be resolved. The double burden is not posed as problematic. For boys, the future expected is generally that of employment in the paid labour market. The personal and emotional needs of self, family, and others are commonly presented as 'incidentals' in men's lives (1993, p. 185).

In recent years, some male writers have focused attention on the idea that, while men undoubtedly benefit from patriarchy, it may also be damaging to them. Anthony Clare has asked why, if patriarchy is so beneficial to men, they:

> …do not seem any the happier. Throughout North America, Europe, and Australia, male suicides outnumber female by a factor of between 3 and 4 to 1. The rise in the number of young men killing themselves in much of the developed world has rightly been termed an epidemic…And these suicide figures are viewed as the tip of an iceberg of male depression, an iceberg hidden because men are seen to be either too proud or too emotionally constipated to admit when their feelings are out of control (Clare 2001, p. 3).

Clare does not deny that we are living in a patriarchy and that men benefit from that. He does question whether or not its effects on men have been properly understood (a number of years ago a student in the Limerick School of Art and Design pointed to the last sentence in the quote from Drudy and Lynch above and suggested to one of us that, if women are socialised in school for a double burden, men seem to be socialised to live 'half lives' – that is, a life that cannot competently deal with the "personal and emotional needs of self, family, and others"). Clare argues that men must learn from the women's movement if we are to find a constructive role for ourselves in a world after patriarchy (2001, p. 217).

In the last number of years, gender issues have been the subject of a number of programmes and campaigns within the education system (*Gender Matters, Gender Science and Technology, Exploring Masculinities*). Given that the studies identified above pre-date many of these programmes it will be interesting to note how they have impacted upon the ideology and practice of schools, if at all.

ETHNICITY AND IRELAND: CHANGE AND CONTINUITY

Economic change in Ireland came at a time when the country was also undergoing substantial social change. Indeed, the two are related, since the first played a part in the latter. Net immigration (i.e. the balance between inward and outward migration) reached an historic highpoint of twenty-six thousand, three hundred in 2001. Returning Irish nationals continue to be the largest immigrant group (between 1995 and 2000 they accounted for fifty per cent of immigration). In that period, US nationals represented seven per cent of immigrants compared with eighteen per cent for the UK and thirteen per cent for the remainder of the EU. Immigrants who are nationals of other countries (including Australia, Canada and New Zealand) accounted for twelve per cent of immigrants during that period (Department of Justice Equality and Law Reform 2002, p. 9).

Ireland is becoming increasingly a country that is attracting foreign nationals to its shores and a growing number of cultural and ethnic groups are visible in the country. These include asylum seekers applying for refugee status in Ireland. In fact, the numbers of individuals seeking asylum in Ireland have risen quite dramatically in the last decade, from just thirty-nine applications in 1992 to ten thousand nine hundred and twenty in 2000 (National Consultative Committee on Racism and Interculturalism 2001; United Nations High Commissioner for Refugees 2001). These asylum seekers have come from a range of different countries, including Nigeria, Romania, Moldova, the Russian Federation, Croatia, the Democratic Republic of the Congo, Lithuania and Poland (United Nations High Commissioner for Refugees 2002, p. 14). Even the range of countries of origin does not show the extent of diversity among asylum seekers: on its own, a country like Nigeria is home to over two hundred separate ethnic groups, languages and cultures.

While a great deal of media attention has focused on the numbers of refugees and asylum seekers coming to Ireland, the last few years have also seen a significant number of people coming to Ireland on working visas. During the boom years around the recent turn of the century, significant labour shortages developed which had a negative impact on economic growth. Although the EU allows for free movement of people, the number of workers from EU countries was not sufficient to meet the economy's labour needs. As a result, work visas were issued to non-EU citizens to fill specified jobs. In the year 2000, about eighteen thousand work visas were issued. This figure rose to over thirty-six thousand in 2001. Apart from EU citizens living in Ireland, significant numbers of migrant workers have come to Ireland from countries such as Latvia, Lithuania, Poland, the Philippines, South Africa and the Czech Republic (Regan and Tormey 2002, p. 212).

The increased visibility of cultural and ethnic diversity in Ireland has meant that cultural diversity has been highlighted recently as an issue. However, it is arguable that Ireland has long had diverse cultures present and that this diversity has not been recognised hitherto. One of the largest ethnic minority groupings in Ireland is the Traveller community. There are an estimated fifteen thousand Travellers in Ireland, while a further twenty-five thousand Irish Travellers live in Britain (Pavee Point 2002). The report of the Government's 1995 Task Force on the Travelling Community (Ireland 1995, p. 71) noted that:

> veller community's culture is distinct and different.
> ly recognise the difference but fail to understand it as
> s is a phenomenon, characteristic of many societies,
> ure sees itself as holding a universal validity or norm
> anings and identity.

Erratum   Page 27:

There are an estimated twenty-five thousand Travellers in Ireland, while a further fifteen thousand Irish Travellers live in Britain (Pavee Point 2002).

only historic minority in Irish society. According to the recent growth in immigration – there were forty-our in Ireland, north and south (McVeigh and Lentin reland also contains a diversity of religious groups. In cent of the population of the island of Ireland were Catholic (Tovey and Share 2000, p. 315). Narrowing the focus to the Republic of Ireland, in 1991 ninety-two per cent of people described themselves as Roman Catholic, three point two per cent described themselves as Protestant, of which two point five per cent described themselves as belonging to the Church of Ireland, two point four per cent described themselves as having no religion, one point nine per cent did not state a religion. Other religions, including Muslims, Jews, and Jehovah's Witnesses, each accounted for a fraction of one per cent (Central Statistics Office 2002). Yet this snapshot does not represent the historic extent of religious diversity in Ireland, since the numbers of some religious groups in Ireland have been in decline. In 1911 Protestants made up ten point four per cent of the population. This fell to seven point four per cent in 1926. This figure continued to fall until the 1991 low point of three point two per cent. The number of Jewish people living in the state has also fallen. Between 1911 and 1945 the number of Jewish people stayed at about three thousand eight hundred people. Thereafter it fell to the 1991 low point of one thousand five hundred and eighty one people (zero point zero four per cent of the population).

Overall then, we can see that the traditional sense of Irishness as being settled and Catholic is one that was always questionable as a description of Ireland. Lentin, for example, argues that it was always naïve to describe Ireland as mono-cultural: "Ireland has been multi-ethnic for a long time now", she writes (2000, p. 5). Lentin argues that the way in which Irishness was understood has excluded many Irish people and also relates the emigration of young Irish Jews to their being made to feel that they do not really belong here. She cites the example of one young Irish-Jewish woman who told her: "I am fourth generation Irish born.

How can I be more Irish other than being Catholic?" (2002, p. 157-158). In a similar way, the idea that 'Irish' means 'settled' has meant that there has been little accommodation for what is distinctive in Traveller culture in Irish society.

RACISM IN CONTEMPORARY IRELAND

The term 'racism' is defined by the UN International Convention on all Forms of Racist Discrimination (1969) (quoted by National Consultative Committee on Racism and Interculturalism 2001) in the following terms:

> Any distinction, exclusion, restriction or preference, based on race, colour, descent, national or ethnic origin, which has the purpose of modifying or impairing the recognition, the enjoyment or exercise on an equal footing of human rights and fundamental freedom in the political, economic, social, cultural, or any other field of public life constitutes racial discrimination.

More detailed explanations of racism offered by various social scientists over the last twenty years have tended to concentrate on two specific aspects, namely:

- individual racism
- institutional racism.

We will look at these in turn.

Individual racism

Individual racism is often manifested in stereotypes about difference and inferiority (The Commission on the Future of a Multi-Ethnic Britain 2000, p. 63). Increasingly, attention is being drawn to the fact that many people living in Ireland experience racism on an ongoing basis. In January 2002 a 29-year-old Chinese man, Zhao Liu Tao, was attacked and beaten to death by youths who hurled racial abuse at him. As McVeigh and Lentin note, this attack "marked a terrible new phase in the evolution of racism and antiracism in Ireland" (2002, p. 1). They also note that this attack is not an isolated incident. In a survey of ethnic minority attitudes in Ireland, seventy-eight per cent of more than six hundred respondents from a variety of ethnic minorities living all over Ireland highlighted that they had been victims of racism, most often in public places like the street or in shops or pubs, and over eighty per cent of the sample tended to agree that racism is a serious problem in contemporary Ireland (Loyal and Mulcahy 2001).

Travellers also experience individual racism in Ireland. The Government's Task Force on the Travelling Community noted:

> Discrimination at the individual level is most common when a Traveller seeks access to any of a range of goods, services and facilities, to which access is denied purely on the basis of their identity as Travellers. Examples abound of

public houses refusing to serve Travellers, hotels refusing to book Traveller weddings, bingo halls barring Traveller women, leisure facilities barring access to Travellers, and insurance companies refusing to provide motor insurance cover. This experience can also include physical and verbal attacks and intimidation (Ireland 1995, p. 79-80).

Anti-Traveller sentiment can be found in newspapers and in statements from public representatives. O'Connell (2002, p. 55), for example, describes how in 1996, a Fianna Fáil Councillor at a Waterford County Council Meeting is reported to have said: "The sooner the shotguns are at the ready and these Travelling people are put out of the county the better. They are not our people, they aren't natives."

Harvey (2002, p. 41) notes that the European Union research body *Eurobarometer* sees Ireland as a 'passively tolerant' society with about fifty per cent of people neither wanting government action against racism, nor wanting members of ethnic minorities assimilated or sent home. Only around thirteen per cent of Irish people had very negative attitudes towards minorities. He goes on:

Support for the outlawing of discrimination against minorities is very low in Ireland, 24%, the lowest in the [European] Union, as is support for promoting equality at all levels of social life, 31%, also the lowest…Irish people are, compared to other Europeans, more prepared to welcome Muslims and people from eastern and central Europe, but less sympathetic to people fleeing human rights abuses or situations of conflict. Asked whether they feel that minorities enrich our cultural life, only 32% of Irish people say yes, compared to 50% of all Europeans. The Eurobarometer survey found a sharp hardening of attitudes to minorities between 1997 and…2000.

Institutional Racism

While individual prejudice and attacks are part of racism, they are not all of racism. McVeigh and Lentin quote Stokely Carmichael who graphically illustrates this:

Racism is both overt and covert. It takes two closely related forms: individual whites acting against individual Blacks, and acts by the total white community against the Black community. We call these individual racism and institutional racism…When white terrorists bomb a Black church and kill Black children, that is an act of individual racism, widely deplored by most segments of society. But when in the same city 500 Black babies die each year because of the lack of proper food, clothing, shelter, and thousands more are destroyed or maimed physically, emotionally and intellectually because of conditions of poverty and discrimination, that is a function of institutional racism (2002, p. 7).

Institutional racism refers to racist structures in society (Epstein 1993, p. 15) and to the social exclusion and marginalisation of particular identity groups because of their ethnic or cultural backgrounds. Institutional racism may be obviously unfair; however, it is not always so. On the surface of it, things identified as institutionally racist may have the appearance of fairness because the same rules and regulations are applied to everyone: however, when one recognises that the rules, in effect, benefit some groups more than others, one can see why they are identified as institutionally racist. Such a situation is called indirect racism. Epstein cites the example of a school that, because it is oversubscribed, offers places first to children who have a sibling there. She notes that this common enough situation:

> ...is likely to disadvantage black children in areas where there have been relatively recent influxes of black people. It is unlikely that such a practice would have originated from the prejudiced intention of reducing the numbers of black pupils, but this will be the effect. It is practices such as these that are defined as 'indirect racism' (1993, p. 15).

According to The Commission on the Future of a Multi-Ethnic Britain (2000, p. 75) the elements of institutional racism include:

- indirect discrimination
- a lack of positive action to promote equality
- a lack of professional expertise or training in dealing with diversity in the organisation
- a lack of systematic data gathering on the impact of policies on minority groups
- a lack of workable facilities for consultation and listening to minority groups.

The report of the Government's Task Force on the Travelling Community identifies that institutional discrimination against Travellers is practised in Ireland through three mechanisms:

- Procedures and practices can reflect a lack of acceptance of Travellers' culture and identity and can involve controls placed on Travellers in excess of those placed on members of the 'Settled' community in similar circumstances.
- Travellers can be segregated in the provision of various services. Segregation is an imposed setting apart of a group. Segregation is therefore different from provision which is designed to advance positive resourcing and affirmative action policies, where participation is by choice.
- Legislation, policy making and provision can be developed without account being taken of their potential impact on a minority cultural group such as the Travellers. In this way, policy and practice can develop in a manner that only reflects the 'Settled' community's culture and identity and can therefore be inappropriate for the Traveller community. The nomadic way of life, though not being named, is marginalised, as resources and services which are provided are inappropriate to this aspect of the Traveller culture and identity (Ireland 1995, p. 80).

Institutional racism can stem from those who have power in institutions ignoring the different ways of life of people. In this respect, treating everyone the same is not the same as treating them equally. The Commission on The Future of Multi-Ethnic Britain notes, one of the fundamental beliefs of a good society is that:

> Since citizens have different needs, equal treatment requires full account to be taken of their differences. When equality ignores relevant differences and insists on uniformity of treatment, it leads to injustice and inequality; when differences ignore the demands of equality, that results in discrimination. Equality must be defined in a culturally sensitive way and applied in a discriminating but not discriminatory manner (2000, p. ix).

McDonagh (1994, pp. 99-108) has identified that evidence of institutional racism against Travellers can be found in government policy concerning Travellers from the 1960s to the 1990s. During the 1960s, Ireland's policy focus was on assimilating Travellers into the settled population, and on denying them opportunities to travel. He cites the boulders and trenches which are designed to prevent Travellers from stopping on roadsides, and the lack of suitable accommodation for Travellers.

He also cites evidence of indirect institutional racism against Travellers within the education system. Into the 1990s, the basic educational policy of the Irish State in relation to Travellers continued to be based on the denial of a right to be nomadic and an insistence on assimilation. While other states found themselves able to provide for children whose circumstance or culture made it difficult for them to attend settled schools (radio-based instruction in the Australian outback, for example), in Ireland, "no provision is made for meeting the educational needs of nomadic children nor...to accommodate nomadic families" (1994, p. 103). Instead, it was assumed that education could be properly offered only to those based in settled accommodation, with the 1980's Report of the Travelling People Review Body warning that 'settled' Travellers ran the risk of "regression to a travelling way of life and consequential negativing of the benefits of permanent accommodation and education" (quoted in McDonagh 1994, p. 103).

Travellers are not the only Irish people who have found that Irish institutions do not reflect their culture. For example, those who are not Roman Catholic have often found it difficult to obtain suitable local education for their children since educational provision is tied so closely to the religion of the majority. Many parents from minority religious groups in Ireland have, throughout the life of the state, been forced to place their children in Catholic education because of the lack of a local realistic alternative (Inglis 1987, p. 53). It is certainly worth asking whether the lack of provision which might reflect the diversity of cultures and religious groups also constitutes evidence of indirect discrimination.

INTERCULTURAL IRELAND

The Irish State has sought to respond to racism in Ireland in a number of ways. In legal terms, provisions in the Employment Equality Act (1998), the Equal Status Act (2000) and the Human Rights Commission Act (2000) present Ireland with comprehensive anti-discrimination legislation covering discrimination related to gender, marital status, family status, age, disability, race, sexual orientation, religious belief, and membership of the Traveller Community, in areas such as employment, education, provision of goods, services and accommodation and disposal of property. The enactment of this equality legislation by the Government has also enabled Ireland to ratify the UN Convention on the Elimination of All Forms of Racial Discrimination.

At a policy level, equality infrastructure has been put in place to give effect to this equality legislation. The Equality Authority was set up as an independent body under the Employment Equality Act (1998) and was formally established in 1999. The purpose of the Authority is to ensure that the provisions outlined in the Employment Equality Act (1998) and the Equal Status Act (2000) are realised. Additionally, the Department of Justice, Equality and Law Reform established the National Consultative Committee on Racism and Interculturalism (NCCRI) in July 1998. The committee consists of a partnership of government departments, agencies and non-government organisations. It was created to provide an ongoing structure to develop programmes and actions aimed at developing an integrated approach against racism and to act in a policy advisory role to the government (National Consultative Committee on Racism and Interculturalism 2001). The choice of the term 'interculturalism' rather than, for example, 'multiculturalism' is quite notable. It indicates the sort of society the Government envisages we should aim to live in: while the term multiculturalism may denote a society in which different cultures live side by side, the term interculturalism is intended to go further, denoting the "belief that we become richer persons by knowing and experiencing other cultures, that we add to our personality because of encounters with other cultures" (Exchange House Travellers Service 2002). In 2002 a National Action Plan Against Racism in Ireland was in the preparation phase, while a Department of Education and Science plan was also in development. The National Council for Curriculum and Assessment were, at the same time, in the process of developing intercultural education curriculum guidelines for both primary and post-primary schools.

CONCLUSION

Education and schooling are not separate from the world: they happen in the world. Ireland is now one of the richest countries in the industrialised world, and also one of the most economically unequal. There are significant gender inequality issues still to be addressed in Irish society and, while minority groups such as Travellers have long experienced discrimination in Irish life, more recent immigrants have also suffered in this way. This is the context within which Irish education happens. It is a context that cannot be ignored by educators.

Education is never neutral. Through teaching people we help to make them what they are. If they are unaware of some of the social justice issues in Ireland, then their capacity to act as responsible, active members of society will be curtailed. If they leave school without ever learning how and where and with what strategies they can make a difference, then their capacity to act as responsible members of a democratic society will be curtailed. It is not sufficient to pass these tasks off to someone else or say, "that is the job of the CSPE teacher, mine is to teach them science". No subject exists outside the world. Paulo Freire once noted that, irrespective of what we teach, education is a political act. Our education either deals with cultural diversity and justice issues or it hides from them. Either way, the choice has consequences for the children before us and for society at large. Freire said:

> This is a great discovery, education is politics! When a teacher discovers that he or she is a politician, too, the teacher has to ask, What kind of politics am I doing in the classroom? (Shor and Freire, quoted in Shor 1993, p. 29).

REFERENCES

Cantillon, S. Corrigan, C., Kirby, P. and O'Flynn, J. (2001) *Rich and Poor, Perspectives on Tackling Inequality in Ireland.* Dublin: Oak Tree Press and Combat Poverty Agency.

Central Statistics Office (2001) *Population and Migration Estimates, April 2001.* Dublin: Central Statistics Office.

Central Statistics Office (2002) *Principal Statistics.* (website address: http://www.cso.ie/principalstats/pristat2.html) (Accessed: 24 September 2002).

Central Statistics Office (2003) *Principal Statistics: Industrial Employment, Earnings and Hours Worked.* (website address: http://www.cso.ie/principalstats/pristat9a.html#earnings) (Accessed: 25 February 2003).

Clare, A. (2001) *On Men: Masculinities in Crisis.* London: Arrow Books

Combat Poverty Agency (2001) *Annual Report 2000.* Dublin: The Combat Poverty Agency.

The Commission on the Future of a Multi-Ethnic Britain (2000) *The Future of Multi-Ethnic Britain; The Parekh Report.* London: Profile Books.

Department of Justice, Equality and Law Reform (2002) *Towards a National*

Action Plan Against Racism in Ireland. Dublin: Department of Justice, Equality and Law Reform.

Department of Social, Community and Family Affairs (2002) *Building an Inclusive Society*. Dublin: Department of Social, Community and Family Affairs.

Drudy, S. and Lynch, K. (1993) *Schools and Society in Ireland*. Dublin: Gill and McMillan.

Epstein, D. (1993) *Changing Classroom Cultures – Antiracism, Politics and Schools*. Stoke-on-Trent: Trentham Books Limited.

Exchange House Travellers Service (2002) *The Danger of Words* (website addres: http://www.exchangehouse.ie/dangerofwords.htm) (Accessed: 21st September 2002).

Freire, P. (1999) *Pedagogy of Hope; Reliving Pedagogy of the Oppressed*. New York: The Continuum Publishing Company.

Harvey, B. (2002) *Rights and Justice Work in Ireland: A New Baseline*. London: Joseph Rowntree Charitable Trust.

Hyland, A. (2002) 'Looking to the Future – Ending Disadvantage?' in Gilligan, A.L. (ed.) *Primary Education: Ending Disadvantage, Proceedings and Action Plan of the National Forum*. Dublin: St. Patrick's College, Drumcondra.

Inglis, T. (1987) *Moral Monopoly: The Catholic Church in Modern Irish Society* Dublin: Gill and MacMillan.

IPA (2003) *Administration Yearbook and Diary 2003*. Dublin: IPA.

Ireland (1995) *Report of the Task Force on the Travelling Community*. Dublin: Government Stationery Office.

Ireland (1997) *The National Anti-Poverty Strategy – Sharing in Progress*. Dublin: Government Stationery Office.

Ireland (1999) *The National Development Plan 2000 – 2006*. Dublin: Government Stationery Office.

The Irish Times (17th April 2002)

The Irish Times (24th July 2002)

Jackson, J. and Haase, T. (1996) 'Demography and the Distribution of Deprivation in Rural Ireland' in Curtin, C., Haase, T. and Tovey, H. (eds.) *Poverty in Rural Ireland, A Political Economy Perspective*. Dublin: Oak Tree Press.

Kellaghan, T., Weir, S., O hUallachain, S. and Morgan, M (1995) *Educational*

Disadvantage in Ireland. Dublin: Department of Education, Combat Poverty Agency and The Educational Research Centre.

Lentin, R. (2000) 'Racialising the other, racialising the 'us': Emerging Irish identities as a process of racialisation' in Lentin, R. (ed.) *Emerging Irish Identities*. Dublin: Ethnic and Racial Studies and Department of Sociology, Trinity College.

Lentin, R. (2002) "Who ever heard of an Irish Jew?' Racialising the Intersection of 'Irishness' and 'Jewishness'" in Lentin, R. and McVeigh, R. (eds.) *Racism and Anti-Racism in Ireland*. Belfast: Beyond the Pale Publications.

Lewis, M. and Kellaghan, T. (1993) *Exploring the Gender Gap in Primary School*. Dublin: Educational Research Centre

Loyal, S. and Mulcahy, A. in association with FAQs Research (2001) *Racism in Ireland: The Views of Black & Ethnic Minorities*. Dublin: Amnesty International Irish Section.

Lynch, K. (1989) 'The ethos of girl's schools; an analysis of the differences between male and female schools' in *Social Studies* Vol. 10, No. 1-2, p. 11-31.

Lynch, K. (1999) *Equality in Education*. Dublin: Gill and MacMillan.

McDonagh, M. (1994) 'Nomadism in Irish Travellers' Identity' in McCann, M., Ó Síocháin, S., and Ruane, J. (eds.) *Irish Travellers, Culture and Ethnicity*. Belfast: Institute of Irish Studies.

McVeigh, R. and Lentin, R. (2002) 'Situated Racisms: A Theoretical Introduction' in Lentin, R. and McVeigh, R. (eds.) *Racism and Anti-Racism in Ireland*. Belfast: Beyond the Pale Publications.

Millett, K. (1977) *Sexual Politics*. London: Virago.

National Consultative Committee on Racism and Interculturalism (2001) (website: http//www.nccri.com) (Accessed 4th September 2001).

O'Connell, J. (2002) 'Travellers in Ireland: An examination of discrimination and racism' in Lentin, R. and McVeigh, R. (eds.) *Racism and Anti-Racism in Ireland*. Belfast: Beyond the Pale Publications.

O'Connor, P. (1998) *Emerging Voices, Women in Contemporary Irish Society*. Dublin: IPA.

Pavee Point (2002) 'Factsheets – Distribution' (website: http//www.paveepoint.ie) (Accessed June 2000)

Power, C. and Tormey, R. (2000) 'Refocusing the Debate: An Examination of the Interplay between Measurement and Intervention in Educational

Disadvantage' *CEDR Occasional Paper No. 2*. Limerick: Centre for Educational Disadvantage Research.

Regan, C. and Tormey, R. (2002) 'Migration and Development; No Papers, No Voice, No Rights..' in Regan, C. (ed.) *80:20 Development in an Unequal World*. Bray and Birmingham: 80:20 and TIDE.

Shor, I. (1993) 'Education is Politics: Paulo Freire's Critical Pedagogy' in McLaren, P. and Leonard, P. (eds.) *Paulo Freire, A Critical Encounter*. London: Routledge.

Tovey, H. and Share, P. (2000) *A Sociology of Ireland*. Dublin: Gill and Macmillan.

United Nations Development Programme (2002) *The Human Development Report 2002*. Oxford and New York: Oxford University Press.

United Nations High Commissioner for Refugees (2001) *Asylum Applications Submitted in Europe, 2000*. Geneva: Registration and Statistics Unit, UNHCR.

United Nations High Commissioner for Refugees (2002) *Trends in Asylum Applications Lodged in Europe, North America, Australia and New Zealand, 2001*. Geneva: UNHCR Population Data Unit.

Walby, S. (1990) *Theorising Patriarchy*. Oxford: Blackwell.

CHAPTER 3

MATHEMATICS EDUCATION IN GLOBAL AND POLITICAL CONTEXTS

Aisling Leavy

In the process of individualising its view of students, it (mathematics education) has lost any serious sense of the social structures and the race, gender and class relations that form these individuals. Furthermore, it is then unable to situate areas such as mathematics education in a wider, social context that includes large programs for democratic education and a more democratic society.
(Apple 1995, p.331)

The purpose of this paper is to challenge many of the assumptions that exist regarding the nature of mathematics and mathematics education. The first part of the paper presents three different perspectives on mathematics education: a) a political perspective, b) global, regional and local perspectives, and c) mathematics education within the perspective of teachers, students and classrooms. The second part of the paper examines the ramifications of ethnomathematics and situated theory for the teaching of mathematics.

POLITICAL ASPECTS OF MATHEMATICS EDUCATION

Recent international curricular statements suggest that mathematics is not a neutral discipline. The potential role that mathematics can play in the achievement of democratic ideals has been referred to by the South African Ministry of Education (South African Ministry of Education 1997), the Columbian General Education Act (*Ministerio de Educacion* cited in Skovsmose and Valero, 2000), the United States Curriculum and Evaluation Standards (National Council of Teachers of Mathematics 1992) and the Curriculum Guidelines in Mathematics of the Danish Ministry of Education (*Undervisningsministeriet* cited in Skovsmose and Valero, 2001). Furthermore, the notion of the existence of an intrinsic resonance between mathematics education and democracy has been suggested (Skovsmose and Valero 2001). Proponents of this view maintain that the study of mathematics provides individuals with the skills to contribute to the technological, political, and socio-economic development of society (Niss 1996).

The notion of mathematics as value-free, amoral or apolitical has been challenged (Bishop 1988; D'Ambrosio 1997; Fasheh 1990; Frankenstein 1987). Evidence exists of the negative influence of mathematics on society, predominantly due to its association with the tools of warfare, disease and environmental destruction (D'Ambrosio 1994). A study of the antidemocratic uses of mathematics paints a poignant picture of its power to isolate and make powerless members of society. Nazi mathematics advanced technological developments that brought about destruction, and the mathematicians themselves were never held accountable for their contributions to the regime (Mehrtens 1993). In South Africa, apartheid education excluded Blacks from mathematics hence excluding them from participation in society. A statement by H. Verwoerd (1954) in his address to the South African Senate questions "the use of teaching the Bantu mathematics when he cannot use it in practice."

Mathematics education has played a less than positive role in promoting the tenets of democracy. The dominant justification for the presence of mathematics education is the role it plays in educating a productive and technologically savvy workforce. However, at the individual level where complex mathematics is not a requirement, the most common reason for teaching mathematics is 'because we use mathematics everyday'. Recent studies are challenging the assumption that school mathematics is put to critical use in our everyday lives. On the contrary, it seems that the mathematical procedures used in everyday situations are not those taught in school (Lave 1977; Lave et al.1984; Nunes et al. 1993). In fact, it has been suggested that a possible reason for the inclusion of certain forms of mathematics is not as a means to equip our students with necessary skills but rather to serve as a "filter restricting the choices for individuals" (Mukhopadhyay and Greer 2001). The role of mathematics education as an "objective judge" (Volmink 1994), differentiating the able from the less able, has lead to differentiation and exclusion. Mathematics education has lead to stratification in educational circles of those who possess mathematical knowledge and those who do not and hence has become a gatekeeper that dictates participation in certain elements of society. The civil rights leader Robert Moses (2001) identifies mathematics education as a civil rights issue. His argument is supported by findings that disproportionate numbers of poor children and children of colour are performing below average on mathematical competency assessments and dropping out of mathematics courses, thus denying them access to skills necessary for economic enfranchisement. He argues

Today ... the most urgent social issue affecting poor people and people of color is economic access. In today's world, economic access and full citizenship depend crucially on math and science literacy. I believe that the absence of math literacy in urban and rural communities throughout this country is an issue as urgent as the lack of Black voters in Mississippi was in 1961. (Moses, 2001, p.5)

As can be seen, mathematics has played a varied role both in the maintenance and destruction of democratic ideals. Mathematics can no longer be conceived as independent of the people who use it. Considerations need to be made as to who uses mathematics, and to what purposes it is used. Whereas previous connotations of mathematics education were associated with students, teachers, and classrooms; more recently, mathematics education has been viewed through a broader lens that takes into account the wider social practices of mathematics and mathematics education. Hence mathematics education research has experienced a shift from a psychologically oriented theoretical framework to frameworks attempting to merge the social and psychological aspects of teaching and learning mathematics, leading to construction of the notion of mathematics education as both an academic activity and a social practice.

GLOBAL, REGIONAL AND LOCAL CONTEXTS OF MATHEMATICS EDUCATION

It is currently accepted that mathematics is becoming the most internationalised subject of higher education, a belief substantiated by the abundance of international organisations (International Commission of Mathematics Instruction), conferences and study groups (International Congress for Mathematics Education, International Group for the Psychology of Mathematics Education, International Organisation of Women and Mathematics Education, World Federation of National Mathematics Competitions), and journals (Journal for Research in Mathematics Education, For the Learning of Mathematics, and Educational Studies in Mathematics). Despite these international links, the discipline of mathematics education remains dominated by Anglo-European voices and opinions, the language of discourse is primarily English, and the visibility of educators from developing countries at conferences and in journal publications is low (Bishop 1992; Clements and Ellerton 1996; Jacobson 1996).

This internationalisation of mathematics education is not a recent phenomenon. The most palpable example comes from the colonisation of developing countries at the conclusion of World Wars I and II. Many of the colonised countries modelled their educational curricula and teacher education programs on that of their mandate country. Organisations such as the United Nations, UNESCO, and the World Bank have sponsored many projects aimed at eliminating illiteracy, projects whose primary focus is on the development of Western-like mathematics education programs (Souviney 1983). Another phenomenon contributing to the internationalisation of mathematics education is that of overseas study. Many developing countries operate education programs sponsoring students to undertake postgraduate studies in many academic areas, including mathematics and mathematics education. However, the skills and information acquired by many of these students is not reaped by their native countries due to the 'brain drain' resulting from the non-return of these academicians (UNESCO 1998).

An increased internationalisation of the mathematics education community has lead to a visible globalisation of mathematics education. This globalisation is evident in the similarity of international curriculum documents in terms of the mathematical content, focus and aims of the mathematics curricula. Reforms of mathematics curricula in developed countries are closely followed by similar reforms in developing countries. This globalisation of mathematics education is not without criticism. Concerns relating to the dominance of Western mathematics and the potential dangers of this dominance in the context of other cultures were voiced at the seventh ICME conference. Mathematics education researchers warned against the globalisation of mathematics education stressing, "our differences provide the best situation for curriculum development and implementation" (Uisiskin 1992, p. 20). Clements (1995, p. 3) aptly highlighted what many international educators have been long aware of when he stated "I have often had cause to reflect that it is western educators who were responsible not only for getting their own mathematics teacher equation wrong, but also for passing on their errors to education systems around the world".

Interestingly, the Western world's attempts to support a move from Western dominated mathematics in order to legitimise and authenticate cultural specific mathematical practices have met with disapproval from several mathematics educators from developing countries. Arguments have been made by the African Mathematical Union (Kuku 1995) and Asian mathematics educators (Sawiran 1995) that a move towards an ethnomathematical or situated curriculum in developing countries would impede students in developing the skills in the types of mathematics that support the economic and technological development of their countries, hence decreasing the ability of developing countries to compete in an increasingly globalised world.

TEACHERS, STUDENTS AND CLASSROOMS

The teaching of mathematics, as we see it in the classroom, does not emulate many of the ideals associated with democracy. An examination of *what* mathematics is taught and *how* it is taught sheds light on what happens to the notion of democracy in mathematics classrooms.

How is mathematics taught? Democratic forms of interaction in mathematics classrooms are only recently becoming more prevalent and at that only in limited educational settings. Many mathematics classrooms remain dominated by forms of authority represented either through teachers, textbooks or tools. The absolutism of these authorities limits the space available for dialogue, student voice, or communication of anything other than esoteric mathematical principles.

What mathematics is taught? The recent emergence of ethnomathematics has focused attention on the types of mathematics being taught in classrooms. In highly technological societies, mathematics is an essential and critical component of development. Mathematical skill, and corresponding technical expertise, lead to technological and economic development. This development leads to a need for greater mathematical expertise to sustain and develop these technological environments, hence leading to greater formalisation and mathematisation of society (Gellert *et al.* 2001). However, the importance of the mathematics being taught in school has become less relevant to the lives of students, as many of the mathematical processes once carried out by hand are now being undertaken by new tools and technologies.

The essential components of mathematical literacy are different now from what they once were. Part of the reason for the change is due to the work of situated cognitivists and ethnomathematicians who have contrasted the institutionalised scientific systems of Western mathematical practices with the integrated cultural practices evident in the mathematics of non-western cultures. Gellert *et al.* (2001) have identified several approaches to mathematics education that challenge previous conceptions of mathematical literacy: teaching modelling, using mathematics for social critique, and using ethnomathematics as cultural critique.

Curricular approaches concerned with teaching modelling and applications of modelling are concerned with equipping students with the skills to allow them use mathematics as a flexible tool that enhances their ability to progress through society. Such curricula use real-world situations as the starting point for mathematics activity (Banu 1991; Bishop 1988; de Vore 1987). Examples of such curricula are Mathematics in Context (National Centre for Research in Mathematical Sciences at the University of Wisconsin/Madison and Freudenthal Institute at the University of Utrecht 1997-1998), and the Quantitative Literacy Project (American Statistical Association and National Council of Teachers of Mathematics 1986).

Curricular approaches that use mathematics for social critique are primarily concerned with preventing the reproduction of school knowledge. This reproduction occurs through the presentation of mathematical tasks and practices that do not reflect the interests of marginalised pupils, and results in the development of an unhealthy relationship with school (Mellin-Olsen 1989). Mathematics, when used as a tool for social critique, should facilitate the questioning of assumptions of how society is structured. This can be achieved through a shift from a focus on technical aspects of quantitative data analysis and a resulting 'number numbness' (Peterson 1995), to a focus on analysis of issues and data of importance to minority populations such as Native Americans.

Ethnomathematics (D'Ambrosio 1985) challenges formal school mathematics, and educators from this perspective argue for the inclusion of culturally familiar contexts and problems in school mathematics. Mathematicians coming from an ethnomathematical perspective emphasise the diversity of mathematical approaches deriving from different cultures and are concerned with moving away from a definition of mathematics as a rigidly defined abstract activity.

The remainder of this paper focuses on the potential contributions of ethnomathematics and situated mathematics to classroom mathematical practices in the Western world. In particular, an examination of several keystone studies of situated mathematical practice is undertaken and their ramifications for the teaching of mathematics identified.

ETHNOMATHEMATICS, SITUATED MATHEMATICS AND EVERYDAY SCHOOL MATHEMATICS

Mathematics is embedded in different cultures and what is defined as mathematics is becoming ever increasingly culturally determined. Interpretations of the term ethnomathematics have caused debate regarding the meaning(s) of the term. Early interpretations (Gerdes 1988, p. 138) viewed ethnomathematics as the mathematics implicit within certain cultures or a "spontaneous, natural, informal indigenous, folk, implicit, non-standard, and/or hidden (ethno)mathematics". This interpretation led to the identification and examination of Western mathematical ideas embedded in non-Western cultural practices. However, ethnomathematics constitutes more than examination of cultural specific (for example, Mayan or Babylonian) counting systems or (Inuit or Navaho) classifications of shapes. Later versions of ethnomathematics took on a socio-political view (Finau et al. cited in Stillman and Balatti 2001; Gerdes 1994; Millroy 1992). The socio-political view of ethnomathematics was described by Gerdes (1994, p. 20) as the study of "mathematics (or mathematical ideas) in its (their) relationship to the whole of cultural and social life". These orientations lead to an examination of the suitability of Western mathematics in non-Western cultures and provided authentication for the hidden mathematics embedded in cultural-economic activity. The more recently accepted definition of ethnomathematics is:

> the mathematics which is practiced among identifiable cultural groups, such as national-tribal societies, labour groups, children of a certain age bracket, professional classes, and so on. Its identity depends largely on focuses of interest, on motivation, and on certain codes and jargons which do not belong to the realm of academic mathematicians (D'Ambrosio 1985, p.45).

The attention of many researchers in the fields of mathematics education and mathematics has focused on the means by which ethnomathematics can enhance the teaching and learning of 'school-based' mathematics. School mathematics represents a narrow subset of the range of mathematical activities. A focus on ethnomathematics can help teachers construct culturally relevant pedagogy and challenge the assumption that mathematics is a product of the intellectual activity of white western men. Much can be discovered about the nature of learning by investigating situations in which individuals appear to be effective problem solvers. One belief is that the information gained from the analysis of out-of-school problem-solving activities can be used to restructure the approach of teaching certain activities in school settings, resulting in practical problem-solving skills similar to those utilised by people in everyday settings (D'Ambrosio 1990).

Several keystone studies investigated the situated (more commonly referred to as 'street mathematics') and ethnomathematical mathematics of people in a variety of cultural contexts. These studies have influenced the way that mathematics educators view the teaching and learning of mathematics. The next section examines the findings of several such studies, provides explanations for the effectiveness of mathematics procedures carried out in situated contexts, and provides suggestions for changes in the teaching of mathematics.

Findings of Situated and Ethnomathematical Studies of Mathematical Behaviours

Children do not utilise school taught algorithms out of the school context. A study carried out by Carraher *et al.* (1985a)[1] found that Brazilian street traders use computational strategies different from those taught in schools. The study involved a tester who acted as a customer and asked the (child) trader to calculate the cost of purchases and amount of change in a normal sales transaction. Despite the fact that the majority of the street traders had received formal instruction on mathematical operations and word problems, none used algorithms or a pen and paper in carrying out calculations. The children used mental computations that were related to the quantities in question (cost and number of items being purchased).

In the school context, children's computational procedures are most effective when they use informal strategies. In a study carried out by Michael Hass (cited in Lave 1997), children were given instruction in specific computational procedures. The children produced correct solutions to answers, however further investigations found that they used counting and regrouping strategies to solve the problem rather than using the new strategy being taught.

The situation in which the problem is presented elicits the strategy/procedure to be used². Carraher *et al*. (1987) found that the context in which mathematical computation problems are presented influences the choice of solution method. Problems were presented in three different situations (i) as a simulated store situation, (ii) as embedded in word story problems, or as (iii) as computation exercises. A significant effect of situation on choice of procedures was found. Oral procedures rather than written procedures were more likely to be used when computational exercises were presented in the form of store problems and word problems. On the other hand, written procedures were more likely to be used when the problems were presented as computational exercises.

Choice of procedure determines success. This outcome, when considered in the context of the previous finding, represents a significant finding in terms of implications for education. The Carraher *et al*. (1987) study found that the number of correct responses was related to the procedures selected rather than the problem context. Oral computation had greater success than written computation. The computational problems were significantly less likely to be solved; hence it seemed that children were significantly more successful when using oral computational procedures than when using written procedures.

Explanations for the Effectiveness of Mathematical Procedures carried out in Real-World Contexts

Mathematics as the central dilemma of ongoing activity. It is useful at this point to turn our attention to what Lave (1997) termed as 'focusing on learning in doing'. Lave describes a study of children in an upper-mathematics group who designed their own mathematical algorithms to provide solutions to problems posed in the classroom situation. However, they disguised their answers to reflect what they viewed as the appropriate method to solve the problems (those methods demonstrated by the teacher). The main dilemmas for the children were performance dilemmas rather than mathematical dilemmas. Lave argues that mathematical problems must be dilemma motivated. Situations such as those described above do not occur in real world contexts because the dilemmas faced are mathematical ones (street vendors calculating the cost of a purchase, supermarket shoppers making price comparisons). The methods normally used are the most efficient one. Hence, the aim for classrooms is to make the mathematical activity authentic, make mathematical activity the central dilemma, and make the outcome of the mathematical problem have significance other than in terms of a grade.

Ownership of a mathematical problem, it would seem, is an important aspect in mathematical problem solving. The problem must pose a real dilemma; otherwise the problem does not pose as a problem, rather as a constraint. School mathematical activities should be dilemma motivated. A problem prevalent in school activity is that the solution to the problem is considered as the endpoint of the activity. This contrasts to real world mathematics activities in which the mathematics problem solving is not an end in itself.

The use of oral procedures. Resulting from the Carraher *et al.* (1987) study, the authors conclude that the superior success rate with oral procedures as compared to written procedures should be given more emphasis and consideration as a way of promoting the development of mathematical understanding. In the study, all cases involving oral computation had greater success. The children solved the problems with ease when utilising oral procedures but experienced difficulties associated with written procedures for the same problems. The authors point out that written procedures have many problems associated with them. Essentially, written procedures involve manipulation of symbols (Lave 1981). The symbols are not connected with any real problems and effective problem solving requires children to carry out a number of manipulations and procedures on the symbols.

The oral procedures utilised by the children, however, are not preset or fixed. They do not involve the manipulation of symbols disconnected from reality. Rather, students work on quantities that are meaningful. This does not result in the type of errors that occur with the use of algorithms i.e. mixing up rules, applying incorrect algorithms.

Mathematics is embedded in a context – this context contains information that helps solve the problem. The Carraher and Schliemann (1985b)[3] study found that problems that were embedded in a context were more easily solved than those not embedded in context. In their study, ninety-eight percent of the items in the informal test (embedded in context) were solved while seventy-three point three per cent of the word problems and thirty-six point eight per cent of the mathematics problems in the formal test were solved. Lave *et al.* (1984) point to the success of the mathematics computation carried out by supermarket shoppers as being attributed to the problems being presented in context. The arithmetic, they claim, was immersed in a context steeped in meaning. The calculations carried out were characterised by the simplification procedures used by the subject. In order to simplify the problem, the shopper needed to understand what she was doing.

Brown *et al.* (1989, p. 36) also speak of the importance of context. School activities, they claim, are not authentic activities. Authentic activities are the ordinary activities of the culture; school activities do not reflect the practices of mathematicians. Hence, the activity in schools is "hybrid ... implicitly framed by one culture, but explicitly attributed to another." This hybrid activity that occurs in schools "limits students access to the important structuring and supporting cues that arise from the context." Removing knowledge from the context often results in removing implicit knowledge from the domain and attempting to make it explicit. This adds to the learning 'load'. In addition, very little of the activity that occurs in practice can be made the subject of explicit instruction. Much of the mathematics remains implicit in the practice itself where it is available for the learner to acquire. In many cases, the implicit knowledge loses its value in the process of being explicated. Another important consideration is that the explicit can become outdated or redundant as the practice evolves but the implicit is dynamic and evolves with practice.

Brown *et al.* (1989, p. 36) refer to the dieters in a Weight Watchers study and the solutions they came up with to the arithmetic problems. The authors mention the advantages of using useful aspects of the task and state that the understanding of the context helps to "limit and to share the representational and computational load."

Suggestions For The Teaching Of Mathematics

Questioning the correct time to begin teaching mathematics algorithms. These findings question the long-held belief that physical and pictorial representations are the most appropriate models to introduce addition and subtraction. Another belief is that children must master addition and subtraction algorithms before they can attempt verbal problems. The meaning and context afforded to addition and subtraction problems by the use of a narrative context has been commented on by Carpenter and Moser (1982). The findings by Carraher *et al.* provide support for Carpenter and Moser's position and raise doubts about the practice of teaching mathematics operations in a disembedded form before applying them to real problems. Carraher *et al.* accept that children have to eventually learn how to carry out algorithms, however their study highlights the central question of "where is the proper pedagogical point of departure?" (1985, p. 28). Findings from situated and ethnographic studies suggest that the proper point of departure is starting with context bound word problems and moving from there to algorithmic problems. Yet, we tend to teach algorithms first and then turn our attention to word problems. Perhaps, we have, as St. Julien (1994 cited in Kirshner and Whitson 1997, p. 270) terms it, "things backwards".

Identify the strategies utilised by children in real world mathematics activities and teach these strategies in the classroom. One strategy utilised by children is manipulation of quantities versus manipulation of symbols. Lave's (1981) study of Vai and Gola tailors identifies two approaches for performing arithmetic operations. The first is the 'manipulation-of-quantities' approach, which is universal (they claim) and represented in terms of counting on fingers, or using objects as tallies. The second approach is the 'manipulation-of-symbols' approach, which stems from western algorithmic manipulations. It is the manipulation of symbols that occurs out of context and 'carries the burden of computation.' Carraher *et al.* (1985a) also found that the daily problem solving carried out by the street traders involved the use of strategies involving the mental computation of quantities[4]. The authors point out that problems presented in the school- type situation involve the manipulation of symbols. This manipulation of symbols carries the extra burden of computation, which divorces even more the operation from any real context.

Another strategy utilised by children was checking adequacy of solutions. The importance of this strategy was highlighted by the Carraher *et al.* study. They state that in all cases where the algorithms were carried out (formal tests in all cases) there was no evidence of the children checking the adequacy of their solutions. In the example of the three coconuts, the child does not realise the inappropriateness of his answer[5]. The lack of attention to the quantity/size of an answer resulting from an algorithmic procedure is particularly obvious in the example cited by Carraher *et al.* (1995a) where the child is presented with a word problem[6]. It doesn't appear strange to the child that the second fisherman caught 36 fish, even though he supposedly caught five times as many fish as the first fisherman (who caught 50 fish).

Identify the specific mathematical heuristics utilised by children in the mathematics contexts and design instruction so as to place focus on these useful strategies. The specific heuristics identified by Carraher and Schliemann (1985b) are based on a qualitative analysis of children's spontaneous oral mathematical procedures. They refer to these oral mathematical procedures as 'heuristics.' Two main types of heuristics were identified. The Decomposing Heuristic involved decomposing some of the numbers presented in the problem into smaller more manageable units. The Repeated Grouping Heuristic was utilised for multiplication and division problems and involves 'chunking' (carrying out multiplication through successive additions or division through successive subtractions).

Examination of ethnomathematical and situated contexts provide insight into the mathematical practices of people for whom mathematics is a fundamental component of their daily work activities. Table 1 provides a summary of the findings resulting from these studies and presents guidelines for designing classroom-based experiences.

Table 1: Creation of classroom cultures that capture the practices of Situated and Ethnomathematical theories

Findings of Situated and Ethnomathematical theories	*Classroom implementation strategies*
Children need to engage in authentic tasks in authentic contexts.	Anchor instruction in a real-world event (authenticity of objects and data).
Children carry out computations with greater ease and success when problems are presented in a context.	Encourage the use of informal procedures in conjunction with the formal mathematical algorithms, so as to maintain the connection with the real context.
The success observed in situated contexts is due mainly to the procedures elicited by the context.	Problems presented must be a means to an end and not an end in themselves (authenticity of problem situation).
Informal (oral) mathematical procedures result in most success.	
Children are more efficient in solving word problems than school algorithmic problems that are disembodied from context.	Teach oral mathematical procedures for problems prior to algorithmic procedures.
The errors resulting from the use of algorithms are senseless errors, often consisting of large numerical quantities.	Increase emphasis on checking answers – particularly, the use of using informal mathematical procedures to check the answers on problems solved using algorithms.

CONCLUSION

Mathematics has developed out of the social and cultural needs of peoples and societies. These needs provide the contexts out of which the central activity in relation to mathematics is meaning making. However, once these mathematical practices are moved into the school environment the mathematics is divorced from the context within which it was developed, making it considerably difficult to make mathematical ideas meaningful to the learners. The construction of links between in-school mathematics and out-of-school experiences helps children see mathematics as a useful and critical tool, facilitates generalisability of mathematics learned within the school context, and makes children more mathematically powerful.

NOTES

[1] Investigation of the oral mathematics procedures carried out by children in a non-school context was the focus of a study carried out by Carraher *et al.* (1985a). They examined the everyday use of mathematics by Brazilian street traders by examining the mathematical practices of five street traders aged 9-15 years old. They presented both an informal test (which was presented in the course of a normal business transaction) and a formal test.

[2] Carraher *et al.* (1987) investigated the oral calculation procedures used by children in schools and contrasted them to the written mathematical procedures used by the same children.

[3] Carraher and Schliemann (1985b) investigated the procedures used by 50 Brazilian school children when solving seven addition and four subtraction problems.

[4] A nine year old street trader was asked the following question while in the running of a normal business transaction (in an informal testing situation):

"Customer: OK, I'll take three coconuts (at the price of Cr$40 each). How much is that?

Child: (without gestures calculates out loud) 40, 80,120." (p. 26)

[5] The street trader (a nine-year-old child) was asked to compute 3 times 40. "The child solves the item 40*3 and obtains 70. She then explains the procedure 'Lower the zero; 4 and 3 is 7'" Pg. 26

[6] "Test item: A fisherman caught 50 fish. The second one caught five times the amount of fish the first fisherman caught. How many fish did the lucky fisherman catch?

Child: (Writes down 50*6 and 360 as the result; then answers) 36.

Examiner repeats the problems and the child does the computation again, writing down 860 as a result. His oral response is 86.

REFERENCES

American Statistical Association and National Council of Teachers of Mathematics (1986). *Quantitative Literacy Series*. Dale Seymour Publications.

Anderson, J.R., Reder, L.M., and Simon, H.A. (1997). 'Situative Versus Cognitive Perspectives: Form Versus Substance'. *Educational Researcher*, 26(1), 18-21.

Apple, M. (1995). 'Taking power seriously: New directions in equity in mathematics education and beyond' in Secada, W.G., Fennema, E. and Adajian, L.B. (eds.) *New directions for equity in mathematics education*. Cambridge, UK: Cambridge University Press.

Banu, H. (1991). 'The importance of mathematical modelling in Bangladesh'. in Niss, M., Blum, W., and Huntley, I. (eds.) *Teaching of mathematical modelling and applications*. Chichester: Ellis Horwood.

Bishop, A. (1988). *Mathematical enculturation. A cultural perspective on mathematics education*. Dordrecht: Kluwer.

Bishop, A. (1992). 'International perspectives on research in mathematics education' in Grouws, D. (eds.) *Handbook of research on mathematics teaching and learning*. New York, Macmillan.

Brown, J.S., Collins, A., & Duguid, P. (1989). 'Situated Cognition and the culture of learning'. *Educational Researcher*, 18, 32-42.

Carpenter, T.P., and Moser, J.M. (1982). 'The development of addition and subtraction problem solving skills' in Carpenter, T.P., Moser, J.M., and Romberg, T.A. (eds) *Addition and Subtraction: A Cognitive Perspective*. Hillsdale, NJ: Lawrence Erlbaum Associates.

Carraher, T.N., Carraher, D.W., and Schliemann, A.D. (1985a). 'Mathematics in the streets and in schools'. *British Journal of Developmental Psychology*, 3, 21-29.

Carraher, T.N., and Schliemann, A.D. (1985b). 'Computation Routines Prescribed by Schools: Help or Hindrance?' *Journal for Research in Mathematics Education*, 16(1), 37-44.

Carraher, T. N., Carraher, D. W., and Schlieman, A. D. (1987). Written and oral mathematics. *Journal for Research in Mathematics Education*, 18(2), 83-97.

Clements, K. (1995). 'Restructuring mathematics teacher education: Overcoming the barriers of elitism and separatism' in Hunting, R., Fitzsimons, G.,

Clarkson, P. and Bishop, A. (eds.) *Regional collaboration in mathematics education*. Melbourne: Monash University.

Clements, K. and Ellerton, N. (1996). *Mathematics Education Research: Past, Present and Future*. Bangkok: UNESCO.

D'Ambrosio, U. (1985). 'Ethnomathematics and its place in the history and pedagogy of mathematics'. *For the Learning of Mathematics*, 5(1), 44-48.

D'Ambrosio, U. (1990). 'The role of mathematics education in building a democratic and just society'. *For the Learning of Mathematics*, 10(3), 20-23.

D'Ambrosio, U. (1994). 'Cultural framing of mathematics teaching and learning' in Biehler, R., Scholz, R.W., Strässer, R. and Winkelmann, B. (eds.) *Didactics of mathematics as a scientific discipline*. Dordrecht: Kluwer.

D'Ambrosio, U. (1997). 'Where does mathematics stand nowadays?' *For the Learning of Mathematics*, 17(2), 13-17.

Fasheh, M. (1990). 'Community education: to reclaim and transform what has been made invisible'. *Harvard Educational Review*, 60(19-35), 2-8.

Frankenstein, M. (1987). 'Critical mathematics education: An application of Freire's epistemology' in Shor, I. (ed.) *Freire for the classroom: A sourcebook for liberatory teaching*. Portsmouth NH: Boynton/Cook.

Gellert, U. Jablonka, E. and Keitel, C. (2001). 'Mathematical Literacy and Commonsense in Mathematics Education' in Atweh, B., Forgasz, H. and Nebres, B. (eds.) *Sociocultural Research on Mathematics Education: An International Perspective*. Mahwah, NJ: Lawrence Erlbaum Associates.

Gerdes, P. (1988). 'Culture and geometrical thinking'. *Educational Studies in Mathematics*, 19, 137-162.

Gerdes, P. (1994). 'Reflections on ethnomathematics'. *For The Learning of Mathematics*, 14(2), 19-22.

Ginsburg, H.P. (1981). 'The Development of Mental Addition as a Function of Schooling and Culture'. *Journal of Cross-Cultural Psychology*, 12(2), 163-78.

Jacobsen, E. (1996). 'International Co-operation in mathematics education' in Bishop, A., Clements, M.A., Keitel, C., Kilpatrick, J., & Laborde, C. (eds.), *International Handbook of Mathematics Education*. Dordrecht: Kluwer.

Kirshner, D. and Whitson, J.A. (1997). *Situated Cognition: Social, Semiotic, and Psychological Perspectives*. Mahwah, NJ: Lawrence Erlbaum.

Kuku, A. (1995). 'Mathematics education in Africa in relation to other countries' in Hunting, R., Fitzsimons, G., Clarkson, P. and Bishop, A. (eds.) *Regional collaboration in mathematics education*. Melbourne: Monash University.

Lave, J. (1977). 'Cognitive consequences of traditional apprenticeship training in West Africa'. *Anthropology and Education Quarterly*, 7, 177-180.

Lave, J. (1997). 'The Culture of Acquisition and the Practice of Understanding' in D. Kirschner and J. Whitson (eds.) *Situated Cognition: Social, Semiotic and Psychological Perspectives*. Lawrence Erlbaum Associates.

Lave, J., Murtaugh, M. and de Rocha, O. (1984). 'The dialectic of arithmetic in grocery shopping' in Rogoff, B. and Lave, J. (eds.) *Everyday cognition: Its development in social context*. Cambridge, MA: Harvard University Press.

Mehrtens, H. (1993). 'The social system of mathematics and social nationalism: A survey' in Restivo, R., Bendegem, J.P. and van Fisher, R. (eds.) *Maths worlds: Philosophical and social studies of mathematics and mathematics education*. Albany: State University of New York Press.

Mellin-Olsen, S. (1989). *The politics of mathematics education*. Dordrecht: Reidel.

Millroy, W.L. (1992). 'An ethnomathematical study of the mathematical ideas of a group of carpenters'. *Journal for Research in Mathematics Education Monograph No. 5*. Reston VA: NCTM.

Moses, R.P. (2001). *Radical equations: Math literacy and civil rights*. Boston: Beacon Press.

Mukhopadhyay, S. and Greer, B. (2001). 'Modelling with Purpose: Mathematics as a critical tool', in Atweh, B., Forgasz, H. and Nebres, B. (eds.) *Sociocultural Research on Mathematics Education: An International Perspective*. Mahwah, NJ: Lawrence Erlbaum Associates.

National Center for Research in Mathematical Sciences at the University of Wisconsin/Madison and Freudenthal Institute at the University of Utrecht (1997-1998). *Mathematics in context*. Britannica, USA.

NCTM (1992). *Curriculum and evaluation standards for school mathematics*. Addenda Serie, grades 9-12. Reston, VA: Author.

Niss, M. (1996). 'Goals of mathematics teaching' in Bishop, A. Clements, K.,

Keitel, C., Kilpatrick, J. and Laborde, C. (eds.) *International handbook of mathematics education*. Dordrecht: Kluwer.

Nunes, T., Schliemann, A.D., and Carraher, D.W. (1993). *Street mathematics and school mathematics*. Cambridge, UK: Cambridge University Press.

Peterson, B. (1995). 'Teaching math across the curriculum'. *Rethinking Schools*, 10(1), 4-5.

Sawiran, M. (1995). 'Collaborative efforts in enhancing globalisation in mathematics education' in Hunting, R., Fitzsimons, G., Clarkson, P. and Bishop, A. (eds.) *Regional collaboration in mathematics education*. Melbourne: Monash University.

Skovsmose, O. and Valero, P. (2001). 'Breaking Political Neutrality: The Critical Engagement of Mathematics Education with Democracy' in Atweh, B., Forgasz, H., Nebres, B. (eds.) *Sociocultural Research on Mathematics Education: An International Perspective*. Mahwah, NJ: Lawrence Erlbaum Associates.

South African Ministry of Education (2001). *National Strategy for Mathematics, Science and Technology Education in General and Further Education Training*. (Website address: http://education.pwv.gov.za/DoE_Sites/Maths%20and%20Science/Maths%20Science%20htm/national_strategy_for_mathematic.htm.) (Accessed 19/02/02).

Souviney, R. (1983). 'Mathematics achievement, language, and cognitive development: Classroom practices in Papa New Guinea'. *Educational Studies in Mathematics*, 14, 183-212.

Stillman, G. and Balatti, J. (2001) 'Contribution of Ethnomathematics to mainstream Mathematics Classroom Practice in B. Atweh, H. Forgasz & B. Nebres (Eds.), *Sociocultural Research on Mathematics Education: An International Perspective*. Mahwah, NJ: Lawrence Erlbaum Associates.

Uisiskin, Z. (1992). 'Thoughts of an ICME regular'. *For the Learning of Mathematics*, 12(3), 19-20.

UNESCO. (1998). *Brain Drain to Brain Gain*. (Website address: http://www.unesco.org/education/studyingabroad/highlights/brain_drain.shtml) (Accessed 19/02/02).

Volmink, J. (1994). 'Mathematics for all' in Lerman, S. (ed.), *Cultural perspectives on the mathematics classroom*. Dordrecht: Kluwer.

de Vore, P.W. (1987). 'Cultural paradigms and technological literacy'. *Bulletin of Science, Technology, and Society*, 7(5 and 6), 711-719.

CHAPTER 4

WHOSE SCIENCE DO WE TEACH? - DEFINING SCIENCE FOR TEACHING SOCIAL JUSTICE ISSUES

Neil Ó Conaill

Teaching about social justice issues inevitably involves the identification of unjust events and practices that shape our society and societies throughout the world. In identifying these practices, and understanding their origins, the use of scientific knowledge is a recurrent theme in any attempt to make sense of where we are now. This paper highlights the value of postcolonial histories of science for giving a more comprehensive reading of historical events and for evaluating the role science has played shaping the tide of history. It also asks if our Science Curriculum provides the scope for teachers to incorporate a social justice perspective in their science teaching. It makes the case that, without a broad definition of science, particularly within an educational context, it is difficult to assess science's responsibility for past events or to map out a positive role for it in future.

Asking the question, 'whose science do we teach', presupposes that there is an accepted body of knowledge or way of working that is universally accepted as science. The question is framed to inform us more of those excluded from the answer than included: as with calling the roll at school, you want to know who is not there as much as who is present. The significance of whose science we teach is determined by the purposes or functions ascribed to the scientific knowledge taught.

Of course, as a way of making sense of our environment, science is universal. If, however, we accept the uncontentious definition of science as making sense of our world, then why is the sense that some cultures make valued more than that of others? This issue of accepted scientific knowledge is important since, as Fuller (1991, p. 177) points out, when a discipline earns the title science it "acquires the authority to promulgate truthful and reliable knowledge, control over education and credentials, access to money and manpower, and the kind of political clout that comes from possessing knowledge that is essential yet esoteric".

It is because of this power yielded by science that it is important to address the definition of science, what knowledge and process is accepted and what is not, and, more crucially, the issue of access to these dynamics. Exclusion is the currency of power as Apple (1996) and Bernstein (1971) have written. Consider how appropriate Apple's assertion is in the domain of scientific knowledge:

> The decision to define some groups' knowledge as the most legitimate, as official knowledge, while other groups' knowledge hardly sees the light of day, says something extremely important about who has power in society (Apple 1996, p. 22).

If science is defined in a particular way in the context of science education, those empowered to define it also have a view regarding its purpose and value.

Harding (1998, p. 21) highlights the significance of this power in the context if an information technology and science-based economy in asserting that:

> ...whoever owns 'nature' and has access to it, whoever has the capital and knowledge to decide just how best they can access nature's resources and how such resources will be used - these are the people [to whom] the benefits of contemporary scientific and technological change largely will accrue.

The issue for Harding is not solely the right of access to 'nature' but also the manner in which the resources will be used and for whose benefit.

This is a post-modernist view of the dominant role science and technology can play in the shaping of culture and society, rather than simply contributing to it. The postcolonial histories of science which have emerged in the last fifty years have revealed how closely related scientific developments in Europe were to countries colonial expansion. The scientific enquiries in the sixteenth and seventeenth centuries were driven by the economic and political opportunities which were offered in the Americas, West Africa and in India. Scientific endeavour was applied to exploit the natural resources and ecology of these areas for the benefit of the West. These cultures were found to be scientifically and technologically advanced, but their advances in areas such as navigational instrumentation, local knowledge of geology, plants, medicine and agriculture were appropriated by the West. Harding (1998) details how the voyages of discovery were fuelled by the ability of science to extract the maximum from new lands, from the Americas to India - from the development of the coffee and indigo crops, to the study of tetanus and anti-malaria treatments. The scientific and technological advancements that accompanied the colonial expansion led to the enrichment of the colonisers but "delivered increases in mortality rates and human bondage" for the colonised (Harding 1998, p. 46).

It could be said that this era of expansion made European science truly multicultural, but modern science refuses to acknowledge the contributions made by other cultures. The effect of this exclusion is both epistemological and cultural since, as Kawagley *et al.* (1998 p.134) point out, its exclusion:

> ...not only diminishes the legitimacy of knowledge derived through generations of naturalistic observation and insight, it simultaneously devalues those cultures which traditionally rely heavily on naturalistic observation and insight.

Cobern and Loving (1998) relate many examples of this traditional ecological knowledge to illustrate multicultural perspectives on science - particularly the anecdote of the conversation between the western scientist and the South Pacific islander. The latter disputed the West's use of the moon to explain the tides. He continued - the ocean rises and falls as the great sea turtles leave and return to their homes in the sand. The ocean falls as the water rushes into the empty nest. The ocean rises as the water is forced out by the returning turtles. If science is making sense of Nature in a systematic way, here then is a genuine constructivist scientist - rejecting explanations that do not conform to his observations. This approach to developing scientific understanding exemplifies *the process as significant as the content* view of science education. Clearly the Irish Primary School Science Curriculum promotes this view as it states:

> What distinguishes a scientific activity from other forms of enquiry is not the sophistication of the ideas used but the process through which these ideas are developed. (Ireland 1999b, p.2)

The postcolonial readings of the history of science are uncomfortable readings for those espousing the dominant ideology which lauds science as society's benefactor. This dominant ideology encourages the pupil to consider science's contribution to culture and society rather than, as postcolonial writers would have it, see how science and technology have shaped society and given us our cultural values. As Siraj-Blatchford (1994, p. 21) points out, unless we are conscious of the applications of science we remain unaware of how science has been able "to mask the real political and economic priorities it has followed".

Amongst the aims of the Science Curriculum (1999a, p. 11) is "to help the child to appreciate the contribution of science and technology to the social, cultural and other dimensions of society". The nuance here is not so subtle, though perhaps if the power relations alluded to by Apple and Harding were different, the emphasis and appreciation would focus on the extent to which society and culture can determine the role and contribution of science.

The 'appreciation of the contribution of science...' espoused by the Science Curriculum is to be achieved in the context of a Social Environmental and Scientific Education curriculum which aspires to "cultivate humane and responsible attitudes and an appreciation of the world in accordance with beliefs and values" (Ireland 1999a, p. 5). Given that the dominant ideology regards scientific achievement as positive and valuable to the point of being a prerequisite for national well-being, one can presume that the 'beliefs and values' will be derived from this ideology, though none are articulated in the curriculum.

The Environmental Awareness and Care strand unit will enable the child to:
• *recognise the contribution of the scientist to society* and
• *recognise and investigate aspects of human activities that may have positive or adverse effects on the environment*

Similarly, an example can be taken from the Caring For The Environment strand unit:
• *come to appreciate individual, community and national responsibility for environmental care*

The curriculum rightly advocates an investigation of the *positive* or *adverse* human activities. However the phraseology here is that science is positive and the action of humans is questionable. Desirable or otherwise, it is unlikely that a primary school teacher working within a 'new' curricular area will adopt a postcolonial perspective to these strand units and refer to the contribution of scientists to colonial expansion and its consequent ecological and economic exploitation either past or present. Another obstacle to the discussion of the *contribution of science to society* is the extent of primary teachers' science subject knowledge and the type of scientific experiences they will create for their classes. As Coates *et al.* (1998 p. 7) point out, more confident teachers are more adventurous in their methodologies and more effective, while those with limited subject knowledge avoid teaching difficult and complex aspects of science and, more importantly in the primary school, "teach in a manner that does not allow children to question and investigate for themselves". Teachers' scientific knowledge and a social context for this knowledge may emerge as factors which curtail the implementation of this aspect of the curriculum.

The above strand units illustrate that the curriculum does give the teacher scope to adopt a postcolonial perspective but this is not easily facilitated. Resources such as *The World in Our Classroom* (Ruane *et al.* 1999) and *Windows on our World* (Hegarty *et al.* 1992) show how a development education perspective can be adopted, but it is ultimately the teacher's decision. There is significant literature on the need to adopt a multicultural perspective in science education and how this can be achieved (Thorp *et al.* 1994; Antonouris 1991; Iram and John Siraj-Blatchford 1991). However the case for such a perspective to be adopted is not helped by the limited scientific knowledge teachers possess and the absence any study of the history or philosophy of science in the curriculum which would introduce pupils to different perspectives of scientific enquiry. Nor is there reference in the curriculum to the contribution other cultures have made to science and an acknowledgement that scientific achievement is not the monopoly of any particular culture. Jarvis and Rennie (2000 p. 16-18) highlight several non-Caucasian men and women scientists whose achievements can be studied with a view to overcoming the stereotypical images primary school pupils hold about scientists and science. These are useful reference points for the study of scientific developments, but also provide a platform for the discussion of the images of scientists at work and discussion of the contributions people of different backgrounds have made to science. While these initiatives are appropriate in the context of ethnically diverse classes, adopting a multicultural perspective and Development Education methodologies may not have the impact intended. Regan and Schagen (1998 p. 9) caution against making claims for Development Education in the absence of further research into its effectiveness, particularly in the context of how successfully it can overcome stereotypical representations of these issues at a wider level and young children's ability to conceptualise the complexities of the issues.

The curriculum is decidedly non-committal when declaring a vision of science and the values it sees coming from science as science *per se* (as distinct from science education). The process of working scientifically does offer opportunities to practice the methodologies of Development Education, but this relates to methodology, not content. The only definition of science offered in the curriculum is:

> Science encompasses knowledge and understanding of the biological and physical aspects of the world and the processes through which such knowledge and understanding are developed. (Ireland 1999a, p.6)

This is not a disputed definition of science, simply a limited one which is developed only in the context of science education and the emphases on the process of learning scientifically and the benefits accruing from a science education. The Department of Education and Training in the Australian Capital Territory define science in a more comprehensive and inclusive manner, as it elaborates:

> The nature and practice of science builds on traditions of inquiry found in many cultures in all parts of the world and has been shaped by people who believe that humans could aspire to understand the real world by observing it. (Department of Education and Training 2002, p. 3)

This is a purposefully intercultural definition of science arrived at through negotiation with several groups. Their rationale and definition includes a section on multicultural science education appropriate for a country keen to acknowledge its aboriginal heritage. Those specifics apart, the Australian Capital Territory Curriculum Framework Document offers a broad definition of science which is useful to the teacher and acknowledges the multicultural nature of scientific knowledge and how it is and has been shaped.

Though our own curriculum gives a limited definition and rationale for science, it emerged from a public debate heavily weighted towards an unquestioning acceptance of the virtues of science (without defining it) and of its centrality to economic development. The NCCA, in its Discussion Paper Science and Technology Education in the Senior Cycle (2000), a discussion paper on the future of science subjects at Leaving Certificate level, define science in terms of knowledge and understanding of our world, but firmly place science education in an economic context quoting from groups such as IBEC, ICSTI, the Expert Group on Future Skills Needs and the Department of Enterprise and Employment, amongst others. Not once in this discussion paper are history of science or the philosophy of science mentioned.

CONCLUSION

In the absence of a broad definition of science which acknowledges the validity of many forms of scientific enquiry and knowledge, the ideology surrounding science and science education will be dominated by groups whose values are representative of just one opinion as to what science is and what is the purpose of its study. These perspectives on science education, though valid, may not easily facilitate teachers advocating a social justice perspective.

When exploring the nature of science with their pupils, examining what is meant by science, scientific knowledge and scientific processes, ultimately, in improving their scientific literacy, teachers are introducing their pupils to issues of social justice. The challenge for initial teacher education and in-service teacher education is to ensure that this dimension of science education becomes central to teachers' classroom practice. By engaging with these issues, the discourse of social justice can prevail in the classroom and, as Foucault (1970) points out, discourse is the power to be seized.

REFERENCES

Antonouris, G. (1991) 'Teaching Science in a Multicultural Society' *Primary Science Review* 17 p3-7

Apple, M. W. (1996) *Cultural Politics and Education* Birmingham: Open University Press

Bernstein, B. (1971) 'On the Classification and framing of educational knowledge' in Young, M.F.D. (ed.) *Knowledge and Control* London: Collier-Macmillan

Coates, D., Vause, J., Jarvis, T. and McKeon, F., (1998) *Mentoring in Primary Science* Leicester: SCIcentre, University of Leicester.

Cobern, W. and Loving, C. (1998) 'Defining "Science" in a Multicultural World: Implications for Science Education' (Website address: www.wmich.edu/slcsp/148.html) (Accessed: February 2002)

Department of Education and Training (2002) *Australian Capital Territory Curriculum Frameworks and Across Curriculum Perspective Statements - Science Curriculum Framework* (Website address: www.decs.act.gov.au/publicat/pdf/science.pdf) ((Accessed: February 2002)

Foucault, M. (1970) *The Order of Things: The Archaeology of the Human Sciences* London: Tavistock

Fuller, S. (1991) *Social Epistemology*. Bloomington, Indianapolis: Indiana University Press

Harding, S. (1998) *Is Science Multicultural?* Bloomington and Indianapolis: Indiana University Press

Hegarty, T., Larkin, T., MacHale,B. and Honan, A. (1992) *Windows on the World - Shaping and Being Shaped by Culture*. Navan: Columban Fathers and Sisters

Jarvis, T., and Rennie, L., (2000) *Helping Primary Children Understand Science and Technology* Leicester: SCIcentre, University of Leicester.

Kawagley,A.O., Norris-Tull D., and Norris-Tull,R. A.,(1998) 'The indigenous worldview of Yupiaq culture: Its scientific nature and relevance to the practice and teaching of science'. *Journal of Research in Science Teaching*, 35(2), 133-144

National Council for Curriculum and Assessment, (2000) *Science and Technology Education in the Senior Cycle - A Discussion Paper*, Dublin: NCCA

Ireland (1999a) *Primary School Curriculum* – Science. Dublin: Stationery Office

Ireland (1999b) *Primary School Curriculum - Science Teacher Guidelines.* Dublin: Stationery Office

Ruane, B., Horgan, K. and Cremin, P. (1999) *The World in the Classroom - Development Education in the Primary Curriculum*, Limerick: Curriculum Development Unit , Mary Immaculate College.

Regan C. and Schagen, S. (1998) *Teaching Justice; A Research and Conference Report on Contemporary Social issues in the Curriculum.* Dublin and Limerick: Network of Curriculum Development Units and Curriculum Network and NFER

Siraj-Blatchford, J., (1994) 'The Nature of Science Education', in Thorp, S., Deshpande, P., and Edwards, C. (eds.) (1994) *Race, Equality and Science Teaching.* (No Place of Publication Listed): The Association of Science Education

Siraj-Blatchford, J., and Siraj-Blatchford, I. (1991) 'Science and Cultural Relevance' *Primary Science Review* 17 p16-17

Thorp, S., Deshpande, P., and Edwards, C. (eds) (1994) *Race, Equality and Science Teaching.* (No Place of Publication Listed): The Association of Science Education

CHAPTER 5

ART AS THE '*SENSUS COMMUNUS*': THE AESTHETIC EXPERIENCE AND TASTE, FACTS AND FICTIONS, PEERS AND PLEBS.

Nora P. Donnelly

Immanuel Kant is the grand old man of Aesthetics. In fact, he is as Kennick says, "its magisterial authority" (1979, p. xi), because few philosophers of his stature devoted as much attention as he to an aesthetic inquiry. It may be said that Kant dropped nothing less that a boulder into the aesthetic pool, and its ripples are still being felt to this day. It is said that all post-Kantian aesthetic discourse is merely "a series of discussions and repudiations of Kant" (Wellek 1970, p. 133), and that one may argue *against* Kant, or *with* him, but never *without* him. Scholars acknowledge Kant as the *fons et origo* of contemporary aesthetics and claim that were it not for his *Critique of Judgement* (1790) aesthetics would not exist in its modern form.

In this seminal text Kant directs the might of his philosophical attention to identifying the nature of the Aesthetic Experience. He undertakes a comprehensive analysis of what it logically involves, as well as making a strong case for its value to human nature, particularly in terms of a '*Sensus Communis*' (a sense that is shared or held in common by all people by virtue of the fact that they are human). He does not, it must be noted, use the term 'Aesthetic Experience' but rather speaks of 'The Judgement of Taste'. In other words, without naming it *per se*, the aesthetic experience is the sum and substance of his argument, while the technical term he employs is the 'Aesthetic Judgement of Taste'.

Turning away from Kant's highly technical use of the term 'taste', it is fair to say that there is little doubt but that, to our ears, the question of 'taste' is a vexed one. To begin with, the notion of 'good taste' – meaning the facility to identify and enjoy, aesthetically speaking, what is of value – denotes a certain supremacy in levels of education, refinement, sensitivity or sensibility. Such a person has the advantage over another because it may be thought that in their *lack* of discernment they have 'no taste' or 'poor taste' since they profess to admire and cherish what those with a delicate sense of taste pronounce tawdry, trashy, and of no aesthetic account.

The idea of 'taste' as a facility of cultured minds or artistic souls who can, for this reason, pass judgement for the rest of us on what *is* and what is *not* of aesthetic merit can raise sociological hackles and, as I hope to show, with very good reason. However, I also propose to reveal the extent to which this type of thinking is anathema to the democratic principles that underpin Kant's aesthetic.

TASTE THEORISTS

The dominant theories of 'taste' were written in the Eighteenth Century by the British Empiricists. For these men (and they were all men) the topic of 'taste' had a special significance since, as Daniel Cottam remarks, "the critical consciousness of that age is a defensive consciousness directed less to arguing what art is or should be than to arguing that it must not and should not be popular – a property of the common people" (1981, p. 367). Consequently, there was a concerted thrust to construct canons, or universal standards of Beauty. These were rigid and fixed and were to be adopted as such by the general populace: in fact they were *imposed* on them. However, these standards were drawn up by a select group of highly influential people of noble birth (two of them peers of the realm) who led lives of ease and indolence. This was important, as it was thought that money, breeding, rank and social privilege were the essential prerequisites for dictating in matters of taste. Conversely, the underprivileged, the socially disadvantaged (and this included all those who had to work for a living), were deemed incapable of experiencing beauty, at least the beauty in the Fine Arts. It is significant to note at this juncture that, as Dickie put it "Taste theories claim that beauty depends in part on a specific kind of object in the external world which is independent of the subject" (1964, p.59). In other words, the emphasis was on identifying categories or particular qualities of objects, rather than the nature of the response of the experiencing subject. In fact, any experience of a work of art, no matter how powerful, was of no consequence if the person who had the experience or who related the experience was uneducated in matters of taste. One could go further and say that, according to the Connoisseurs of the day, such a person was actually incapable of the aesthetic experience. Lord Kames, writing in 1762, states baldly that:

> Those who depend for food on bodily labour are totally void of taste: of such a taste at least as can be of use in the fine arts. This consideration bars the greater part of mankind: and of the remaining parts many by a corrupt taste are unqualified for voting. The common sense of mankind must then be confined to the few that fall not under these exemptions (cited in Cottam 1981, p. 368).

In his *Of the Standards of Taste*, first published in 1757, David Hume explains that 'One obvious cause why many feel not the proper sentiment of Beauty is the want of delicacy of imagination which is requisite to convey a sensibility of these fair emotions' (cited in Cottingham 1996, p.551)

These men not only controlled aesthetic discourse; they also coerced aesthetic opinion. It could be said, with some justification, that the ruling class kept the rest of mankind in a tyrannical stranglehold; disempowering and disenfranchising them and silencing any critical voices but their own. By proscribing the qualities of an object that make it fitting to be called 'beautiful', they contrived to subvert the capacity to judge in all outside the *sanctum sanctorum*. Further, in the event that the vulgarians *do* claim to experience aesthetic pleasure, it is said of them that their taste is 'corrupt' and they are 'in error'.

Such elitism was considered to be necessary because it erected impenetrable barricades that not only served to mark the occupied territory but also to keep the uninformed louts at bay. To put it another way, principles of taste were a deliberate attempt to keep the ill-bred rabble in their place. They served not only to support class difference by repression but also were considered as an effective way of preventing social disorder. Jonathan Richardson, writing in 1792 declares that: "There are certain suppositions that the civilised imagination will automatically reject on the grounds that they would violate distinctions and differences which form the very basis of social order", adding that the advance of popular culture in art represents "an approach of the commonality to the aristocracy that must be rectified if the proper government of a society is to be maintained" (cited in Cottam 1981, p. 369).

In order to redress this state of affairs, and to shed some hopeful philosophical light on what is a rather grim and gloomy prospect, let us now turn to Kant's text.

KANT AND THE QUESTION OF TASTE

"Taste" for Kant is just that. It is a personal 'tasting', an immediate, direct hands-on sampling. He says that, "One of the chief reasons why this faculty of Aesthetic Judgement has been given the name of Taste…[is that] I must try out the dish with *my own* tongue and palate and pass judgement according to their verdict" (Kant 1952, p. 140). Far from depending on critical opinion, Kant again and again emphasises the fact that "every judgement which is to show the taste of the individual, is required to be an independent judgement of the individual himself" (Kant 1952, p. 137). In the event that the opinion of the savants, or those whom he calls "virtuosi in matters of taste" (1952 p. 157) should differ from our own, then we simply disregard them. Kant waxes lyrical on this, saying:

> If anyone read me a poem, or brings me to a play, which, all said and done, fails to commend itself to my taste, then let him adduce … famous critics of taste, with all the rules laid down by them, as a proof of the beauty of his poem; let certain passages displeasing to me accord completely with the rules

of beauty, (as set out by these critics and universally recognised): I stop my ears; I do not want to hear any reasons or arguments about the matter. I would prefer to suppose that those rules of the critics were at fault, or at least have no application than to allow my judgement to be determined by *a priori* proofs. I take my stand on the ground that my judgement is one of taste, and not one of understanding or reason (1952, p. 140).

The above passage makes Kant's position *vis a vis* the immediacy of the aesthetic experience quite clear. However, it also introduces certain technical terms such as the judgements of 'taste', 'understanding' and 'reason', which require elucidation at this juncture.

According to Kant, there are three ways of relating to the world; each calling on a different judgement. One is interested in *knowing* the object (which has to do with 'Understanding'); one *desires* it (which refers to 'Reason'); or one simply takes pleasure in it (which marks the judgement as aesthetic) (1952, p. 15-16). 'Understanding' and 'Reason 'are "our higher cognitive faculties" (1952, p. 15-16) and both employ the 'Logical Judgement'. Reason is will-related. It covers all practical knowledge. It *evaluates*. Understanding has to do with the acquisition of all theoretical knowledge, and *identifies*. Both operate in what Kant terms the 'Logical Judgement' insofar as both apply concepts *qua* rules.

The Logical Judgement

The logical judgement pronounces on what Kant calls the 'Good' and he further distinguishes between "that which is *good for something* (useful) and that which is *good in itself*"(1952, p. 46).

For example, it is Understanding that pronounces, 'This is a jug', since the object conforms to the definitive jug criteria (capable of holding and pouring liquid, spout, handle). It further classifies it (a mason's ironstone jug; a wine carafe; a cream ewer). Reason can say either, 'This is a good jug' (does not dribble, handle sustains weight of jug when full); or effect a comparative evaluation ('As jugs go, this is a cracker'). Both apply a system of laws or concepts to the object: both pronounce a verdict on the object. In other words both speak of the object; they do not reveal what you, as subject, feel about it. Both require the imagination, since this is what supplies the data of experience, being the binding force between sensation and thought. Imagination (also a cognitive faculty) apprehends the given object, and without it sense experience cannot be related to concepts. However, in the Logical Judgement, the imagination is strictly governed by Reason or by Understanding.

The Aesthetic Judgement

Kant describes two types of Aesthetic Judgement: that of 'Sense' and that of 'Taste'. The object of the Aesthetic Judgement of Sense he calls the 'Agreeable'. Chicken Chasseur, chilled Chablis or the action of stroking your Siamese cat may be, for Kant, the 'Agreeable'. It is a sensory experience and the accompanying pleasure here is purely sensual. The object of the Aesthetic Judgement of Taste is the 'Beautiful'. It shares certain characteristics with the Judgement of Sense insofar as both are immediate: i.e. based on a personal (unmediated) experience. However, as will become clear, the judgement of taste involves quite a different mode of thought to that of Sense. By the same token the pleasure of the judgement of taste has an entirely distinctive character. Unlike the British Empiricists, it is with the response of the subject that Kant is concerned, rather than with concepts of what constitute aesthetic value in the object. He states quite clearly that "beauty is, apart from any reference to the subject, nothing" (1952, p. 59) and that the Judgement of Taste denotes nothing in the object, but is a feeling the subject has of itself and of the manner in which it is affected by the representation (1952, p. 42).

This criterial condition of the Judgement of Taste has a two-fold implication. Kant has, at one fell stroke, enfranchised both the subject and the object of aesthetic experience. He has delimited the object: it does not matter if it is a common cross spider, a Gilbert and George performance, a concrete mixer, an elegant rugby tackle or Whistler's Mother as long as the subject experiences it as aesthetic. He has, at the same time delivered the subject from the necessity of validating his/her judgement as one of Taste by referring to properties of the object or deferring to any sort of 'Good Guide'.

The Non-Cognitive Nature of the Aesthetic Judgement

Kant makes a clear distinction between the 'Logical Judgement' and the two 'Aesthetic Judgements' on the grounds that the former is conceptually determined whereas neither of the latter are. This notion includes two further aspects of Kant's aesthetic.

The Harmony of the Cognitive Faculties

In the Logical Judgement, as we have seen, the imagination is necessary. However, it plays a minor role. It is guided and organised by the Understanding. It is concept-bound, concept-based, concept-led. However, in the Judgement of Taste, it is quite a different matter. Here the imagination is free, no longer "compelled to follow a course laid down for it by a definite law" (1952, p. 86). This is what Kant calls "The Cognitive Powers in Free Play" (1952, p. 58) and is one of the crucial characteristics of the aesthetic experience, since it is what begins to mark the possibility of setting up a claim for the *'Sensus Communus'*. In Kant's words:

> Only when the imagination in its freedom stirs the understanding, and the understanding, apart from concepts, puts the imagination into regular play, does the representation communicate itself, not as a thought but as an internal feeling (1952, p. 154).

Free from concepts, not "in subjection to the laws of association" (1952, p. 86), it soars and swoops freely over forms, playing with them, inventing and reinventing images. And the accompanying pleasure is the definitive signal that the cognitive faculties are in free play. And *this* is the aesthetic experience. It is also another vital step in the argument for a *'Sensus Communus'*.

The imagination is the keystone of Kant's aesthetic experience. It is productive. It plays a game, and we recognise that it is at play because we are fully aware of our own pleasure. According to Kant, the aesthetic experience "invigorates the mind by letting it feel its faculty – free, spontaneous and independent of determination by nature" (1952, p. 191-192). It is, as Eagleton puts it: "a pleasurable free wheeling of our faculties, a non-referential pseudo-cognition which does not nail down the object to an identifiable thing" (1990, p. 86).

Because the Aesthetic Judgement is not determined conceptually it tells you nothing about the object. It does not identify, classify, categorise, compare with like objects, and it does not evaluate. You may say 'This is beautiful' or 'This is delicious' but the 'This' does not apply to the object because the aesthetic judgement is neither grounded on nor determined by the object, as we have seen. Kant points out that, "If we wish to discern whether anything is beautiful or not we do not refer the representation of it to the Object by means of understanding...but to the subject and its feeling of pleasure or displeasure" (1952, p. 41). Certainly, you do not say, 'This is a beautiful rose/whale/painting'; as to do so is to attempt to identify features which makes the object a beautiful one of its kind. This requires you to link in to the concepts that govern beauty in roses/paintings/whales and compare them to roses/paintings/whales in general. In fact, because of its non-cognitive nature, the aesthetic experience is devoid of cultural and knowledge-based references which means that Kant, in effect, dismantles the notion of the *haut monde*, thereby democratising not only the object but also the experience itself – another steeping stone in building up the case for a *'Sensus Communus'*.

The Form of Finality

Kant's 'Form of Finality' (sometimes translated as the more cumbersome 'Purposiveness without purpose') means that we regard the object as 'final' for perception. In other words, we do not think of it in terms of a purpose or use other than to be perceived. We regard natural forms as if "they seem to be planned entirely with a view to outward appearance" (1952, p. 217), and Art forms as if "Their sole function …is to be looked at" (1952, p. 188). Derrida, speaking of this aspect of Kant's Aesthetic, says: "We admire nature which displays itself in beautiful products…'as it were' designedly, but in aesthetic experience the purpose or end of this purposiveness does not appear to us" (1981, p. 14).

We may be fully cognisant that it has some purpose, but this does not play any part in our aesthetic consideration. It also means that we are precluded from using the object for our own particular ends or from abusing it. In Kant's words we "feel quite at home" (1952, p. 70) in a world that is somehow designed to accommodate our humanity, and which we experience as if it is ordered and designed for no other purpose than to be "grasped in the imagination" (1952, p. 70).

We have ascertained that the imagination is the *primum mobile* of the aesthetic experience: that the judgement is not determined solely by the intellect. It is this aspect of Kant's theory that may be the most problematic in Education.

Educators, who purport to deal with the cognitive, may look askance at the notion of using an aesthetic theory that makes no claims for cognitive value. And Kant remains obdurate on this point. The aesthetic object (be it a clump of Deadly Nightshade or El Greco's *The Burial of Count Orgaz*) "represents nothing" and has "no intrinsic meaning" (1952, p. 72). The aesthetic experience "affords no knowledge of anything" (1952, p. 207). This may not present a problem in the case of the Deadly Nightshade, but it is a different story with the El Greco. Nonetheless, Kant's aesthetic is not to be compromised or manipulated into a cognitive framework. You may not depend on concepts, but Kant's aesthetic experience is not mindless. Nor is it irrational or illogical. Its lack of determinate concepts is not its drawback: it is its virtue (but what that particular virtue is, is the subject for another paper on another day).

The single distinction that Kant draws between the Aesthetic Judgement of Taste on one hand, and both the Logical Judgement *and* the Aesthetic Judgement of Sense on the other is that, while the former is disinterested, neither of the latter are.

The Judgement of Taste is Disinterested

"Every interest vitiates the judgement of taste and robs it of its impartiality" (1952, p. 64). Disinterestedness means neither that the subject is *uninterested* nor that the object is *uninteresting*. Of course the subject must be 'interested' - in the sense of 'paying attention to', or even 'being intrigued by', the object. Rather is it a filtering device that blocks out extra-aesthetic concerns.

The concept of disinterestedness has a crucial role to play as a base on which Kant continues to build up and strengthen his case for establishing universal validity and the *'Sensus Communus'*.

The disinterested subject is unbiased since, as Kant says, he abstracts from "personal conditions to which his own personal self might be party" (1952, p. 51). There are no dictates or laws (as there are with the 'good') and no predilective hankerings (as is the case with the 'agreeable'); the subject is "completely free in respect of the liking he accords to the object" (1952, p. 49). As interest - in Kant's aesthetic - has to do with *desire*, the disinterested subject is freed from need, want or "any inclination of the subject" (1952, p. 51). This notion is significant in terms of the *Sensus Communus* since it means (as Guyer and Cohen point out), that the judgement is devoid "from all possible conditions which would necessarily distinguish the judge from other people" (1982, p.12). Kant himself says that "If the judge is independent of any interest he should look on the object as one containing a ground of delight for all men" (1952, p. 50).

Disinterest also means that in the aesthetic experience we are required to abstract from the functional value of the object. It cannot be perceived as useful, as this would indicate that, in Kant's terms, the judgement is now logical rather than one of taste. This may suggest that the object is *useless*, and this type of thinking has overtones - (particularly in the context of the work of art) – of the aestheticism of Gautier, Baudelaire, Valerie or Oscar Wilde (whose infamous, 'All Art is quite useless', epitomises the tenets of aestheticism). The aura that surrounds aestheticism, the implication that art is the province of the select few, is one to which Kant is positively hostile. His is not an 'Art for Art's sake' aesthetic, but an 'Aesthetic Experience for Humanities sake'. He is, as we have seen, scathing about the extravagant affectation of the Connoisseur. He would never subscribe to Vigny's notion of the 'ivory tower'.

Universal Validity: the *Sensus Communus*
At this stage, when we pull the threads of Kant's argument together, we find that he has established the fundamental grounds of a *Sensus Communus*.

In insisting on the disinterestedness of the judgement of taste, Kant has effectively disposed of elements that may be divisive among people such as bias, prejudice, personal preference, bigotry, likes and dislikes. By eliminating the cognitive element in aesthetic experience, he dispenses with knowledge-based factors that otherwise may deem people either deficient or privileged in this regard. Since the aesthetic experience is devoid of factors that would necessarily distinguish one spectator from another on the grounds of education, scholars, historians, academics are no more advantaged that those less well instructed or well informed. By the same token, the relation between the spectator and the object is devoid of cultural and conceptual referents that may distinguish one person from another of a different background. His 'Harmony of the Faculties' relies on what Kant describes as common to all people: the constitution of the human mental faculties. For Kant, it is insofar that we are human beings, and insofar as *being human* means that we function cognitively in a particular way, that we can point to the existence of a 'common' sense. Because the judgement of taste calls on the subjective condition necessary to cognition, it can be attributed to every knowing person. Being *in* one mind, we are *of* one mind.

Kant does not say that all people are equal. Far from it. In fact he refers specifically to difference in the context of a *Sensus Communus* as follows:

> The art of reciprocal communication of ideas between the more cultured and ruder sections of the community…that bridge[s] the difference between the amplitude and refinement of the former and originality of the latter … as a sense common to all mankind (1952, p. 227).

He does, however, subscribe to the notion that all people are equally capable of experiencing aesthetically *in virtue of the fact that they are human*. In fact, he says that when the individual makes a judgement of taste he/she speaks with a "Universal voice" (1952, p. 56).

By establishing that the judgement is made by calling on what people have in common, rather than on that which divides them, Kant shows that it is trans-cultural, trans-societal. In a word Kant offers an aesthetic experience that transcends what Haskins terms "all class and educational barriers" (1989, p. 46) Taking this notion one step further, we can see, as Hofstader says, that Kant envisages a "genuine human communion" (1975:182). Eagleton says that, in the judgement of taste, "We exercise a precious form of intersubjectivity, establishing ourselves as a community of feeling subjects linked by a quick sense of our shared capacities" (1990, p.74).

It must be remembered that it is the *judgement* that is universally valid: not the *object*. Kant is certainly not saying that beauty (which we attribute to the object) has universal appeal, but the ability to feel the particular pleasure of the aesthetic experience (which is the Harmony of the Faculties in the Finality of Form) is one shared by all people. There are no grounds for exclusion as the ability to experience aesthetically is a mark of our common humanity (*qua* 'common sense'). Far from dismissing minorities, local viewpoints or marginal groups, Kant's 'Universal Voice' embraces all, and the exercise of the judgement of taste is a unifying force which bonds people in their awareness of their common humanity.

CONCLUSION

However much we may vehemently object to the scathing indictments of the British Empiricist gentry, I would argue that the we, in the early days of the twenty-first century, are still haunted by the ghosts of their thought. This is particularly evident when new forms of art are shown, either locally in the gallery next door or internationally as we read in the Sunday supplements or see on Channel Four. There is an unwillingness to rely on a personal response and to look instead towards those who are 'in the know' about such matters. A dependence on the opinion of someone who, by virtue of specialist knowledge, is considered to be a competent authority in the area, must surely lead to the suppression of one's immediate or intuitive reaction and even to the feigning of a favourable - or unfavourable - judgement. How sad! To be denied the right, as many people feel they are, to an unmediated aesthetic experience and the accompanying pleasure because one feels that one does not have a sufficiently broad knowledge base is certainly a relic of Eighteenth Century thought.

Kant has successfully debunked this myth. He has enunciated a more important and profound truth. He has not merely indicated the way towards a freedom of ownership in our experience of Artistic/Aesthetic value, but he has also constructed a very powerful argument that shows not only that we *own our own* aesthetic experience, but further that we have the right to *own that we own it*.

REFERENCES

Cottam, D. (1981) 'Taste and the Civilised Imagination'. *Journal of Aesthetics and Art Criticism*, v.39 pp.367-380.

Cottingham, J. (ed.) (1996) *Western Philosophy*. London: Blackwell.

Derrida, J. (1981) 'Economimesis' *Diacritics* vol. 11, pp.3-25.

Dickie, G. (1964) 'The Myth of the Aesthetic Attitude' *American Philosophical Quarterly*. No.1, pp.56-65.

Eagleton, T. (1990) *Ideology of the Aesthetic*. Oxford: Basil Blackwell.

Greene, (1865) *The Works of Joseph Addison Volume 5*. New York:

Guyer, P. and Cohen, T. (eds.) (1982) *Essays in Kant's Aesthetics*. Chicago: University of Chicago Press.

Haskins, C. (1989) 'Kant and the Autonomy of Art' *Journal of Aesthetics and Art Criticism*. Vol. 47, pp. 43-54.

Hoftstadter, A. (1975) 'Kant's Aesthetic Revolution' *Journal of Religious Ethics*, vol.3, pp.171-191.

Kant, I. (1952) *The Critique of Judgement*. Translated by James Creed Meredith. Originally published 1790. New York: Doubleday.

Kennick, W.F. (ed.) (1979) *Art and Philosophy: Readings in Aesthetics Second Edition* New York: S. Martin's Press.

Wellek, R. (1970) *Discriminations: Further Concepts of Criticism*. New Haven and London: Yale University Press.

CHAPTER 6

DECOMMISSIONING THE CANON: TOWARDS A DECONSTRUCTION OF THE GIVENS OF THE LITERARY CANON

Eugene O'Brien

One day when Father Butler was hearing the four pages of Roman History, clumsy Leo Dillon was discovered with a copy of *The Halfpenny Marvel*. 'This page or this page? This page? Now, Dillon, up. "Hardly had the day"... Go on! What day? "Hardly had the day dawned"... Have you studied it? What have you there in your pocket?' Everyone's heart palpitated as Leo Dillon handed up the paper and everyone assumed an innocent face. Father Butler turned over the pages, frowning. 'What is this rubbish?' he said. '*The Apache Chief*! Is this what you read instead of studying your Roman History? Let me not find any more of this wretched stuff in this college. The man who wrote it, I suppose, was some wretched fellow who writes these things for a drink. I'm surprised at boys like you, educated, reading such stuff! I could understand it if you were... National School boys. Now, Dillon, I advise you strongly, get at your work or...'
(Joyce 1994, pp.12-13)

Here we see the hegemonic imperative of the literary canon in essence. The connection which underwrites Father Butler's comments is that between literature and education; between certain works which are self-evidently of value, a canon, and others which are inimical to such notions of value. If one examines the context of Father Butler's criticism, however, problematic questions arise. Both texts, the Roman history book and *The Halfpenny Marvel*, deal with the structures of imperialism and resistance. In one, it is seen as culturally valuable to learn about the imperial practices of the Roman Empire. It is culturally valuable to learn about the imposition of an empire on people who may have had little choice in participating in that empire. The essential core of Roman history is a description of battles fought and tribes vanquished. *The Apache Chief*, in contrast, is deemed culturally lacking in value. It is seen as 'wretched stuff', inspired by a drunken writer and not worthy of study. Yet it, too, deals with an imperialistic history of conquest and colonisation. It too, outlines the struggles of individuals in wartime conflict and it too speaks of the history of a people. It too, deals with battles fought and tribes vanquished.

Of course, there are situational and cultural factors to be taken into account here. Roman history and literature carry significations of Empire, civilisation and the Roman Catholic religion with them as part of their cultural baggage. Occupying a culturally hegemonic position, this literature is something to which people feel they should aspire in terms of cultural capital. At a racial and indigenous level, on the other hand, the Apache is associated with nomadism, primitivism and, given the binary oppositional role of the native American, or Red Indian, to use the term in commonest contemporary usage, with obscurantist opposition to the civilising mission of the white race. It is a classic example of Said's notion of positional superiority as expressed in *Orientalism*:

> The colonised are thereby constrained to assert a dignified self-identity in opposition to a discourse which defines them as, variously, barbarian, pagan, ape, female; but always subordinate and inferior. Hence 'positional superiority' puts the coloniser in a whole series of possible relationships with the colonised...without ever losing him the relative upper hand (Said 1978, p.7).

The canon in literature provides cultural validation for this positional superiority in terms of the accrual of cultural capital, to use Bourdieu's term. Cultural capital, in its institutionalised state, provides academic credentials and qualifications which create a "certificate of cultural competence which confers on its holder a conventional, constant, legally guaranteed value with respect to power" (Bourdieu 1986, p.248). These academic qualifications can then be used as a rate of conversion between cultural and economic capital, and it is this conversion rate that Father Butler is enforcing in the above extract from Joyce. Roman history is a validation of the cultural capital that attaches to middle and upper class Irish Catholic societal values and, as such, is canonically validated by the educational system. *The Apache Chief*, on the other hand, has little cultural capital attached to it, and is hence a signifier of non-value.

This notion of a canon, an *organon* of literary works selected according to purely aesthetic criteria, has long been central to the educational procedures of Western culture. That there are certain works which occupy a transcendental position within the culture, due to self-evidently superior aesthetic, stylistic and moral qualities, has been almost a truism in the study of literature. The very term 'canon' derives from scripture where it signifies the set of those biblical books officially accepted by any of the Christian Churches as genuinely inspired; or any collection or list of sacred works accepted as genuine. In this sense, a secular canon takes on this connotative dimension, being seen as an almost self-selecting order of great works which are studied on purely aesthetic and moral grounds and which serve to enculturate new generations into high, or middle-class culture as well as enunciating values and practices which are enshrined as desirable qualities in our culture.

As well as embodying the content of these great works, the canon has also come to stand for a particular attitude towards the study of literature, an attitude encapsulated by Christopher Norris in the following quotation:

> Literary critics interpret texts. By and large they get on without worrying too much about the inexplicit theories or principles that underwrite their practice. Some of them very actively resist the idea that such theories can be found, or that bringing them to light could serve any useful purpose. (Norris 1985, p.1)

Where Norris himself stands on the issue of the validity of theory in literary criticism can be gauged from his observation that "one needs theory to avoid reading stupidly, accepting language at face value" (Norris 1988, p.11), as well as from his closely argued studies of the interrelationships of theory, philosophy and postmodernism. Perhaps a classic example of the type of thinking which I have termed 'canonical' is to be found in the work of F.R.Leavis, who begins his book, *The Great Tradition*, with the ringing assertion that the "great English novelists are Jane Austin, George Eliot, Henry James and Joseph Conrad" (Leavis 1972, p.9). For Leavis, the term 'Literature' (the capital 'L' is symptomatic, as is the adjective 'great' in the book's title) is a given, not to be questioned in any way. That its 'value' is cultural and societal, as Rick Rylance has noted, is clear from the example of Leavis's pamphlet *Mass Civilization and Minority Culture*, wherein he "sought a way to moral and cultural health through...literary traditions" (Rylance 1987, p.2).

Leavis saw the act of reading as inevitably intuitive, and when asked by René Wellek to defend the philosophical choices inherent in his position, he refused to be drawn into abstract debate on the basis of the radical distinction between literature and philosophy (Widdowson 1982, p.129). His attitude to theory, and it is an attitude shared by some contemporary critics, was that it is outside the brief of the critic. For Leavis, theory was for philosophers, and he professed that he was "no philosopher" as he had "pretensions – pretensions to being a literary critic" (Leavis 1976, pp. 211-212). The problem with this attitude is that, like Father Butler, there is no verifiable ground upon which to challenge the assumptions that give rise to the particular set of texts that are deemed to constitute the canon. In effect, groups of writers and readers become radically disenfranchised through their work being deemed to posses little cultural capital, and these groups have no right (write) of appeal in terms of their lack of standing. To claim that such choices are not theoretically based is disingenuous to say the least. It is useful to call to mind a wry assertion of Terry Eagleton's, namely that "hostility to theory usually means an opposition to other people's theories and an oblivion of one's own" (Eagleton 1983, p.viii).

In her discussion of the use of theory in *Critical Practice*, Catherine Belsey argues that Leavisite 'common sense', which seems to be anti-theoretical, is in fact based on an unstated theoretical model. The 'assumptions' about which Leavis expressed himself so reluctant to theorise, have been summarised by Belsey as drawing on the theory of 'expressive realism'. This theory proposes "a *humanism* based on an *empiricist-idealist* interpretation of the world" (Belsey 1980, p.7). Belsey details the theoretical premises of this philosophy noting the "humanist assumption that subjectivity, the individual mind or inner being, is the source of meaning and of action" (Belsey 1980, p.3). The power of this argument is that it draws attention to the theoretical basis of all forms of criticism; the only difference is that some theories are explicitly stated, while others remain a series of shared assumptions, ideas and impressions. In her view 'common sense' itself is ideologically and culturally constructed; it is produced in specific societies by the discursive practices employed by that society.

Criticism, like other modes of societal discourse, is theoretically based; therefore, this theoretical base, be it explicit or implicit, can be studied in the light of its mode of production. Linguistic, philosophical, psychoanalytic and ideological factors are intertwined at both extrinsic and intrinsic levels, and all can be subjected to theoretical critique. Hence, the canon, as a form of knowledge, is implicated in Foucault's dictum that knowledge is a factor in the maintaining of a precarious system of power, as it is part of a "relation of distance and domination" (Foucault 1994, p.12).

Looked at from such a theoretical perspective, canonicity functions very much as an example of what Louis Althusser termed ISAs or Institutional State Apparatuses. These are the socio-cultural devices which allow for the enculturation of the next generations into the norms and default positions of the hegemonic group which controls the society. RSAs, or Repressive State Apparatuses, such as the police, courts of law and the military, are the ground on which compliance is enforced, but the ISAs – education, media, religion – are more subtle in their operation as they draw people's assent to the hegemonic standards that are in force. In this sense, the identification with a cultural artefact, such as literature, can have a huge effect on the aspirational identity of different groups, races and genders (Althusser 1977, p.152).

Given that the term canon is religious in derivation, and that it has been defined in the OED as "the set of those biblical books officially accepted by any of the Christian Churches as genuinely inspired"; or as "any collection or list of sacred works accepted as genuine", notions of origin are often elided in terms of the criteria which determined the inclusion or exclusion of certain texts. However, in the light of recent theory attention has come to focus on precisely those criteria which motivated the choice of individual works. In Foucault's terms, issues of knowledge can never be separated from their contextual framework: "knowledge is always the historical and circumstantial result of conditions outside the domain of knowledge" (Foucault 1994, p.13). In other words, there are ideological factors involved in the choices which determine what is canonical and what is not: issues of canonicity are imbricated with societal control and hegemony.

Traditionally, then, canonical choices involve a classic binarism of 'either/or' choices: whether a work is canonical, and hence attaches some form of cultural capital, or it is non-canonical and hence of little cultural value. The canon here forms a coherent centre around which the edifice of a hegemonic culture can be established. However, in the context of Jacques Derrida's work on deconstruction, the whole epistemological structure of centrality has been brought into question.

Derrida has discussed the concept of centrality in 'Structure, Sign and Play in the Discourses of the Human Sciences' (Derrida 1978, pp.278-293). He makes the point that the centre in terms of any structure functions by limiting the 'play' of the structure (Derrida 1978, p.278). He goes on to define typical conceptions of centrality based on the Cartesian view of the transcendental subject as positioned anterior to language:

> Thus, it has always been thought that the centre, which is by definition unique, constituted that very thing within a structure which, while governing the structure, escapes structurality...the centre is at the centre of the totality, and yet, since the centre does not belong to the totality (is not part of the totality), the totality has its centre elsewhere....The concept of centred structure is in fact the concept of a play based on a fundamental ground, a play constituted on the basis of a fundamental immobility and a reassuring certitude, which itself is beyond the reach of play (Derrida 1978 p.279).

The centre could no longer be thought of as a form of self-presence, existing anterior to the structure in question; it, like the subject referred to earlier, became a function in which "an infinite number of sign-substitutions came into play", and this process of sign-substitutions, which can be called 'discourse' became the constituent factor in the existence of the "central signified, the original or transcendental signified" which is never absolutely present "outside a system of differences" (Derrida 1978, p.280).

The desire to find a centre which conflates land and language, is deconstructed by Derrida's notion of *différance*:

> Every concept is inscribed in a chain or in a system, within which it refers to the other, to other concepts, by means of the systematic play of differences. Such a play, *différance*, is thus no longer simply a concept, but rather the possibility of conceptuality....*Différance* is the non-full, non-simple, structured and differentiating origin of differences (Derrida 1982, p.11).

In this context, the issue of choice becomes all important: if there is more than one centre, then, by definition, there will be more choices to be made in terms of which centre one should choose. The Joycean example demonstrated the hegemonic force that a binary choice can enforce on notions of literature, culture and social class. In a deconstructionist context, such choices are now subject to as much interrogation as are their results. The motivating factors of such choices, what Foucault terms the interactions of power and knowledge (Foucault 1994, p.85) are in as much need of conceptual unpacking as are the choices themselves.

For Derrida, choices can no longer be outlined in simplistic terms of "this nor that; but rather this and that (e.g. the act of differing and of deferring) without being reducible to a dialectical logic either" (Derrida 1981b, p.161). The emancipatory effect that such a paradigm can bring to bear on issues of canonicity and, by extension, of social inclusion and of cultural validation, is immense. Foucault's notion of an epistemic shift in the seventeenth century, when the classical mind analysed things in terms of 'identity' and 'difference' (Foucault 1970, p.52) is a useful analogue here. The canon, as an unexamined cultural 'given', exercises a conservative and limiting force, maintaining a form of cultural control through a hegemonic structure of literary choice. On the other hand, once the criterion of sameness is replaced with that of difference, then new possibilities of transformation and pluralist engagement with literature and culture emerge.

Once notions of sameness and centrality have been replaced by those of difference and a decentred perspective, then the canon, as repressive cultural implement, can be decommissioned, and replaced by a pluralistic and transformative set of choices which will allow new forms of expression to accrue cultural capital and, hence, to enfranchise different social, cultural, economic and racial groups. Temporally, this means that the criteria which determine the canon can be seen to alter, and that structures of exclusion can no longer be maintained indefinitely. To extend the Joycean example, Joyce's *Ulysses* was banned by the American and British censors as a dirty book. In this case, Joyce's work was being equated with *The Apache Chief* in terms of its cultural value, or lack of value. Yet now, its status as a piece of literature is unchallenged. The text has remained unchanged, pace the Joyce wars; what has altered is the societal habitus, or *Weltanschauung*, which made these choices.

I would contend that such transformations of issues of value and cultural capital are an important part of the ethical function of literature and literary theory in terms of the ability to change the cultural and, by extension, social structures within which we live, and would adduce the work of Seamus Heaney to underscore this point:

> I tended to conceive of English and Irish as adversarial tongues, as either/or conditions rather than both/and, and this was an attitude that for a long time hampered the development of a more confident and creative way of dealing with the whole vexed question – the question, that is, of the relationship between nationality, language, history and literary tradition in Ireland. (Heaney 1999, p.xxiv)

In terms of Derrida's already discussed notion of *différance*, the similarity in phrasing and in epistemology is striking, with the process of *différance* being governed by a similar logic of 'this *and* that' as opposed to 'this *or* that'; of 'both/and' as opposed to 'either/or'. Clearly, both writers have come to the conclusion that only by some form of structure which accommodates selfhood and alterity within itself, can the complexities of identity be given an ethically correct enunciation.

Derrida has made the point, in *Of Spirit*, that the origin of language is responsibility (Derrida 1989, p.132), and Heaney is discharging his responsibility to a complex sense of interaction with the English language and culture through this act of translation and transformation. In terms of issues pertaining to the canon, and to notions of exclusivity contained therein, Heaney's analysis of a book setting out the canon of Pastoral poetry is worthy of study in terms of the liberating and emancipatory value of a deconstructive critique of the strictures of canonicity with a view to enabling a new type of canon, which is more fluid and less rigid.

For Heaney, the epistemological force of literature is complex and multi-layered, involving the granting of voice to different perspectives, as well as setting up cognitive and intellectual structures which allow for their interaction. In an essay entitled 'In the Country of Convention', in *Preoccupations*, about a collection of English pastoral verse, he is critical of what he sees as an oversimplification of response on behalf of the editors to the notion of what they term 'the pastoral vision'. Barrell and Bull (1975) see this vision as being ultimately false, because it posits a simplistic unhistorical relation between the land-owning class and the workers, which mystifies and obscures the actuality of working conditions. Heaney notes the influence of Raymond Williams on this point of view,[1] and goes on to criticise this "sociological filleting of the convention" as being guilty of a "certain attenuation of response" which curtails the consideration of the poems as "made things" as "self-delighting buds on the old bough of a tradition" (Heaney 1980, p.174).

The complexity of his position may not seem at first obvious in this essay; there is a polarity seemingly set up between what we might term intrinsic and extrinsic, or aesthetic and sociological criticism. While deploring the simplification of response, Heaney is also willing to grant the benefit of sociologically-driven criticism as "a bracing corrective" to what could prove an "over-literary savouring" of the genre as a matter of "classical imitation and allusion" (Heaney 1980, p.174). He is obviously not against extrinsically driven criticism *per se*; rather he is against any form of 'attenuation of response', any thinning of the plurality and complexity of the notion of literature. He sees the relationship between the internal dynamics of the poems, and their reflection, refraction, and transformation of external societal and cultural factors, as far too complex to allow the 'Marxist broom' to sweep aesthetic considerations aside in favour of the societal and economic. In terms of the construction of a canon, the issue which is the core of this essay, Heaney is arguing, in a Foucauldian manner, that the factors influencing choice are necessarily intertwined: there is a need to take into consideration both the extrinsic and the intrinsic, the sociological and the aesthetic, text and context, in determining these criteria.

Heaney's notion of the relationship between text and context is far more complex and fluid. It could be seen as an example of the rhetorical figure of *anastomosis*, as cited by J. Hillis Miller in *The Ethics of Reading*, in terms of notions of 'penetration and permeation'. Miller is also speaking about the relationship between text and context, and sees this notion of context as hovering "uneasily" between "metonymy in the sense of mere contingent adjacency and synecdoche, part for whole, with an assumption that the part is some way genuinely like the whole" (Hillis Miller 1987, p.6). It is here that he cites the trope of anastomosis, adverting to Joyce's verbal example 'underdarkneath' [2]as well as Bakhtin's view of language as a social philosophy which is permeated by a system of values "inseparable from living practice and class struggle" (Hillis Miller 1987, pp.6-7). [3]One could just as easily see 'con-text' as a similar case, with one word, 'text' penetrating or permeating the other, 'context'.[4] Here both words intersect and interfuse, but perform the dialectical action of remaining separate as well as blending. In terms of the canon, the parameters which structure the decisions are similarly interwoven. Canonical structures must, of necessity, be amalgams of their respective aesthetic, historical, political and sociological constituents, and it is the task of literature and theory to constantly interrogate and problematise these categories, as opposed to reifying them.

Heaney's reading sets up a further contextual aspect of this dialectical structure which, far from attenuating our response, will thicken and enable it. Heaney laments the decision of the editors not to print translations of Theocritus, Virgil, Horace, Mantuan, and Marot,[5] as these were the 'informing voices that were "modified in the guts of the living"'(Heaney 1980, p.175), which underwrote the pastoral poetry of Spenser, Milton, Pope and Thomson as they attempted to 'adorn and classicise' the native literature. He feels that such a 'classical penumbra' was automatic cultural capital for these writers, and thinks it a pity that the "ancient hinterland, the perspectives backward, are withheld" (Heaney 1980, p.175). Here, the textual-contextual anastomosis becomes more intricate, as this withholding delimits our reading of the pastoral genre, and of the specific English writing of this genre, as well as the complexities inherent in the title of the book, as well as decommissioning the canonical structure that the book itself initiates.

What is set out as *The Penguin Book of English Pastoral Verse*, with all the canonical, imperial, and culturally homogenous connotations that are implied by the proper adjective *'English'*, becomes something different when placed in a dialectical relationship with these classical antecedents. Such external influences, in this case, far from attenuating the response to the lyrical impulse of the pastoral, thicken our reading of these works by complicating and interrogating how *'English'* this genre actually is. This 'perspective backwards' is also a perspective outwards, pointing up the dependence of what is seen as the English poetic canon on generic and conventional borrowings from continental Europe. It is also a perspective inwards, as these extrinsic features have had a major influence on stylistic and thematic considerations, as well as on the aesthetic objectives of the genre. Here, the anastomosis between text and context is enacted in the permeation and intersection of the poems in the book and the poems which preceded them; of the English language and Latin and French; of Latin and French and translation; of classical pastoral convention and the English version of it and finally, of the texts that are present in the book, and those enabling translations from the classics, which are absent.

This complex interrogation of the categories of text and context calls to mind a similar interrogation in the work of Derrida who, in *Limited Inc.*, has noted that "nothing exists outside context", and that, consequently, the "outside penetrates and thus determines the inside" (Derrida 1988, p.153).[6] Derrida has made a similar point in *Positions*, where he speaks of how each seemingly simple term is marked by the trace of other terms, so that the 'presumed interiority of meaning' is constantly being 'worked on by its own exteriority. It is always already carried outside itself' (Derrida 1981a, p.33). Heaney's project will also demonstrate a view of poetry which stresses the transformative and interpenetrative mode of action through which poetry achieves its ends of breaking down opposed binary positions.

Having noted these points, one returns to the title, 'In the Country of Convention', and realises that this title is, like the essay, less simple than it might seem. While the country in question is England, as denoted by the proper adjective of the sub-title, *'English* Pastoral Verse', the essay draws out the connotations of the diverse influences, literary, linguistic and political, that are present in the pastoral convention. The constituent factors of this genre are not English, but Latin and French in language, as well as in tone and theme. The 'convention' of the title derives from classical pastoral literature but, as translations of this literature are absent, the presentation of the 'country' in question is consequently attenuated.

As much of the poetry shares Thomson's notion of "England as an after-image of Augustan Rome" (Heaney 1980, p.178), Heaney has accurately pointed out the weakness of the book, while at the same time providing a strong reading of the genre itself through an interrogation of this absence. Thus, Heaney allows the classical context to imbricate his reading of the English texts in the book, and both present text and absent context permeate and penetrate each other in a fuller exploration in the essay than is given in the book itself. Heaney's reading can be seen, in the terminology of Mikhail Bakhtin, as heteroglossic, in that different voices and different languages are allowed to confront each other and achieve some kind of dynamic interaction, or dialogisation (Bakhtin 1981, 263).

Here Heaney pluralises the title of the essay so that the 'country of convention' opens its borders to other countries, other languages and other literary traditions. Just as Heaney's reading of this book sees text and context interpenetrate each other, so, by implication, the genre of English pastoral has also set text and context in a dialectical relationship, a relationship which ultimately calls into question the separateness of the English poetic canon as such. Heaney's reading of conventionality has become unconventional in its dislocation of the ground on which the epistemological premises of the book are based. In this reading, there is an obvious similarity with a reading by Derrida of Shelley's *The Triumph of Life*. Here, Derrida also questions the borderlines of a text, suggesting that a text is no longer:

> a finished corpus of writing, some content enclosed in a book or its margins, but a differential network, a fabric of traces referring endlessly to something other than itself, to other differential traces. Thus the text overruns all the limits assigned to it so far (not submerging or drowning them in an undifferentiated homogeneity, but rather making them more complex, dividing and multiplying strokes and lines) (Derrida 1992a, p.84).

This is precisely the process of reading undertaken by Heaney in this essay; he takes the assumptions imposed by the title and format of the book, points to the attenuation of response that the selection criteria impose, an attenuation that has an analogous relationship to the Marxist broom and sociological filleting already mentioned, and proceeds to make them 'more complex, dividing and multiplying strokes and lines'. He furthers this process towards the end of the essay by wondering whether the temporal and spatial limits imposed by the editors on poets who were included in the book are valid.

He questions whether the editors 'brisk dismissal' of the further possibilities of pastoral are well-founded, and goes on to suggest valid reasons for the inclusion of other writers – Edward Thomas, Hugh MacDiarmid, David Jones, A. E. Houseman – and also wonders about Louis MacNeice's eclogues which "represent the form as an enabling resource" (Heaney 1980, p.180). Finally, he further extends the limits of his critique by multiplying some 'strokes and lines' which figure as political borders, and asks whether such seminal works as Synge's *Aran Islands* (pastoral),[7] Kavanagh's *The Great Hunger* (anti-pastoral), and Montague's *The Rough Field* are "not to be regarded just as 'occasional twitches'" before finishing the essay with the ironic question "Or are these latter works held at bay in the term 'frontier pastoral'?" (Heaney 1980, p.180).

This final irony is instructive, as his earlier dialectical interpenetration of text and context demonstrated that the English pastoral had already crossed temporal, political and linguistic frontiers in appropriating Latin and French translations from classical antiquity into a specifically English landscape. However, to adopt another 'perspective backwards', the origin of the master trope of the pastoral was, as Barrell and Bull (1975) have noted, the Eden myth, which, together with classical dreams of a Golden Age "lies behind most versions of pastoral" (Heaney 1980, p.175). Here again, frontiers of language and culture have been crossed by the genre. So his question is, why stop at this particular frontier? If the genre has been sufficiently fluid to engage with the classics and the Bible, perhaps it is also capable of engaging with more modern sensibilities. The frontier, denotative of a spatial binary opposition between one notion of place and another, functions here as both a borderline of the anthology and, at the same time, as a point of possibility which will allow the 'English' pastoral as genre, to develop. In a further expansion of these limits, this development would necessitate an ongoing problematisation of the notion of Englishness in the title as, now, some form of 'Irishness' would be included. Of course, as Heaney has already noted, the final poem in the anthology is Yeats's *Ancestral Houses* (Heaney 1980, p.177), so there has already been a crossing of the 'frontier pastoral'. It becomes clear, then, that his reading of the conventions of the pastoral becomes quite unconventional in its implications and in its reading practice. What we see are what Hillis Miller, in his discussion of anastomosis, terms a variety of "crossings, displacements, and substitutions, as inside becomes outside, outside inside, or as features on either side cross over the wall, membrane or partition dividing the sides" (Hillis Miller 1987, p.7), and I will argue that such transgressive and transgenerative crossings of frontiers are a central feature in Heaney's epistemology of poetry.[8] They are also a crucial aspect of a deconstructive and theoretical reading of canonicity.

Hence, for Heaney, the two poles of an opposition, as exemplified here by text and context, are never simply set down in isolation; nor are they placed in a dialectic which produces a definite synthesis. Instead, his work produces readings which set up a relationship which is fluid and interactive, and in which both terms interact and reflect each other.[9] This relationship is what Theodore Adorno would term a *Kraftfeldt* (force-field), which contains transactional and dialectical interplay of different, and sometimes opposing, forces, and which comprises of juxtaposed clusters of changing elements that, according to Martin Jay, "resist reduction to a common denominator, essential core, or generative first principle" (Jay 1984, p.15). In this essay, that is precisely the structure that is envisaged for a deconstructive notion of the canon: a forcefield which is deliberately chosen, and whose choices are, themselves, subject to verification and justification – that Roman history and literature should be part of a canonical structure is not necessarily to be disputed. However, that *The Apache Chief* also deserves a place in a parallel canon, constituted under different intersections of power and knowledge, is the point of this essay.

In a manner that is strikingly similar to the thinking of Heaney, Derrida has described a similar process, in *Positions*, where what he terms 'undecidables' inhabit an opposition, "resisting and disorganising it, *without ever* constituting a third term, without ever leaving room for a solution in the form of speculative dialectics" (Derrida 1981a, p.43). The answers which Heaney's enabling searches find are often similar 'undecidables', which encourage us to probe the interstices of the text, and to the "network of textual referrals to *other* texts" where each term is "marked by the trace of another term" (Derrida 1981a, p.33).

Perhaps the most important dimension of this deconstructionist reading of the canon is that of temporality. Traditional forces of canonicity were rooted in decisions from the past – the canon was always a retrospective structure, which delimited participation as opposed to encouraging new enunciations of culture and literature. All of the verbal map-readings offered in this discussion participate in one of literature's primary responsibilities, namely that their "concept is linked to the to-come" (Derrida 1992b, p.38). By asking questions of the choices that are creative of the canon, by noting the structured, and hence motivated, nature of these choices, the canon has become many canons, perhaps of smaller calibre, but definitely of greater inclusiveness. It is now becoming common to speak of a postcolonial canon, a feminist canon, canons devoted to racial and class-based literature, gay and lesbian canons and various theoretical canons. The restrictive and conservative function exercised by literature through unthought and untheoretically grounded canonical assumptions has been replaced by a plurality of canons, hence allowing for the free movement of cultural capital in terms of different groups within society.

In *Spectres of Marx*, Jacques Derrida discusses what he terms *hauntology*, in answer to his question: "*[w]hat* is a ghost?" (Derrida 1994, p.10). In this book, he discusses the spectrality of many areas of meaning, seeing ghostly hauntings as traces of possible meanings. One might compare his *hauntology* to the different alternatives that have been repressed by the canon but which have now come into being in the alternative canons under discussion. This is not to say that notions of canonicity should be consigned to history: indeed, quite the contrary. The purpose of decommissioning the canon is to decommission the outdated binary 'either/or' mode of selection and rejection and to replace this modality with the more inclusive paradigm of 'both/and'. As Derrida has put it, it is important for a community to "know its limit – and for its limit to be its *opening*" (Derrida 1995, p.355).

This paper attempts this process of seeing canonical limitations as openings to alternative notions of canonicity. By examining the choices which underpin the canon, and which are themselves related to their societal and cultural contexts, issues of validation and of participation in the activity of literature are interrogated from a perspective which is aware of issues of social justice. The imbrication of text with context, of canonical and non-canonical, of aesthetic and culturally sanctioned choices allows for the voicing, in what Bourdieu terms dominant cultural formations, of the hitherto unvoiced: women, people of colour, the colonised and those whose stories, like that of *The Apache Chief*, were only told as indices of non-value. Such canonical decommissioning deconstructs the rigid thinking that we saw at the beginning of this essay, where reading *The Apache Chief* was seen as inimical to notions of being educated. In a deconstructive paradigm, inclusion, as opposed to exclusion, choices governed by the logic of 'both/and' as opposed to 'either/or', and the ability to enjoy, and critique, studies about ancient Romans and more recent Native Americans, is the desired index of education.

NOTES

[1] Raymond Williams wrote of pastoral poetry and conventions in broadly similar terms in his The *Country and the City*, and Heaney sees this book as in many respects a 'companion volume', incorporating "most of the texts he refers to and underlining or extending his discussion of them" (Heaney 1980, p.174). This aside demonstrates one aspect of the literary-political *nous* that becomes all the clearer as we read the essays and articles; he is ever-aware of the complications and connections between the world, the text and other critics.

[2] Hillis Miller's Joycean example of 'underdarkneath', in *The Ethics of Reading* (Hillis Miller 1987, p.6), captures concretely the interpenetration of one word by another; the traces of the original ontologies of the words, and the neologistic relationship which is brought into being between syntax and semantic value through the anastomosis in question. He sees this as one of the generating linguistic tropes which brings about the crossings, displacements and substitutions between the non-linguistic and language (Hillis Miller 1987, p.7).

[3] The Bakhtin quotation comes from *Marxism and the Philosophy of Language* (Volosinov 1973, p.471).

[4] Strictly speaking context is a cognate of text, but I feel that the example is still a valid one, working as it does both syntactically, semantically and etymologically with 'text' deriving from the Latin for fabric or structure while 'context' derives from the Latin for 'to weave together' or 'compose' (Myers and Simms 1985, 64, 307).

[5] In later essays, the whole issue of translation is discussed in similarly complex

terms, especially in the context of translations from the Irish language; see *The Government of the Tongue, An Duanaire*, and also translations from Eastern European poetry.

[6] This point, made in the 'Afterward' of *Limited Inc.*, is part of what can be seen as a redefinition of one of deconstruction's central axioms *'Il n'y a pas de hors-texte'* (Derrida 1976, p.158) as *'Il n'y a pas de hors contexte'* (Derrida 1988, p.136). Simon Critchley has an informative discussion of this point in his *The Ethics of Deconstruction* (Critchley 1992, pp.31-43).

[7] In a parenthetic aside, directly after mentioning Synge's text he notes '(prose, granted)', a point which underlines my own view that prose, while generically distinct, should not be factored out of any equation in terms of the study or analysis of a writer who is more celebrated within a different generic frame. If Heaney sees the prose of Synge, a playwright, as being important, this bolsters my own case for seeing the prose of Heaney as being worthy of a central place in his canon. It is also a further example of his stretching the borderlines of the book under review by questioning the automatic association of the pastoral with poetry.

[8] Henry Hart makes a similar point in connection with Heaney's volume of prose poems, published in 1975, entitled Stations, in his book *Seamus Heaney: Poet of Contrary Progressions*, (1992, p. 99-118). I would argue that this *modus agendi* of Heaney's can be seen as a driving force in all of his work. Hart's study, which is an excellent, theoretically aware reading of Heaney's poetry, pays comparatively little attention to his prose.

[9] As we shall see, there are often more than two terms brought into the equation.

REFERENCES

Althusser, L. (1977) *Lenin and philosophy and other essays. Second Edition.* London: New Left Books.

Bakhtin, M. (1981) *The Dialogic Imagination: Four Essays.* Translated by Caryl Emerson and Michael Holquist. Austin: University of Texas Press.

Barrell, J. and Bull J (eds). (1975) *The Penguin Book of English Pastoral Verse*, London: Harmondsworth.

Belsey, C. (1980) *Critical Practice.* London: Methuen.

Bloom, H,. de Man, P., Derrida, J., Hartman, G. and Hillis Miller, J. (1992) *Deconstruction and Criticism.* New York: Continuum Press.

Bourdieu, P. (1986) 'The Forms of Capital' in Richardson, J. (ed.) *Handbook of Theory and Research for the Sociology of Education.* New York: Greenwood Press.

Critchley, S. (1992) *The Ethics of Deconstruction: Derrida and Levinas*. Oxford: Basil Blackwell.

Derrida, J. (1976) *Of Grammatology*. Translated by Gayatri Chakravorty Spivak. London: Johns Hopkins Press.

Derrida, J. (1978) *Writing and Difference*. Translated by Alan Bass. London: Routledge.

Derrida, J. (1981a) *Positions*. Translated by Alan Bass. London: Athlone.

Derrida, J. (1981b) *Dissemination*. Translated by Barbara Johnson. First published: Paris (1972) Chicago: Chicago University Press.

Derrida, J. (1982) *Margins of Philosophy*. Translated by Alan Bass. Chicago: Chicago University Press.

Derrida, J. (1988) *Limited Inc*. Translated by Samuel Weber and Jeffrey Mehlman. Evanston, Illinois: Northwestern University Press.

Derrida, J. (1989) *Of Spirit: Heidegger and the Question*. Translated by Geoffrey Bennington and Rachel Bowlby. Chicago: Chicago University Press.

Derrida, J. (1992a) 'Living On – Borderlines' in Bloom, H,. de Man, P., Derrida, J., Hartman, G. and Hillis Miller, J. (1992) *Deconstruction and Criticism*. New York: Continuum Press.

Derrida, J. (1992b) *Acts of Literature*. Edited by Derek Attridge. London: Routledge.

Derrida, J. (1994) *Spectres of Marx: The State of the Debt, the Work of Mourning & the New International*. Translated from the French by Peggy Kamuf. Introduction by Bernd Magnus and Stephen Cullenberg. London: Routledge.

Derrida, J. (1995) *Points...Interviews, 1974-1994*. Edited by Elizabeth Weber. Translated by Peggy Kamuf and others. California: Stanford University Press.

Eagleton, T. (1983) *Literary Theory: An Introduction*. Oxford: Blackwell.

Foucault, M. (1970) *The Order of Things: 'An Archaeology of the Human Sciences'*. Translated by Alan Sheridan-Smith. New York: Random House.

Foucault, M. (1994) *Power. Essential Works of Foucault 1954-1984. Volume 3*. Faubion, J.D. (ed.) Translated by Robert Hurley and others. London: Penguin.

Hart, H. (1992) *Seamus Heaney: Poet of Contrary Progressions*. New York:

Syracuse University Press.

Heaney, S. (1980) *Preoccupations: Selected Prose 1968-1978*. London: Faber.

Heaney, S. (1999) *Beowulf*. London: Faber.

Hillis Miller, J. (1987) *The Ethics of Reading: Kant, de Man, Eliot, Trollope, James, and Benjamin*. The Welleck Library Lectures. New York: Columbia University Press.

Leavis, F.R. (1972) *The Great Tradition*. Harmondsworth: Penguin.

Leavis, F. R. (1976) *The Common Pursuit*. Harmondsworth: Penguin.

Jay, M. (1984) *Adorno*. Fontana Modern Masters. General editor Frank Kermode. London: Fontana

Joyce, J. (1994) *Dubliners*. Introduction by Anthony Burgess. London: Secker and Warburg. First published 1914.

Myers, I. and Simms, M. (1985) *Dictionary and Handbook of Poetry*. London: Longman.

Rylance, R. (1987) *Debating Texts*. Milton Keynes: Open University Press.

Norris, C. (1985) *The Contest of Faculties*. London: Methuen.

Norris, C. (1988) *Deconstruction and the Interests of Theory*. Leicester: Leicester University Press.

Said, E. (1978) *Orientalism*. Harmondsworth: Penguin.

Volosinov, V. N. (1973) *Marxism and the Philosophy of Language*. Translated by Ladislav Matejka and I. R. Titunik. New York: Seminar Press.

Widdowson, P. (ed.) (1982) *Re-Reading English*. London: Methuen.

CHAPTER 7

RELATIVISING IMAGES OF SELF AND OTHER IN THE
INTERCULTURAL LITERATURE CLASSROOM

Sabine Egger

Our world is characterised by internationalisation and fragmentation. Traditional
certainties about social class, ethnic, national and other groupings and identities
are being challenged. As there is more ambivalence, more negotiation is needed
in communication processes. This has been reflected in recent years in the
growing emphasis on the teaching and learning of 'Intercultural Competence' in
Foreign Language (FL) methodology (Roberts *et al.* 2001, p. 10). Intercultural
competence is based on knowledge about other cultures and, more importantly, on
the speakers' awareness of their own patterns of perception. Focusing on the
concept of 'critical intercultural awareness' employed by Michael Byram (1997),
I will discuss how intercultural approaches to the teaching of literature in the
third-level FL classroom may help learners to develop intercultural awareness by
encouraging them to reflect on culturally constructed perspectives and images of
their own and other cultures. Intercultural education in this sense refers to a
process of decentring, of relativising Self and Other in an effort to view both from
a 'third' point of view. After outlining the theoretical background within a
constructivist framework, I will briefly refer to some examples from the third-
level teaching of German as a FL in Mary Immaculate College, particularly to the
use of Turkish-German *Migrantenliteratur*.

THEORETICAL CONSIDERATIONS

The Current Interest in Intercultural Learning

The current interest in the role of culture in language teaching has resulted in the
revision of third-level FL curricula, including novel approaches to literature and
cultural studies in FL teaching - in Irish universities as much as elsewhere
(Fischer 1992; 2001; Roberts *et al.* 2001, pp. 7-8; Rost-Roth 1996, p. 2; Zarate
1997). This 'cultural turn' in FL teaching is, on the one hand, based on pragmatic
considerations, i.e., the assumption that it is not possible to effectively

communicate in a foreign language, even with excellent language skills, without understanding its underlying specific socio-cultural values and conceptualisations (House 1996, p.4). On the other hand, there are more global reasons for the growing interest in intercultural learning in general, and the establishment of the area of *Interkulturelle Germanistik* (intercultural German studies) since the 1980s, in particular, with its focus on '*Fremdverstehen*' (understanding the Other) (Krusche 1985; Thum 1985; Wierlacher 1985; 2000):

> Increased contact with other cultures [...] makes it imperative for us to make a concerted effort to get along with and understand other people who are vastly different from ourselves. The ability, through increased awareness and understanding, to coexist peacefully with people who do not necessarily share our backgrounds, beliefs, values or life styles can not only benefit us in our own neighbourhoods, but can also be a decisive factor in forestalling nuclear annihilations. (Samovar and Porter 1988, cited in Harden and Witte 2000, p. 1)

What Samovar and Porter have suggested rather dramatically in 1988, probably applies to an even greater extent today, since more and more of us inhabit an increasingly globalised and migratory world, in which we have to constantly negotiate between several cultures. Ireland, for example, is currently developing from a monocultural into an increasingly multicultural society. Having traditionally been a country of high emigration, this has radically changed, due to the growth of the Irish economy in recent years, and Ireland is now experiencing growing levels of immigration, both with regard to asylum seekers and foreign workers (Fischer 2001, p. 224). The number of work permits issued to non-nationals, for instance, has trebled between 1999 and 2000, and the overall number of immigrants predicted for the next six years is three hundred and thirty six thousand (*The Irish Times*, 24 January 2001). Limerick City alone now has residents from one hundred and thirty different nationalities, according to the local Immigration Office. Since the 1980s, there has been a growing awareness in international research in education, the humanities and social sciences that 'acculturation' is a 'bilateral or multilateral' process (Auernheimer 1995, p. 28), involving the 'natives' as much as the 'foreigners', and is based on a willingness on all sides to learn from the Other. Paul Cullen in his recent book, *Refugees and Asylum Seekers in Ireland*, however, criticises what he sees as a failure of the Irish government to develop and implement policies which allow for acculturation in this sense:

> It isn't just asylum-seekers who need education and assistance with integration; there is evidence that much more needs to be done to educate Irish people about other cultures and the challenges of living in a multi-cultural society. The authorities need to take a more pro-active role in countering the negative images and stereotypes propagated by the media and, yes, government departments. (2000, p. 59, cited in Fischer, 2001)

While there is clearly a need for the further development of intercultural awareness in various sectors of Irish society, this need has been addressed in different disciplines in tertiary education, as well as in Irish primary and post-primary school curricula for different subject areas, including FL teaching. 'Cultural awareness' is stated as one of the three main objectives in the *Draft Curriculum Guidelines* of the 'Pilot Project on Modern Languages in the Primary School' (NCCA 1999, p. 5), and is also mentioned in the Language Syllabus for Secondary Schools (Harden 2000, p. 117).

Intercultural Learning in the Context of FL Learning

The learning of a foreign language may provide a particularly suitable context for intercultural education, because communication in FL teaching is, by definition, concerned with interaction that is interlingual as well as intercultural, that involves mediating and establishing relationships between one's own and other cultures, and the confrontation with arising questions of identity and 'alterity', i. e., perceived Otherness (Albrecht and Wierlacher 2000, p. 296). Opinions differ, however, as to how and where intercultural learning in the context of FL acquisition can best take place. While some, such as Theo Harden, maintain that real intercultural learning can only take place during a prolonged period of immersion in a FL and cultural environment, where one has to question and adjust one's cultural assumptions as a matter of survival, and cannot be achieved in a classroom situation (Harden 2000, pp. 120-121), the majority of researchers propose a combination of methods within the FL classroom, including, to varying degrees, the use of new media, literature and area studies, role-play, the simulation and discussion of authentic every-day situations and, in recent times, the use of ethnographic methods in preparation for and during placement periods abroad (Christ 1996; House 1996; Kramsch 1995; Roberts *et al.* 2001). Like Dore Fischer, in her recent article 'Irish Images of Germany', I would like to suggest the FL literature classroom as a place of intercultural learning (2001). While she does not explain, within a coherent theoretical framework, how this process may take place and why literary texts may have particular merits with regard to intercultural learning, I will attempt to do so, with a focus on the development of learners' critical awareness of culturally constructed images of Self and Other, based on the comparative approach of '*Komparative Imagologie*' (image studies) (Dyserinck 1988; Leersen 1999; Schwarze, 1998, pp. 232-234).

Literature, Culture and Identity: The Constructivist Perspective

Image studies are informed by a broad definition of culture, based on the assumption that human beings collectively construct their social and cultural reality (Schmidt 1987; Hansen 1993, p.11). 'Culture' or 'cultural programme' refers, according to semiotics and constructivism, to the totality of ideas, patterns of perception, values and meanings, generated by a group of human beings, and expressed in symbolic systems (Geertz 1993). This includes the way people see themselves and others, as every individual and collective Self has discourses on its own identity, as well as on the identity of some Other against which it defines itself (Albrecht and Wierlacher 2000, p. 296; Fischer 1987; Giesen 1991, pp. 9-18). The assumption that systems of individual and collective images of Self and Other have a bipolar structure, is central to any analysis based on image studies: In the example given below, a 'Turkish' hetero-image of the 'German' mainstream culture would be analysed with regard to its explicit representation of the 'Germans', but the aspects portrayed would at the same time express relevant aspects of 'Turkish' reality, i.e. implicitly reflect the values and norms of the group that has produced the image in question. A collective Self can comprise of a national culture or a smaller ethnic, gender or social group. This model allows for both intra- and intercultural relationships, because cultures are not monolithic blocks, but rather consist of a complex network of ethnic, regional, social and gender-specific subcultures and their discourses (Bennett 1998, p. 23-24). Also, the larger units of 'national cultures', providing the primary focus in FL education, influence each other in a variety of ways (Auernheimer 1995, p. 2; Kramsch 1995, pp. 5-6). Comparable to language as a 'symbolic system', literature is seen as a specific form of generating versions of reality, within particular cultures, rather than simply 'reflecting' them. The formal qualities of literary texts may thus be seen as particular forms of generating ideological fictions, patterns of perception, of thinking and feeling. Within a constructivist framework based on Foucault, literature can be regarded as an '*elaborierter Interdiskurs*' (elaborated interdiscourse), since it tends to incorporate themes and conventions of different specialised discourses (Link 1984, p. 65). Because of this 'interdiscoursive' quality, it is even more suited than other manifestations of culture to give an insight into the cultural programme.

Intercultural Learning: A Constructivist Definition

Intercultural learning encompasses the acquisition of 'intercultural awareness' (Byram 1997), or 'intercultural understanding' (Harden and Witte 2000). These terms are largely synonymous and, in my view, preferable to the widely used 'intercultural communicative competence' (Fischer 2001, p. 226; Roberts *et al.* 2001), because the latter implies, by analogy with the concept of linguistic competence, that there is a fixed set of rules to be acquired as to how to behave in intercultural communication. Such communicative situations, however, are characterised by the complex interaction of a variety of factors, including levels of affective, as well as rational, behaviour (Neuner 2000, p.42). The development of intercultural awareness is the result of a number of dialogical, dynamic and reflective processes (Harden and Witte 2000, pp. 13-15). Firstly, the individual is only able to position and construct him-/herself in dialectic communication with others, as is apparent from the theoretical considerations above. This does not, however, reduce him or her to a passive receptacle of collective ideas:

> As a speech actor he or she creates meanings in the actual production of speech shared by all members of a given culture, but the elements of speech are filled by the speaker with particular meaning which to a certain degree is not communicable because everyone within a culture appropriates words in slightly different ways. (Harden and Witte 2000, p. 15)

Secondly, meaning is never fixed, but always in the process of emerging. If one accepts the idea of a dynamic construction of the self within a highly complex network of socio-cultural, mental and linguistic representations underlying constructivist approaches, then it follows, thirdly, that the basic mechanisms of understanding the FL and culture are the same as understanding one's own language and culture. Intercultural learning is a reflective practice: The more the learner understands about the foreign language and culture, the more he or she becomes critically aware of his or her own language categories and culturally moulded patterns of cognitive construction. The critical discussion of the home culture thus becomes an important element of FL classes. The process of understanding the Other is inextricably linked to the simultaneous process of alienating the familiar.

Changing Places, Changing Perspectives

Intercultural learning, as envisaged here, refers to a process of decentring, of relativising Self and Other in an effort to understand both on their own terms, an ability to adopt a flexible, rather than ethnocentric, perspective, even to be able to see the world temporarily through the eyes of others. The assumption that one is actually able to put oneself into somebody else's place is debatable. It is, in my opinion, more realistic to work with the concept of a dynamic 'third place' as suggested by Claire Kramsch, drawing on Homi Bhaba's ideas outlined in 'Post-colonial authority and post-modern guilt' (1992) and *The Location of Culture* (1994), to replace the binarism of Us versus Them, or Self versus Other that essentialises and reduces people to one or the other of their many cultural dimensions (Kramsch 1995, p. 89). It implies firstly an awareness that the distinction between the other and one's own culture is not ontological but relational, and that this relationship is dynamic and constantly changing and, secondly, an understanding of the social, economical and historical factors involved in the development of perspectives on the collective Self and Other (Christ 1996, p. 15). The most fundamental insight to be gained is, therefore, that perspectives or patterns of perception are not naturally given and, as it would appear from an ethnocentric point of view, that cultural barriers are not insurmountable, but that they are collectively constructed and changeable. This is a precondition for the potential acceptance of other perspectives as different, but equally valid as one's own, and thus a step outside rigid binarisms and toward intercultural awareness. The analysis of images of Self and Other in literary texts can help learners in this process, since it develops an awareness of the existence of different patterns of perception, especially if the textual analysis is complemented by activities that encourage learners to reflect on their own patterns of perception. This leads to an understanding that a relationship of alterity, manifested in a binary set of interdependent images of Self and Other, is neither a purely subjective, nor objective phenomenon, but rather the product of both subjective and collective processes. Intercultural awareness further presupposes an understanding of the 'diachronic context' of the relation between Self and Other (Kramsch 1995, p. 83), since cultural patterns of perception are embedded within historical relations of power and authority; they are the result of a long personal and collective development (Halbwachs 1950). It is, therefore, not sufficient that learners formally recognise the frames of reference, in which they live, think and communicate. They must also be connected with their social and historical contexts and contents in order not to remain empty and abstract (Christ 1996, p. 15). A mere stating of existing culturally different patterns may even have the adverse effect of reinforcing the stereotyping and essentialising of people in one or other of their cultural dimensions - as 'German, 'Turkish', 'woman', or 'Muslim'. Intercultural theorists agree that the rational level of awareness must be complemented, by a level of 'empathy', i.e., the emotional reaction of the Self to the feelings and perceptions of the Other (Schinschke 1995, p. 45). They differ, however, with regard to the relative significance they assign to 'affective' or 'empathic' aspects on the one hand, and cognitive aspects on the other, in the learning process (Geertz 1976, p.224; Ropers 1990, p. 118; Schwerdtfeger 1991). While affective factors obviously play a significant role in the perception of Self and Other, the process of decentring and relativising described above, must be based on the rational reflection of such - often affectively acquired - perceptions.

Implementing Literary Texts in Intercultural Learning

Literary texts are particularly useful in FL teaching in third-level in general: they encourage learners to develop 'a feeling for language' and offer a wide variety of tasks for speaking and writing in the FL (Bredella 2000, p. 160). However, they can play a particular role in intercultural learning, because literature, as an elaborated interdiscourse, incorporates themes, perspectives, and ways of expression from a variety of discourses in a particular culture. The fourth point of the following list, compiled by Lothar Bredella, refers - albeit in different words - to this generic quality of literature (2000, p. 160):

- they are a document of the foreign culture which can easily be brought into the foreign language classroom,
- they need the co-operation of the learners so that the process of understanding is at the centre of our attention,
- they encourage different responses and interpretations and thus reflect on the process of understanding,
- they present or represent experiences and conflicts which are relevant for the foreign culture,
- they present experiences which encourage the reader to relate them to their own experiences,
- they offer us models for discussing what it means to recognise or misrecognise others.

What is further implied, rather than stated clearly in Bredella's list, is that literary texts lend themselves to an intercultural approach which is concerned with particular ways of seeing or patterns of perception, because they often foreground subjective and collective patterns of perception or points of view - for example with regard to the point of view of a narrator or characters in a novel. Contrasting perspectives of characters associated with different cultures in a text provide an opportunity for the discussion of characters', as well as learners', perspectives in class. In a culturally diverse group readers will respond in different ways to the same text (Ehlers 1994, p. 310; Gollner 2001, p. 11). In a third-level seminar, learners usually include male and female students, mature and younger students, students from urban and rural backgrounds, from different social classes, and different regions in Ireland, as well as International Students from a number of European countries. Even if the primary thematic focus in my example is on Turkish-German, therefore ethnic relations, factors such as social, regional and gender difference must be taken into account. Literature can help to involve affective channels of learning, for, as Claire Kramsch has put it: "it is literature that opens up 'reality beyond realism' and that enables readers to live other lives - by proxy" (1995, p. 86). While it is important to recognise others in their Otherness and respect their collective identities, this "must be supplemented by a hermeneutics of complementarity", an awareness of those things we have in common, most essentially our humanity (Bredella 2000, p. 156). Identification of the reader with a character from a different culture in a text, allows for the raising of awareness for shared human - or gender-, age-, or class-related - properties and difficulties, especially when made explicit in the intercultural classroom. What finally distinguishes literary from other kinds of discourse, and adds even more to the potential of literature for intercultural learning, is its 'auto-referentielle Textstruktur' (self-referential textual structure) - the way literature draws attention to its thematic and formal qualities (Göllner 2001, p. 18). Literary texts often question, or even deconstruct images of Self and Other by juxtaposing different perspectives, by criticising particular ways of perceiving and thinking, by means of irony or through exposing the subjective nature of perception as such. In a class which aims at combining literary and intercultural studies, rather than employing literary texts merely as a source of content information about a foreign culture, it is challenging to analyse and discuss *how* particular poetic strategies are employed in literary texts in order to give shape and meaning to particular cultural experiences.

MIGRANTENLITERATUR IN THE INTERCULTURAL CLASSROOM: A PRACTICAL EXAMPLE

The Choice of Texts

The choice of suitable texts and the questions raised with regard to them thus depends on the group of learners involved. In a third-level course with a focus on images of Self and Other, these may include questions such as: What traditions of images of a particular group can be found in the literature of another group? How do individual authors make recourse to them? How do they use known stereotypes? Do they discuss them explicitly in the text? Do they use techniques such as irony to deconstruct stereotypes? Ehlers, Hunfeld and Schinschke discuss different approaches to reading foreign language texts in the intercultural classroom in further detail (Ehlers 1994; Hunfeld 1990; Schinschke 1995). *Migrantenliteratur*, i.e., literature written by migrants, is particularly suitable for intercultural learning on this level, since its central theme is the situation of people living 'between' or 'with two cultures' that are not easily reconcilable, and the associated issues of identity, language, home, estrangement and stereotypical perceptions (HSM 1983, p. 16). German-Turkish writing, or the work of German authors of Turkish descent, or of Turkish authors writing in the German language, belongs to this body of literature. The problems arising from attempts to categorise this literature, illustrate the influence of different perspectives on the choice of such labels, and is an obvious topic for discussion within the course. The analysis of the chosen literary texts, with a particular focus on literary representations of 'Turkish Germans' and 'German Germans', in a literature seminar should be complemented by a lecture/seminar about social, economic, historical and institutional aspects of German-Turkish relations in contemporary Germany. This component should not be reduced to a one-way communication of factual information, but also include the discussion of relevant auto- and hetero-images in visual and other non-literary media. Allowing for a dialogical process, involving learners' and teacher's perspectives, the learning process in both components should be largely student-centred. The structure of the course is loosely based on the experience of an intercultural module on German-Jewish relations in Mary Immaculate College (Egger 2002). The learners in this module were mostly Irish students who had completed an Off-Campus placement of either six or twelve months' duration in a German-speaking country during the previous academic year. The remainder of the group consisted of international students from Germany, Austria and Poland. These students can easily relate aspects dealt with in the chosen texts, such as questions of individual and cultural identity, and the confrontation with stereotypes, to their own experience of the year abroad. The course structure and content, however, can also be adapted to groups of learners with a lower level of 'intercultural experience' and linguistic competence. The theme of Germany as a multicultural country, with a particular focus on the Turkish as the biggest ethnic minority, was also chosen with a view to challenging dominant - Irish - perceptions of Germany as synonymous with either 'Aryan'-type Nazi soldiers, recurrently appearing in feature and documentary films in Irish television, and plain-looking engineers advertising for 'Vorsprung durch Technik', or Bavaria and the Oktoberfest, as well as the growing relevance of multicultural issues in the Irish context.

Addressing the Learners' Critical Awareness

Since the main aim of the course is to achieve a greater understanding of patterns of perception and cultural construction, of stereotypes and the processes of stereotyping, apart from an insight into methods of literary analysis, it is important for the students to become aware of their own categories and patterns. The first literature seminar should therefore be spent with group activities directly relating to the students' experience. The following example from the previous German-Jewish seminar can easily be adapted to the current theme. Groups of four were asked to make a list of their associations with and impressions of Germany - for the majority of participants a foreign culture - on a large sheet of paper. If the number of international students allows it, they may be put into separate groups, thus increasing the chance of culturally different perceptions and images finding expression. The listed statements were collected and compared in a class discussion (Egger 2002, p.8). Stereotypical statements were written on the whiteboard by the lecturer, in tabular form, ordered according to negative or positive connotations. The students were then asked to rephrase the listed statements in such a way, that the negative ones became positive and vice versa. During the listing of the items on the whiteboard, a discussion developed, further encouraged by the lecturer, regarding the 'truth' of particular statements, as well as parallels and discrepancies between them. The students were thus able to identify ideas and perceptions which tend to differ to some extent in a culturally diverse group. Differences and parallels in perceptions and evaluations showed that these were cultural constructs. These outcomes, and possible reasons for the development of different perceptions, were the subject of further class discussion. Without prior theoretical knowledge, the students mentioned the influence of different historical experience as a cause for different perceptions, the role of media and the fact that both individual and collective factors seemed be of significance here. At the end of the class, the students, again in groups, worked out a preliminary definition of 'stereotype'. To prepare for the next seminar, they were asked to read a short theoretical introduction into image studies. Students' critical awareness can also be addressed by their confrontation with a portrayal of their own culture in texts of the target culture in one of the initial sessions of an intercultural seminar series, before focusing on the particular Turkish-German theme. As examples may serve Heinrich Böll's *Irisches Tagebuch* (Irish diary), originally published in 1957, and Hugo Hamilton's short story 'Nazi Christmas' in his 1996 collection *Dublin Where the Palm Trees Grow*. Dore Fischer lists further examples of suitable Irish texts in English in her article (2001, pp. 231-232). Böll paints a romantic picture of a poor but largely idyllic Ireland in the 1950s, drawing on existing stereotypes, and in turn, exerting significant influence on German perceptions of Ireland until today (Dohmen 1994). Hamilton, a younger Dublin writer of Irish-German parentage, writes about xenophobic Irish reactions to his bicultural background at the time of the Eichmann trial in Israel. While Böll's stereotypical image is bound to be in obvious contrast with Irish students' perception of Ireland and the Irish, as well as, to differing extents, to perceptions of contemporary Ireland of international students, thus bound to provoke debate about these images, Hamilton's 'Nazi Christmas' depicts a similar, but reversed, process of perception in terms of stereotypical images:

> It began with the man in the fish shop saying "Achtung!" and all the customers turning around to look at us [...]. We were exposed. Germans. War Criminals using Ireland as a sanctuary. There was a chance they might have overlooked the whole thing if it wasn't for the man in the fish shop trying out some more of his German. All the stuff he had picked up from films like *Von Ryan's Express* and *The Great Escape*. "Guten Morgen", he said leaning over the counter, then leaning back with an explosive laugh that acted as a trademark for his shop. Our mother was shy of these friendly, red-faced Irishmen. She smiled back at all the people in the shop and they smiled back silently. That was the thing about Ireland. They were all so friendly [...]. "Halt! We must not forgetten der change." [...] It was as though the man in the fish shop had let out this profane secret about us. The word was out. Our assumed identity as Irish children was blown. Everywhere we went, the German past floated on the breeze after us. "Heil Hitler!" we heard them shout, on the way to Mass, on the way to school, on the way back from the shops [...]. (Hamilton 1996, pp. 9-10)

Not only does Hamilton confront the reader with stereotypical images of a German Other, and an Irish Self, probably shared to a certain extent by the Irish students, but he also subverts simplistic notions of monolithic identity by inviting the reader to share and reflect on the protagonist's experience of having to live with two identities and the reductionist perceptions of him by his surroundings.

Working With Texts in the Target Language

The texts discussed in the following literature seminars should be in German, such as, for example, Nevfel Cumart's poem 'Lanu' (given here with an English translation). On the one hand, having to read a literary text in a foreign language poses an additional barrier for the reader attempting to gain access to the text. On the other hand, however, the 'alienness' of the language serves as an additional signal for the reader to read the text more carefully, as well as forcing him/her to read more slowly, and to be more perceptive to other aspects of the text's form and content. The reader's awareness of his/her linguistic lack of competence can help raise his/her awareness of a similar lack of intercultural competence in understanding the culturally 'alien' perspective that the text confronts him/her with (Krusche 1985, p. 139). This is a precondition for an intercultural understanding that does not simply seek to assimilate the Other within one's own frame of reference, but aims at a relativising of perspectives. Nevfel Cumart's poetry is, like Hamilton's, concerned with the complexity of individual and collective identities. Cumart, a member of the second generation of Turks living in Germany, writes about the cultural tug-of-war between the very different worlds of his parents and his German peers, the loss of sense of self arising from this identity crisis, the stereotyping of his ethnic group and the crippling effect of being socially marginalised. The love poem 'Lanu' ironically points to the problem of stereotyping through a thematic twist in the three concluding lines:

meine freundin lanu	my girlfriend lanu
sehr gut noch	I can still remember her
kann ich mich an sie erinnern	very well
mit ihren unzähligen sommersprossen	with her countless freckles
den weizenblonden haaren	her wheat-blonde hair
einem gesicht	her face
engelsgleich	like an angel's
manchmal verängstigt	sometimes frightened
aber stets neugierig voller vitalität	but always curious and full of vitality
schelmisch lächelnd immerzu	with a roguish smile all the time
und niemals	and never
in all den nächten	in all those nights
niemals	never
ertappte ich sie beim gähnen	did I catch her yawning
meine freundin lanu	my girlfriend lanu

ich sehe sie genau vor mir	I see her clearly before me
wie wir im kalten morgengrauen	as in the cold first light of dawn
still und heimlich	quietly and furtively
meinen wagen	we pushed my car
vom haus ihrer eltern	away from her parents' house
wegschieben	soundlessly
geräuschlos	so as not
um ja nicht	to wake up her father
ihren vater zu wecken	her father
ihren vater	who was secretly plagued by the
den insgeheim der alptraum plagte	nightmare
ich würde ihm seine tochter lanu	that I would want to buy his daughter lanu
für vierzehn kamele abkaufen wollen	from him for fourteen camels

    (Cumart 1998, pp. 14-15)

Many of Cumart's poems are quite accessible to the foreign language reader, due to their simple language and structure. Prose texts by writers such as Emine Sevgi Özdamar or Zafer Senocak, as well as the short texts or Rap lyrics by a variety of authors in anthologies such as Irmgard Ackermann's or Feridun Zaimoglu's, present a variety of aspects of the Turkish-German experience, by means of different formal techniques, from the points of view of men and women, of narrators and speakers belonging to different generations and social backgrounds (Ackermann 1983; Zaimoglu 1999). It is generally advisable, for an intercultural FL literature class, to choose texts with an explicit thematic focus on ethnic or other intercultural issues in the broader sense, i.e., a 'littérature engagée', addressing concrete socio-political themes, rather than texts foregrounding their experimental form (Montua 1991, p. 67).

CONCLUSION

Images of Self and Other are not restricted to particular cultural spaces. They rather illustrate the multiple relations and interdependences between cultures - and subcultures. Most intercultural relations are determined by economic relations of domination and dependence - those between the rich North or West and the poor South/East, between 'natives' and 'foreigners', the settled community and Travellers. These relations of inequality must be taken into account in intercultural pedagogy, since there is a danger otherwise that they are interpreted in an essentialist way - as has been the case, for example, with regard to the glossing over of social or economic inequality in the public discourse about Islamic Fundamentalism in recent years. Intercultural pedagogy must be informed by an awareness of the extent to which it is influenced by economic factors and by subjective attitudes toward these. While image studies do not primarily focus on the socio-economic conditions of alterity, their theoretical framework allows for the potential inclusion of such factors. Armin Nahessi, for example, shows how the 'foreigner' becomes an 'enemy', when perceived, within the binary grid, as a competitor for limited resources (1995, p. 458). Such a detailed analysis of socio-economic factors, however, exceeds the scope of intercultural foreign language studies and should be left to the social sciences.

While FL educators find themselves under political pressure to help solve the social and economical problems of our times due to, at times diametrically opposed, educational and ideological motives, their ability to do so is necessarily limited. I hope to have shown, nonetheless, to what extent the use of literature in intercultural FL education can contribute to the development of an intercultural awareness in students, which is not restricted to their ability to communicate successfully with members of their FL target cultures, but that also allows them to bring a better understanding of diversity to their everyday lives in their increasingly multiethnic, multilingual communities.

REFERENCES

Ackermann I. (ed.) (1983) *In zwei Sprachen leben. Berichte, Erzählungen, Gedichte von Ausländern*. Munich: Dtv.

Albrecht, C. and Wierlacher, A. (2000) 'Benötigt wird profundes Fremdheitswissen' in Wierlacher, A. (ed.), *Kulturthema Kommunikation: Konzepte - Inhalte - Funktionen. Festschrift und Leistungsbild des Instituts für Internationale Kommunikation und Auswärtige Kulturarbeit (IIK Bayreuth) aus Anlass seines zehnjährigen Bestehens 1990-2000*. Möhnesee: Residence.

Auernheimer, G. (1995) *Einführung in die interkulturelle Erziehung*. Darmstadt: Wissenschaftliche Buchgesellschaft.

Bennett, T. (1998) *Culture. A Reformer's Science*. London: Sage.

Bhabha, H. (1992) 'Postcolonial Authority and Post-Modern Guilt' in Grossberg, L., Nelson, P. and Treichler, P. (eds) *Cultural Studies*. London: Routledge.

Bhabha, H. (1994) *The Location of Culture*. London: Routledge.

Böll, H. (1957) *Irisches Tagebuch*. Cologne: Kiepenheuer & Witsch. (Trans. By Vennevitz L. (1984) *Irish Journal. A Traveller's Portrait of Ireland*.

London: Sphere Books.)

Bredella, L. (2000) 'The Significance of Intercultural Understanding in the Foreign Language Classroom' in Harden, T. and Witte, A. (eds) in collaboration with Riou, J. *The Notion of Intercultural Understanding in the Context of German as a Foreign Language*. Oxford: Lang.

Byram, M. (1997) *Teaching and Assessing Intercultural Competence*. Clevedon: Multicultural Matters.

Christ, H. (1996) 'Fremdverstehen und interkulturelles Lernen'. *Zeitschrift für Interkulturellen Fremdsprachenunterricht* [Online], Vol. 1, No. 3, pp.1-22 (http://www.ualberta.ca/~german/ejournal/christ/htm) (Accessed on 10th April 2002)

Cullen, P. (2000) *Refugees and Asylum Seekers in Ireland*.Cork: Cork University Press.

Cumart, N. (1998) *Waves of Time/Wellen der Zeit*, trans. by E. Bourke. Düsseldorf: Grupello.

Dohmen, D. (1994). *Das deutsche Irlandbild: Imagologische Untersuchungen zur Darstellung Irlands und der Iren in der deutschsprachigen Literatur* (Studia Imagologica, 6). Amsterdam & Atlanta, GA: Rodopi.

Dyserinck, H. (1988) 'Komparatistische Imagologie: Zur politischen Tragweite einer europäischen Wissenschaft von der Literatur' in Dyserinck, H. and Syndram, K.U. (eds), *Europa und das nationale Selbstverständnis. Imagologische Probleme in Literatur, Kunst und Kultur des 19. und 20. Jahrhunderts*. Bonn: Bouvier.

Egger, S. (2002) 'Komparatistische Imagologie' im interkulturellen Literaturunterricht. *Zeitschrift für Interkulturellen Fremdsprachenunterricht* [Online], Vol. 6 No. 3, pp. 1-22. (http://www.ualberta.ca/~german/ejournal/imagologie.htm) (Accessed on 10th April 2002)

Ehlers, S. (1994). 'Literatur im aufgabenorientierten Fremdsprachenunterricht. Vorschläge für eine interpretative Methodologie'. *Jahrbuch Deutsch als Fremdsprache*, Vo. 20, pp. 303-322.

Fischer, D. (1992) 'Intercultural Communication and Language Teaching'. *Journal of the Modern Language Association of Northern Ireland*. Vol. 22, No. 7, pp. 22-31.

Fischer, D. (2001) 'Irish Images of Germany: Using Literary Texts in Intercultural

Learning'. *Language, Culture and Curriculum*. Vol. 14, No.3, 224-234.

Fischer, M. (1987) 'Literarische Imagologie am Scheideweg: Die Erforschung des Bildes vom anderen Land' in Blaicher G. (ed.) *Erstarrtes Denken: Studien zu Klischee Stereotyp und Vorurteil in englischsprachiger Literatur*. Tübingen: Narr.

Geertz, C. (1973) *The Interpretation of Cultures*. New York: Basic Books.

Geertz, C. (1976) 'From the Native's Point of View: On the Nature of Anthropological Understanding' in Basso, K. H. and Selby, H. A. (eds) *Meaning in Anthropology*. Albuquerque: University of New Mexico Press.

Giesen, B.(ed.) (1991) *Nationale und kulturelle Identität: Studien zur Entwicklung des kollektiven Bewußtseins in der Neuzeit*. Frankfurt/M.: Suhrkamp.

Göllner, T. (2001) *Sprache, Literatur, kultureller Kontext. Studien zur Kulturwissenschaft und Literaturästhetik*. Würzburg: Königshausen & Neumann.

Halbwachs, M. (1950) *La mémoire collective*. Paris: Presses Universitaires de France.

Hamilton, H. (1996) *Dublin Where the Palm Trees Grow*. London: Faber & Faber.

Hansen, Klaus P. (1993). 'Die Herausforderung der Landeskunde durch die moderne Kulturtheorie' in Hansen, K. (ed.), *Kulturbegriff und Methode: Der stille Paradigmenwechsel in den Geisteswissenschaften* (S. 95-114). Tübingen: Narr.

Harden, T. (2000) 'The Limits of Understanding' in Harden, T. and Witte, A. (eds) in collaboration with Riou, J. *The Notion of Intercultural Understanding in the Context of German as a Foreign Language*. Oxford: Lang.

Harden, T. and Witte, A. (2000) 'Introduction' in Harden, T. and Witte, A. (eds) in collaboration with Riou, J. *The Notion of Intercultural Understanding in the Context of German as a Foreign Language*. Oxford: Lang.

Holzbrecher, A. (1997) *Wahrnehmung des Anderen. Zur Didaktik interkulturellen Lernens*. Opladen: Westdeutscher Verlag.

House, J. (1996). 'Zum Erwerb interkultureller Kompetenz im Unterricht des Deutschen als Fremdsprache'. *Zeitschrift für Interkulturellen remdsprachenunterricht* [Online], Vol. 1, No. 3, pp. 1-21. http://www.ualberta.ca/~german/ejournal/house.htm) (Accessed on 10th April 2002)

HSM (1983) 'Zwischen zwei Stühlen' in Ackermann I. (ed.) *In zwei Sprachen leben. Berichte, Erzählungen, Gedichte von Ausländern* (pp. 16-17). Munich: dtv.

Hunfeld, H. (1990) *Literatur als Sprachlehre. Ansätze eines hermeneutisch orientierten Sprachunterricht.* Berlin: Langenscheidt.

Kramsch, C. (1995) 'The Cultural Component of Language Teaching'. *Language, Culture and Curriculum,* Vol. 8, No. 12, pp. 83-92.

Krusche, D.(1985) *Literatur und Fremde. Zur Hermeneutik kulturräumlicher Distanz.* Munich: Iudicium.

Leersen, J. (1999) On Imagologie/image studies in Leersen, J. (ed.) Images [Online] (http://www.hum.uva.nl/images/info/ologie.html. (Accessed on 10th April 2002).

Link, J. (1984) 'Über ein Modell synchroner Systeme von Kollektivsymbolen sowie seiner Rolle bei der Diskurs-Konstitution' in Link, J. and W. Wülfing (eds.) *Bewegung und Stillstand in Metaphern und Mythen.* Stuttgart: Metzler.

Montua, M.-C. (1991) 'Textes de littérature engagée: Lecture pour le cours de langue'. *Praxis des neusprachlichen Unterrichts.* Vol. 1 , pp. 67-73.

Nahessi, A. (1995) Der Fremde als Vertrauter: Soziologische Beobachtungen zur Konstruktion von Identitäten und Differenzen. *Kölner Zeitschrift für Soziologie.* Vol. 47, No. 3, pp. 443-463.

National Council for Curriculum and Assessment (1999) *Pilot Project on Modern Languages in the Primary School: Draft Curriculum.* Dublin: Brunswick Press.

Neuner, G. (2000) 'The 'Key Qualifications' of Intercultural Understanding and the Rudiments of Intercultural Foreign Language Didactics and Methodology' in Harden, T. and Witte, A. (eds) in collaboration with Riou, J. *The Notion of Intercultural Understanding in the Context of German as a Foreign Language.* Oxford: Lang.

Roberts, C., Byram, M., Barro, A., Jordan, S and Street, B. (2001) *Language Learners as Ethnographers.* Clevedon, Buffalo, Toronto & Sidney: Multilingual Matters.

Ropers, N. (1990) 'Vom anderen her denken. Empathie als paradigmatischer

Beitrag zur Völkerverstandigung' in Steinweg, R. and Wellmann, C. (eds) *Die vergessene Dimension internationaler Konflikte: Subjektivität.* Frankfurt/M.: Suhrkamp.

Rost-Roth, M. (1996) 'Deutsch als Fremdsprache und interkulturelle Kommunikation: Relevanzbereiche für den Fremdsprachenunterricht und Untersuchungen zu ethnographischen Besonderheiten deutschsprachiger Interaktionen im Kulturvergleich'. *Zeitschrift für Interkulturellen Fremdsprachenunterricht* [Online], Vol.1, No.1, pp. 1-19. (http://www.ualberta.ca/~german/ejournal/archive/rost11.htm) (Accessed on 10th April 2002)

Schinschke, A. (1995) *Literarische Texte im interkulturellen Lernprozess. Zur Verbindung von Literatur und Landeskunde im Fremdsprachenunterricht Französisch.* Tübingen: Narr.

Schmidt, S. J. (1987) *Der Diskurs des radikalen Konstruktivismus.* Frankfurt/M.: Suhrkamp.

Schwarze, M. (1998) 'Imagologie, komparatistische' in Ansgar Nünning (ed.), *Metzler Lexikon. Literatur- und Kulturtheorie* (pp. 232-234). Stuttgart: Metzler.

Schwerdtfeger, I. (1991) 'Kulturelle Symbole und Emotionen im Fremdsprachenunterricht. Umriss eines Neuansatzes für den Unterricht von Landeskunde'. *Info DaF*, Vol.18, pp. 237-251.

Seeber, U. (1987) 'Zur Rolle von Klischee und Stereotyp in der englischen Literaturkritik und Literaturtheorie des 20. Jahrhunderts' in Blaicher, G. (ed.) *Erstarrtes Denken: Studien zu Klischee, Stereotyp und Vorurteil in der englischsprachigen Literatur.* Tübingen: Narr.

Thum, B. (1985). Auf dem Wege zu einer interkulturellen Germanistik. *Jahrbuch Deutsch als Fremdsprache*, Vol. 11, pp. 329-341.

Wierlacher, A. (ed.) (1985) *Das Fremde und das Eigene. Prolegomena zu einer interkulturellen Germanistik.* Munich: Iudicium.

Wierlacher, A. (2000) 'Konturen und Aufgabenfelder kulturwissenschaftlicher Xenologie' in Wierlacher A. (ed.) *Kulturthema Kommunikation: Konzepte - Inhalte - Funktionen. Festschrift und Leistungsbild des Instituts für Internationale Kommunikation und Auswärtige Kulturarbeit (IIK Bayreuth) aus Anlass seines zehnjährigen Bestehens 1990-2000.* Möhnesee: Résidence.

Zaimoglu, F. (1999) *KanakSprak. 24 Misstöne vom Rande der Gesellschaft.* Hamburg: Rotbuch.

Zarate, G. (1997) 'The Intercultural Dimension: Definition, Objectives and Evaluation' in Council of Europe (ed.) *The Sociocultural and Intercultural Dimension of Language Learning and Teaching* (pp. 11-16). Strasbourg.

CHAPTER 8

PHILOSOPHY AND INTERCULTURAL PEDAGOGY – A CASE STUDY IN MEDIEVAL ISLAMIC THOUGHT

Jones Irwin

Students of philosophy in most Western universities might be forgiven for thinking that speculation on the meaning of life, at least in a systematic and meaningful form, has been exclusively a tradition of the West. Beginning in Greece in 500BC, does not the development of philosophy show an unswerving devotion to European cities with, in more recent times, some short excursions to the American mainland? One thinks of Plato and Aristotle in Athens, Augustine in Rome, Aquinas in Paris, Kant in Königsberg and Wittgenstein in Cambridge (and Connemara). However, more careful scrutiny of this development shows at the very least a substantial contribution from Eastern culture and thinkers to this allegedly mono-cultural tradition. To locate the very origins of philosophical thought in Greece is to neglect that philosophy started in what is present day Turkey. Moreover, Plato's metaphysics was said to have been very influenced by his trips to Egypt and, undoubtedly, his debt to unknown Egyptian thinkers and works. The later 'Greek' neo-Platonist, Plotinus, was actually an Egyptian and that great 'father of the West', Augustine, was an Algerian. Generally speaking, the teaching of philosophy takes little account of such details, deeming them to be of no substantive philosophical significance. Indeed, in my own undergraduate philosophical studies, such details went unmentioned in a rather whitewashed narrative of the philosophical (Christian) West.

This whitewashing becomes particularly significant when one comes to study the epoch of medieval philosophy. The tradition in Irish philosophy departments up until the last twenty years was to present the philosophy of Thomas Aquinas, Thomism, as the *perennial philosophy*.[1] While clearly a result of clerical hegemony within these departments, this strategy had effects beyond the mere issue of Christian dogmatics. It also had the effect of presenting the development of medieval philosophy as being perfected in the system of a late medieval Western Christian thinker. This obscured not simply the huge contribution of Augustine's African perspective (if Augustine was mentioned, he was not considered African but European) but, more importantly, the seismic importance of Eastern Islamic and Jewish philosophies to the development of the so-called *perennial philosophy*. In this paper, I want to offer some redress for this obscurantist bias through a focus on the specific significance of medieval Islamic philosophy.

Since September 11, there has been a renewed interest in the nature of Islamic doctrine and thought. Many commentators have pointed to the fact that 'fundamentalism' is only one aspect of Muslim thought, albeit presently a powerful and influential strand. However, despite such qualifications, little attention has been paid to the historical basis of this claim, i.e. the presence of a rationalist tradition in Islam. In this paper, I will look at a paradigmatic example of such Islamic reason, the philosophy of Averroes (1126-1198AD). Averroes' radical application of rationalistic methods to the analysis of the Koran was severely opposed by the more traditionalist wing of Islamic philosophy as well as by more conservative Muslim theologians. Nonetheless, he was far from being an isolated figure and his thought can be seen as the logical extension of more moderate rationalism in earlier Islamic philosophy and the rationalist Mu'tazila School of theological interpretation.

I will also highlight the significance of Averroes (and wider Islamic thought) for the development of rationalism within the Christian tradition, a factor that has been a major influence on the development of the West as such. At this point, most especially in the Islamic kingdom of Spain but also in the East, Islamic culture was by and large tolerant and affirmative of religious diversity within its own boundaries. This made for a rather impressive *intercultural* intellectual milieu, where Islamic philosophers and theologians discussed and clarified their faith alongside similar representations from Christian and Judaic thinkers. Cordoba in southern Spain, the then capital of the Moorish empire, is perhaps the most impressive example of such intercultural diversity. Here, Muslim translations and commentaries on Aristotle from Greek into Arabic were translated by Jewish scholars into Hebrew and by Christian scholars from Hebrew into Latin. This led to an extraordinary degree of mutual dependence and influence between the three religious traditions, and by today's standards, a surprising level of respect and friendship between Islamic philosophers and their counter-religionists. Thus, for example, the formidable Jewish philosopher Moses Maimonides declared himself a disciple of the Muslim Averroes, while an influential (although heretical) grouping called the Christian Averroists also sprung up in Paris, declaring their debt to Averroes the Master. No less a figure than Thomas Aquinas also owed a huge debt to Averroes, although this debt was not always so explicitly acknowledged.

My focus on Medieval Islamic thought in this case study will, thus, hopefully serve a dual purpose. In the first case, it will serve to present a counter-narrative to the most dominant narrative concerning the history of Western philosophy, in the process serving to symbolize a paradigm of an intercultural philosophical tradition rather than a mono-cultural one[2]. Second, perhaps more importantly, it will exemplify the intercultural resources present within the Islamic cultural milieu itself, the venerable Islamic tradition of dialogue and tolerance of other faiths. If Averroes is correct concerning his interpretation of the Koran, this intercultural community represents the most faithful Islamic pedagogy.

PHILOSOPHY EAST AND WEST

Before looking at Islamic philosophy more specifically, I will first attempt to give some historical context to the conditions that brought about such a unique and fertile mix of philosophical and theological cultures in the medieval period. The origins of philosophy were in Greece in 500BC but by 300BC Athens was already being rivalled by Alexandria in Egypt as the cultural centre of the ancient world. The great leader of Neo-Platonism, Plotinus, although often viewed as a Greek philosopher, was actually an Egyptian. The eclipse of Greek philosophy, however, began with the closing of the School of Athens by the Byzantine Emperor, Justinian, which heralded an eastern migration of Greek thought to Persia, which was more sympathetic to philosophers at this time (Fakhry 2001, p. ix). This heralded a period of great ignorance of Greek philosophy in the West, with Plato's *Timaeus* and Aristotle's logical treatise, alongside the work of neo-Platonism being the only extant works of the original masters. This loss of the original Greek texts is the real source of the term 'the dark ages' and not, as is often suggested, the fact that philosophy became more linked to theology at this time.

The next historic period of philosophy that concerns us here is the so-called Arab-Islamic period, which began in 750 (and lasted until 1258), when Baghdad inherited from Alexandria and Athens the title of cultural centre of the world. Through Baghdad in the East and the western capital of the Islamic empire, Cordoba in southern Spain, Islamic thought was to exert a massive and determining influence on the history of civilisation.

MEDIEVAL ISLAMIC PHILOSOPHY BEFORE AVERROES

Any analysis of medieval philosophy must take account of the extraordinary relationship that existed between philosophy and theology during this entire period. Although standard interpretations present Christianity as the dominant theological influence in this context, a fairer analysis must point to the constant inter-relationship and co-dependence that existed between the respective theological traditions of Islam, Judaism and Christianity. Moreover, this strong influence did not lead to philosophy becoming the 'handmaiden' of theology, as many critics claim. In many instances, to the contrary, the philosophical tendencies of medieval thinkers led them to interpret their own theological beliefs in specific ways. The initial fusion between philosophical and theological elements in the medieval period takes place most especially through Early Christianity (although another powerful example is Philo of Alexandria's Jewish philosophical theology). Augustine is here the major figure of note but it is worth pointing out that his more sympathetic attitude to philosophical influence is countered by a more fundamentalist strain within Christianity (which foreshadows the more well-known Islamic fundamentalism and also remains a source for some contemporary examples of Christian fundamentalism). The most vehement example of such a Christian fundamentalism or traditionalism is Tertullian, who refused any attempt to rationalise or explain theological faith, declaring: "I believe in Christ because it is absurd".

With Augustine, however, one gets a very different approach, schooled, as he was, in the pagan philosophy (having converted only at age 33) of neo-Platonism, Manicheanism and Stoicism. Thus, for example, the influence of Plato's philosophical criticisms of art (outlined most clearly in *Republic* Book 10) can be seen at work in Augustine's view of the imagination as profane. Additionally, one can wonder as to whether Augustine's view of original sin would have been so negative if he had not imbibed the Platonic conception of the 'fall of the soul'. The fusion of Hellenic and Biblical elements made Christian philosophy, particularly in its Augustinian guise, a subtle and influential metaphysic both in the medieval period and well beyond (for example, both Calvin and Luther were to cite Augustine as a major precursor). However, it is an undeniable fact that the most profound development of Christian philosophy took place under an external influence, that of Medieval Islamic thought.

Whereas Early Christianity was primarily Platonic in orientation (under the influence of both Plato's works and those of his neo-Platonic disciple, Plotinus), later medieval thinking began to look to Plato's successor, Aristotle, for philosophical guidance. Centres of Greek learning in Mesopotamia, Syria and Egypt were responsible for the survival of Aristotle's works in the West during this time. Most texts were translated from the original Greek into an intermediate Syriac version and then into Arabic. When many of the original Greek texts were later lost, it was these Arabic translations which were to provide the foundation for re-translation back into late Medieval Latin. When one considers the immense influence of Aristotelianism on later medieval Christianity and Judaism and, indeed, on succeeding Western history, it is instructive to remember this historical debt to the East. But the real intellectual contribution of medieval Islam to Western culture is less in terms of translation and more in terms of independent philosophical analysis.

There are three great Islamic philosophers before Averroes: Alfarabi (870-930), Avicenna (980-1037) and Algazali (1058-1111)[3]. Alfarabi is the least important of these, primarily significant because he is a pioneer in the invocation of Aristotle as a philosophical authority (thus paving the way for the Golden Age of Muslim Aristotelianism). He is said to have believed in the unity of the thought of Plato and Aristotle and his work shows a confluence of their theories, for example, in his claim that God is simultaneously identical with the Neoplatonic One and Aristotle's Self-Thinking Thought. With Avicenna however, one has the development of a Muslim philosophy more independent of theological constraints and an Aristotelianism less apologetic to Platonic doctrine. Thus, Avicenna rejects the conception of a divine creation of the world in time (God is contemporaneous with the world) and follows Aristotle in considering the primary aim of philosophy to be the study of being *qua* being.

Algazali, writing at the end of the eleventh century, represents a critical backlash against the Aristotelianism of Avicenna within the Islamic tradition. In his famous *The Incoherence of the Philosophers*, he attacks the inconsistency of the philosophical positions of Alfarabi and Avicenna with orthodox Koranic interpretation. What makes this work philosophically significant is that it does not rule out the possibility of philosophy *de jure*, but rather points to the misuse of philosophy by both of his predecessors. In particular, he was concerned with the philosophical theories of the eternity of the world and the denial of bodily resurrection, theories which he regarded not simply as theologically heterodox but as the result of a misapplication of Aristotelian logical methods. For reasons that are more political however, to do with power struggles between various Islamic sects, Algazali's defence of theological orthodoxy was to become associated with a form of theological traditionalism, which refused to enter into dialogue with theological or philosophical rationalism. Thus, Algazali's philosophy and theology are an important influence on the movement that will later be termed Islamic fundamentalism. It can also be said that the upshot of Algazali's and his followers' influence in Baghdad was the virtual death of philosophy in the East, although it was soon to receive a new lease of life in the Western part of the Islamic kingdom. This was primarily to be through the work of Averroes.

AVERROES AND PHILOSOPHY

Averroes (1126-1198) is generally regarded as the greatest of the Islamic philosophers of the medieval period and one of the greatest philosophers of the medieval period as a whole. Nicknamed 'The Commentator' (because of his incisive commentaries on Aristotle), Averroes' thought has two main strands. On the one side, he seeks to rid Islamic Aristotelianism of what he reads as a Neoplatonic bias which conflates the very different philosophies of Plato and Aristotle. Here, he is critical of both Alfarabi and Avicenna. It is important to note here in sympathy to these early Islamic philosophers that part of their difficulty in interpreting Aristotle lay in the incorrect attribution of some neo-Platonic texts to

Aristotle; thus works of both Plotinus and Proclus became known as works of Aristotle and thus led to a misconception of his thought as inconsistent. It is also worth noting here, however, that Averroes was the first philosopher to point out that these texts were wrongly ascribed to Aristotle, given their inconsistency with Arisotle's general thinking.

Averroes is, however, not simply in conflict with preceding Islamic philosophy but also with a kind of theological traditionalism present in Algazali's criticisms of Aristotelianism, which Averroes seeks to undermine. In his ironically titled (but nonetheless intently serious) response to Algazali, *The Incoherence of the Incoherence* (a direct response to Algazali's *Incoherence of the Philosophers*) Averroes seeks to philosophically defend a consistent Aristotelianism, freed from Neo-platonic residue and theological prejudice. In so doing, he creates a complicated relation between his philosophy and his religious tradition.

In defending a consistent Aristotelianism, Averroes is critical of philosophical compromises made in the name of theological orthodoxy. What is most significant about this defence of philosophy is that Averroes defends it through recourse to the Koran. The study of philosophy, Averroes argues, is imperative according to Islamic doctrine. He begins by defining philosophy as "the investigation of existing entities insofar as they point to the Maker, I mean insofar as they are made, since existing entities exhibit the Maker" (Fakhry 2001, p. 2). He then cites two passages from the Koran, verse 59:2, which urges "people of understanding to reflect" and verse 7:184, which asks: "have they not considered the kingdom of the heavens and the earth and all the things God has created?" (Fakhry 2001, p.50). He also, importantly, distinguishes between two different kinds of passage in scripture; those that the Koran refers to as "unambiguous" (which must be interpreted literally) and those that are "ambiguous" (Fakhry 2001, p. 3), which must be reflected on and interpreted. The Koran refers to the interpretation of ambiguity as "imperative" and also clarifies that this interpretation can be done by "only God and those well-grounded in knowledge".

This phrase allows Averroes to introduce his very important distinction between different discourses on truth and interpretation, his so-called three-tiered conception of truth. This privileges what he terms 'demonstrative truth' (i.e. philosophical truth) over what he terms 'dialectical' and 'rhetorical' truth (both the latter being under the province of theology). Simply described, it is only philosophical or demonstrative discourse that proceeds from first principles; theological or dialectical discourse proceeds from assumptions, while rhetorical discourse refers to the use of allegory or narrative to make difficult truths palatable to the public at large. Here Averroes again resorts to the Koran for justification, citing verse 16:125: "call to the way of your Lord with wisdom and mild exhortation and argue with them in the best manner" (Fakhry 2001, p. 7). It is also worth noting here that this threefold division of discourses is a development of Aristotle's own classification of discourses and truths in the *Topics* and the *Rhetoric*.

Algazali, for Averroes, confuses the category of religious or even rhetorical truth with that of philosophical truth, seeking to subordinate the category of reason to the category of revelation. But this is simply to repeat the dogmas of Islamic theology, with little philosophical relevance. For example, Averroes rejects Algazali's defence of a divine creation of the universe in time. Although many Koranic verses seem to suggest the creation in time, here, according to Averroes, Scripture has resorted to what he terms 'sensuous representation', that is the third category of rhetorical discourse which frames truths in terms palatable to the many (in this context, rhetorical embellishment is required because the idea of creation out of nothing is an idea which common people are unable to grasp, according to Averroes). Similarly, Averroes rejects Algazali's orthodox claim of the personal immortality of the soul after death, again arguing that the philosophical truth consists in impersonal immortality, but this has to be made more bearable for the common people who find it difficult to accept that their individuality doesn't survive death. Averroes in both these cases is defending Aristotle's claims; both that the universe is eternal and not created in time and also that the soul is only impersonally immortal, but also significantly claiming that these views are compatible with Islamic orthodoxy insofar as the real truth of the Koran lies not in theological embellishment but philosophical rationalisation (we will see below how these views also bring Averroes into conflict with Aquinas in the context of Christian orthodoxy and its relation to Aristotle's thought).

In contrast to Algazali's work, the work of Alfarabi and Avicenna lays claim to philosophical relevance and seeks to distance itself from the mere repetition of theological orthodoxy. Nonetheless, according to Averroes, the philosophical systems of Alfarabi and Avicenna both fall into the category of theological rather than philosophical truth. This is perhaps more clearly the case with Alfarabi, whose work shows a certain caution in its attempt to be consistent with Islamic orthodoxy (this is most notable in Alfarabi's defence of the doctrine of creation of the world in time). However, Avicenna had already begun to distance himself from these theological residues and, for example, is explicit in his avowal of the Aristotelian theory of the eternity of the world.

Despite this apparent philosophical progression, Averroes remains critical of what he sees as implicit deferral to orthodoxy on crucial philosophical points. Thus, he censures Avicenna's theory that essence precedes existence. Rather, for Averroes, existence precedes essence. He is also critical of Avicenna's proofs of the existence of God from the relation of necessity to contingency, as this argument imports too much metaphysical baggage for Averroes' liking. Rather, any proofs of God's existence must avoid metaphysics *de jure* and rely on physical causation alone. In both these cases, it is arguable that Avicenna is in fact closer to the literal meaning of Aristotle's original texts than Averroes and that Averroes is already moving beyond mere commentary on Aristotle, to something approaching an independent philosophical system.

Whatever the truth of this hypothesis, it is undeniable that Averroes certainly succeeded in releasing Islamic philosophy from the fetters of Islamic theological dogma. In this context, it is perhaps not surprising to find that Averroes did not find too many disciples within Islam itself. In fact in later life he was accused of 'irreligion' and temporarily exiled from Morocco, where he had gone to live, and sent back to Spain. However, this was less the result of intolerance of philosophy and more the result of infighting between Islamic tribal factions. Averroes was eventually pardoned although in the meantime his books had been burned and his exile used as an excuse to ban the study of Aristotle. In general, however, he was allowed to express his views freely and with influence. In the immediate future his influence was nonetheless to be greater beyond the boundaries of his own culture than within it, in particular as it influenced the later development of Christian philosophy and it is to this influence on Christianity that I now turn.

AVERROES AND CHRISTIANITY

In hindsight, it is clear that Averroes was too radical a figure to be compatible with any of the religious orthodoxies of the medieval period. His work, which privileges philosophical reason (what he terms 'demonstrative truth') over theological revelation ('dialectical' and 'rhetorical' truth), looks forward to the modern paradigm of an independent rational enquiry; that is, for Averroes, reason is superior to faith, although in principle they should always reach compatible conclusions. Nonetheless, the influence of his work was powerfully felt in the later medieval period, albeit rather negatively. An understanding of this negative reaction is crucial to an understanding not simply of the development of later medieval thought (in particular, that of Christianity), but to an understanding of the formation of the modern Western identity.

The crucial figure in understanding Averroes in the context of later medieval thought is Siger of Brabant (1240-1284). Siger is referred to as a 'Christian Averroist', a phrase which perfectly captures the assimilation of Islamic thought into later Christianity. The Christian Averroists represented the most radical assimilation of Muslim Aristotelianism, adhering to Averroes' supremacy of reason over revelation and the theory of the eternity of the world. Such heterodox views brought Siger and the Averroists into conflict with the Established Church and many of their propositions were rejected in The Condemnation of 1277.

What is doubly significant is that several of the theories of the more orthodox (and historically influential) Thomas Aquinas (1225-1274) were also condemned in 1277. The condemned Thomistic propositions were exclusively those which

Thomas himself had assimilated from Islamic thought, in particular the view that individuation depended on matter rather than form. Apart from the explicitly condemned propositions, however, it is clear that the 1277 Condemnation is an admission of the extraordinary 'contamination' of pure Christian dogma by Christian philosophy (under the influence of Islamic thought). Without Islamic Aristotelianism there would certainly be no Christian Aristotelianism, and although the 1277 Condemnation is an attempt to reinforce the Augustinianism of earlier Christianity, it is the Aristotelianism of Thomas Aquinas that eventually wins the day (being today, for example, the orthodox Catholic philosophy). I think it is interesting to thus look at some of the points of affinity and dissonance between Averroes and Aquinas.

It is clear, for example, that Aquinas was very critical of the Christian Averroists, but it is also clear that they represented a radicalisation, if not a distortion, of Averroes' original thinking. For example, the Christian Averroists affirmed the theory of the 'double truth' (which was also condemned in 1277), the view that one view could be held in philosophy while simultaneously holding to its contradiction in theology, for example, that philosophically one could hold to the eternity of the world thesis while theologically one could hold simultaneously to the view that the universe was created by God in time. The Averroists claimed to derive this view from Averroes' own three-tiered conception of truth, but it is clear that this represents a distortion of his original meaning. Averroes rather claimed that if 'creation in time' was a theological claim (for example in the Koran) that this could not be true but rather was an attempt to make a rather difficult philosophical conception of eternity more acceptable to the general population. This is not a double-truth theory; there is only one truth for Averroes – that the world is eternal.

Thomas Aquinas, as the other great interpreter of Aristotle in the medieval period, also faced difficulties reconciling Aristotelian philosophy with his own, in this case, Christian orthodoxy. The influence of Averroes on Aquinas's own rationalism is clear. As Etienne Gilson has observed:

> rationalism was born in Spain in the mind of an Arabian philosopher, as a conscious reaction against the theologism of the Arabian divines...he bequeathed to his successors the ideal of a purely rational philosophy, an ideal whose influence was to be such that, by it even the evolution of Christian philosophy was to be deeply modified (1962, p. 25).

Indeed, Ernest Renan in his pivotal text, *Averroes et l'Averroesisme*, (1935) goes as far as to refer to Aquinas as the first authentic disciple of Averroes.

This is, in my view, to go too far but the important influence is nonetheless undeniable. The two areas where Aquinas and Averroes differ most are in relation to the 'creation in time' principle and the conception of intellect, Aquinas arguing for the notion of creation as against eternity, and arguing for the individuality of each intellect and thus personal immortality. But on the positive side, Aquinas' thesis of the compatibility of theological and religious truth owes a large debt to Averroes' three-tiered conception of truth. Averroes' philosophical defence of the idea that God knows each individual is also adopted wholesale by Aquinas as is Averroes' defence of an immanent causality in the world and his conception that 'being is to essence as actuality is to potentiality' (Fakhry 2001, p. 142).

The influence of Averroes (and also of Avicenna) on the development of later medieval Christian thought, therefore, is unequivocal. But this intellectual debt to Islam is very rarely mentioned in our times. When one considers the further development of the modern West, based on a paradigm of rational enquiry, it is Averroes who seems to best anticipate this model within the medieval epoch. On both these counts, it seems clear that Averroes truly was a philosophical visionary, anticipating and also influencing progressive developments far beyond his own milieu.

NOTES

[1] This was not simply an isolated Irish phenomenon. Respected historians of philosophy such as Etienne Gilson (1962) and most especially Frederick Copleston (1960) presented all other philosophy through a Thomistic lens, including modern and contemporary thought.

[2] Although the history of philosophy is nothing other than intercultural, the explicit topic of 'interculturalism' has been late to develop in philosophy as a discipline. The writings of Paulo Freire (*Pedagogy of the Oppressed* [1968]) and Frantz Fanon (*The Wretched of the Earth* [1961]) have been seminal in this regard.

[3] For a good critical commentary on each of the Medieval Islamic philosophers in addition to a selection of their most important writings see Hyman (1973) *Philosophy in the Middle Ages*.

REFERENCES

Aristotle (1980) *The Metaphysics*. London: Penguin.

Augustine (1975) *The City of God*. New York: Random House.

Augustine (1990) *The Confessions*. London: Penguin.

bell hooks (1994) *Teaching to Transgress: Education as the Practice of Freedom*. New York: Routledge

Chicago CSG (1994) 'Critical Multiculturalism' in Goldberg, D. (ed.) *Multi-Culturalism: A Critical Reader*. Oxford: Blackwell

Copleston, F. (1960) *History of Philosophy Vols 1-9*. London:Hackett.

Derrida, J. (2003) *Who's Afraid of Philosophy? The Right to Philosophy Vol 1*. New York:Standford University Press.

Fakhry, M. (2001) *Averroes: His Life, Works and Influence*. Oxford: Oxford University Press

Fanon, F. (1961) *The Wretched of the Earth*. London: Penguin.

Freire, P. (1968) *Pedagogy of the Oppressed*. London: Penguin.

Gilson, E. (1962) *Reason and Revelation*. London: Penguin

Giroux, H. E. (1994) 'Insurgent Multiculturalism and the Promise of Pedagogy' in Goldberg, D. (ed.) *Multi-Culturalism: A Critical Reader*. Oxford: Blackwell

Hyman, A (ed.) (1973) *Philosophy in the Middle Ages: The Christian, Islamic and Jewish Traditions*. Indianapolis: Hackett.

Irwin, J. (2003) 'Deconstructing God: Defending Derrida Against Radical Orthodoxy' in Deane-Baker, P. (ed.) *Explorations in Continental Philosophy of Religion*. New York/Amsterdam: Rodopi.

Plato (1970) The Republic. London: Penguin.

Renan, E. (1935) *Averroès et l'Averroesisme*. Paris: Calmann-Levy

Taylor, C. (1994) 'The Politics of Recognition' in Goldberg, D. (ed.) *Multi-Culturalism: A Critical Reader*. Oxford: Blackwell

CHAPTER 9

DEVELOPMENT EDUCATION IN INITIAL TEACHER EDUCATION: THE MARY IMMACULATE COLLEGE EXPERIENCE

Anne Dolan and Paddy Fullam

Education has a fundamental role to play in alerting young people to the complex world they live in and the global forces which impinge on their lives. Educational initiatives ought to help in creating informed and active citizenry at local, national and global levels (Gundara 1997).

Initial teacher education has a crucial role to pay in meeting the educational, social and economic needs of the twenty first century. Mary Immaculate College, Limerick, founded in 1898, is a third-level college of education and the liberal arts. Academically linked to the University of Limerick, Mary Immaculate College offers undergraduate and postgraduate degrees in Education and the Arts to approximately 2,000 students on campus. This paper proposes to focus specifically on the college's approach to development education in the context of its initial teacher education programme. Mary Immaculate College's long-term aim is to develop a centre of excellence in development education. Therefore, the range of development education experiences currently available for students is somewhat unique in the context of initial teacher education.

DEVELOPMENT EDUCATION: A DEFINITION

According to *The World in The Classroom*, "development education seeks to promote the knowledge, skills and attitudes necessary to enable young people to participate actively in their own development and in that of their own community at local and global levels" (Ruane *et al.* 1999, p.1). Colm Regan describes development education as "justice education with a global perspective" (Regan 1996, p.5). Audrey Osler, who has written extensively about development education and world studies in the context of teacher education, highlights key elements of development education, namely a focus on North-South solidarity in the context of interdependence and a concern with development issues at all levels, local, national, regional and global (Osler 1994). Development education in the context of the UN definition is "concerned with issues of human rights, dignity, self-reliance and social justice in both developed and developing countries" (Osler 1994, p.1). More importantly it "encourages the linking of ideas with action for change and a radical approach to the issues we all face working for a new international, social and economic order" (Osler 1994, p.2).

DEVELOPMENT EDUCATION AND INITIAL TEACHER EDUCATION

Several development education programmes, resource packs, in-service programmes and resources have been designed for primary teachers. The philosophy and methodologies advocated by development educators also provide many opportunities for those involved in initial teacher education. Teaching contemporary social issues, the preparation of children for living as citizens in our world, and the development of critical, reflective teachers and learners are key concerns for development education. These concerns are also reflected in the Government's White Paper on Education: *Charting Our Education Future*:

> The formulation of a national education policy in a Western democracy, as the twenty first century approaches, must be firmly set in an international context. Ireland as a sovereign state in a world community of interdependent nations must have an education policy which prepares its young people for the challenges which will face people everywhere at this era in world history (Department of Education 1995, p. 203).

While development education has a specific focus on the nature of development and underdevelopment, the Third World dimension, links to overseas groups and action for change, it has much in common with other areas relating to social justice. The Development Education Commission[1] highlights the common ground shared by development education and other cognate areas such as human rights, antiracist, environmental, peace, multicultural and gender education. However, according to the Commission, "the overall impact of these 'educations' has been limited and they remain marginal. At an educational level, the fragmentation of approach has been debilitating"(Development Education Commission 1999, p. 29). The Commission recommends an evolvement of this common ground based on a key set of dispositions, such as a sense of social responsibility, a commitment to learning, respect and caring for self and others, a sense of human rights and responsibilities and so on. This integrated, holistic approach is also advocated by curriculum development specialists. According to Kevin Kelly:

> it is becoming increasingly apparent to such specialists that further progress will require a fundamental challenge to the basic 'partitionist' and unidisciplinary structures in which the curriculum is located and a shift to more interdisciplinary, holistic, whole school approaches (Development Education Commission 1998, p.71).

Kelly believes that if these changes are made the impact of development education and human rights education will be much more focused and apparent in our education system. Nevertheless, the formal education system has adopted many of the principles and approaches of development education.

According to Kelly "significant inroads have been made in mainstreaming development education in curriculum design, in-service training and educational policy development" (Development Education Commission 1998, p.70). This is further evidenced by references to underdevelopment and our global society in the White Paper on Education.

> An important component of the international dimension of education is making young people aware of the nature and causes of underdevelopment in the world and what needs to be done to bring about change in relation to the imbalance in wealth between rich and poor countries. The horrific degradations being suffered by children, women and men in the third world – the victims of war and famine – underline the importance of creating an awareness of development issues at all levels of the education system.

> An aim informing policy formulation, educational practice and curriculum development at the different levels will be to create an awareness of global issues, including the environment and third world issues. The objective will be to stimulate a commitment by individuals and society as a whole to necessary actions to respond to specific crises and equally importantly to search for and promote long-term solutions to the underlying problems'. (Department of Education 1995, p.210)

In 1999, the Development Education Unit in Ireland Aid (formerly known as NCDE, National Committee for Development Education) published the report *An Evolving Agenda: The Role of the Tertiary Sector in Development Education*. This report reviews the status of teaching and research in development related areas in a number of third-level institutions. According to the author, Professor Joe Remenyi:

> ...impressive progress has been made in the decade past in integrating development education into the taught curricula in Ireland's universities and colleges of higher education, especially in the undergraduate liberal arts and in taught postgraduate programmes in development studies, international studies, equality studies, cultural studies and peace studies (Remenyi 1999, p.5).

However, one of the gaps identified by the author in a national context is "a continuing absence of any systematic focus on the needs of teachers in development education" (Remenyi 1999, p.30). Notwithstanding this trend, Mary Immaculate College is noted as one of the notable exceptions in terms of its approach to development education (Remenyi 1999, p.23).

Mary Immaculate College's institutional commitment to development education is visible in both its formal and non-formal programmes for students. Development education themes and approaches are included in course content, in a range of campus activities focusing on global and justice issues, through opportunities for students to complete some teaching practice in Africa, and through the involvement of staff in establishing links with colleagues and colleges in developing countries.

The philosophy of development education is part of the college's ethos, a philosophy that is clearly stated in Mary Immaculate College's mission statement: "MIC respects cultural diversity. It strives to promote equity in society and to provide an environment where all have freedom and opportunity to achieve their full potential".

DEVELOPMENT EDUCATION: MARY IMMACULATE COLLEGE'S APPROACH

Mary Immaculate College offers a three-year Bachelor in Education (B.Ed.) programme and an eighteen month Post-Graduate Diploma in Education programme. The duration of these programmes may be extended following the 2002 review of initial teacher education. The programmes in education place a very strong emphasis on knowledge of primary curricular areas; pedagogical content and skills; and foundation studies, which includes philosophy, sociology and psychology.

Some study of development-related areas is included in a number of academic subjects e.g. Geography, Media Studies and Theology. Development education is explicitly included in both the SESE (Social, Environmental and Scientific Education) and SPHE (Social, Personal and Health Education) programmes. However, contact time with students for these curricular areas is limited, therefore the amount of development education coverage is minimal. This pressure on the curriculum, which has a detrimental impact on development education in teacher education, is not unique to Ireland. According to Meighan and Harber (1999), curriculum overload tends to marginalise contemporary social and educational issues or exclude them altogether. This is also true both for the curriculum in schools and in colleges of education.

There are thematic elements relevant to development education in the pedagogy of certain areas e.g. art, religious education, history, geography, science, social, personal and health education, sociology etc. Students are actively encouraged and supported to plan thematically and to adopt development education approaches and methodologies in their teaching practice.

Each third year B.Ed student has an opportunity to study intensively one pedagogical area. These pedagogical options or curriculum studies electives include a range of curricular areas in the primary curriculum, cross-curricular approaches (early childhood education, for example) and specific learning methodologies (such as through Information Technology). These courses involve fifty-two hours direct contact time with students over a fifteen-week semester. A curriculum studies elective in development education has been offered to B.Ed. students since 1991. This course currently focuses on development education and local studies. The inclusion of local studies provides a framework through which both local and global issues can be analysed. This course is designed to equip students with the skills necessary to generate greater understanding and appreciation of our local and global environments. It includes an analysis of various contemporary, social issues; field trips; inputs by guest speakers; environmental audits; etc. Assessment is based on attendance, participation and project work.

However in the spirit of partnership and democracy, the content and assessment models for this course are openly negotiated with the students. Meighan and Harber (1989) explore democratic practices in teacher education and suggest a link between the values underpinning teacher education courses and the values which student teachers subsequently adopt in their own teaching. This sentiment is echoed by Nicholson, who advises that teacher educators should practice what they preach! According to Nicholson, "democratic and interactive teaching and learning styles encourage greater student involvement in course design, delivery and evaluation. They are compatible with the wish to provide student opportunities, which are prerequisite for globally aware practice in schools"(Nicholson 1996, p.81).

Over the past few years, several students have had the experience of teaching in primary classrooms in a number of African countries including Zambia, The Gambia, Kenya, South Africa, Tanzania and Ethiopia. This experience results in tremendous personal transformation for each of the students involved. Their views of Africa are radically revised, from a somewhat stereotypical negative view of Africa, to a much more positive image of resilient African people with proud cultures and traditions involved in the daily miracle of providing education within the constraints of access to the most meagre resources. Many of the students who have completed this teaching practice maintain links with teachers and schools in Africa and, in some cases, links have been established on a school-to-school basis. As a result of their experience, the students look forward to teaching development issues in their classrooms. Their experiences in Africa will be portrayed in many classrooms all over Ireland and will influence thousands of children, when they commence their teaching career.

The potential benefits of AEE (Additional Educational Experience) in Africa are numerous, including the professional and personal development of all participating students and staff, the development of the multicultural nature of the College and the potential for developing sustainable links with partner institutions in a developing country.

DEVELOPMENT EDUCATION AND CURRICULUM PLANNING: THE CURRICULUM DEVELOPMENT UNIT IN MARY IMMACULATE COLLEGE

The Curriculum Development Unit of Mary Immaculate College was established to promote and undertake research into the curriculum and methodology of the primary school. The projects that are conducted under the auspices of the Unit are of three principal types:

• The design and implementation of curricular programmes in areas that do not form part of the standard curriculum.

• The investigation of different aspects of the established primary school curriculum in order to evaluate its effectiveness, to identify constraints to its proper implementation, and to propose approaches aimed at overcoming these problems.

• The development of resource materials that will support teachers and other professionals in implementing all aspects of the curriculum.

Development education has been a primary focus for the Curriculum Development Unit since the 1980s.

A strategic partnership between Mary Immaculate College and Trócaire, the Catholic Agency for World Development, gave rise to *The Primary School Development Education Project*. This initiative involved a number of in-service courses for teachers in various regions. In 1989, a thematic, bilingual teaching pack *Ar Scáth a Cheile* was produced. In 1994, *Team Planet* was published. Team Planet consists of a set of four work packs on Social and Environmental Studies, with an underlying emphasis on the importance of achieving sustainable development. The programme explores and develops the key concepts of Nurturing, Dependence, Interconnections and Sustainable Development. (Horgan 1994)

> With a focus on child-centred and activity-based learning, Team Planet: seeks to engage pupils' hearts and minds in active processes of analysis, synthesis, debate and decision-making. It seeks to promote their awareness of global environmental issues, to help them develop their personal code of environmental ethics and, above all, to provide direction as they seek their own path towards a more harmonious relationship with the planet and all its people (Horgan 1994, p.2).

In 1999 the NCCA (National Council for Curriculum and Assessment) launched the revised Primary School Curriculum. While some development educators would like to see a stronger emphasis on development education, nevertheless there are ample opportunities for teachers to integrate global and justice perspectives into their teaching.[2]

The Primary Curriculum is divided into seven curricular areas: Language, Mathematics, Social Environmental and Scientific Education (SESE), Arts Education, Physical Education, Social Personal and Health Education (SPHE) and Religious Education. The language area includes English and Gaeilge. SESE incorporates history, geography and science while the arts area includes visual arts, music and drama. In each curricular area, the content is divided into strands. These are further divided into stand units, each focusing on specific areas of learning.

While all curricular areas lend themselves to the inclusion of development education themes, notable opportunities exist within Social Environmental and Scientific Education (SESE), Social Personal and Health Education (SPHE), and Religious Education.

The publication of *The World in The Classroom* coincided with the introduction of the revised Irish Primary Curriculum. (Ruane *et al.* 1999) *The World in the Classroom* explores each curricular area for every class level indicating a range of suggestions and resources for incorporating justice and global perspectives into the curriculum. This publication seeks to:

- provide a rationale for the inclusion of development education in the work of primary schools.
- highlight the opportunities for development education in the Primary School Curriculum.
- support teachers and school in planning and implementing a development education programme on a whole school basis (Ruane *et al.* 1999, p.1).

The Curriculum Development Unit is currently planning to publish a SESE resource for infant teachers that will include lesson material for history, geography and science with a specific focus on justice and global themes.

Mary Immaculate College also participated in the Network of Curriculum Development Units in Development Education, along with St Mary's College, Belfast, the City of Dublin VEC Curriculum Development Unit, Shannon Curriculum Development Centre, 80:20 Educating and Acting for a Better World and Trócaire. This Network has conducted various research studies into specific aspects of development education and has promoted its integration into primary and post-primary curricula.

CROSS-CURRICULAR APPROACHES

Development education is not a curricular area in its own right. It represents a cross-curricular approach that integrates justice and global perspectives into the curriculum. Inman and Wade argue that if initial teacher education seriously aims to prepare young people to live in this complex, interdependent world, then development education must become a central component of the curriculum. (Inman and Wade 1997)

Many curriculum specialists and development educators agree that development education should not be an independent curricular area in its own right as much of the content concerned with justice and global perspectives is already included in core content. Catherine Coxhead believes that what is required instead is:

> ...a shift in emphasis towards the values messages which should underpin much of children's learning - a sense of obligation towards others, respect for the cultures and lifestyles of all people and a willingness to challenge inequality and injustice, racism, bias and ethnocentrism (Centre for Research and Curriculum Development, St. Mary's College Belfast 1997, p3).

John Hammond strongly argues that there should not be a separate syllabus in development education. According to Hammond, "its very nature as a process and perspective requires that development education should not be confined as an area separate from other subjects with which it is intrinsically involved, like Geography, Religious Education, History, Science, English etc" (Hammond 1991, p.7). He argues that the potential for development education "exists at the core of all subjects" (Hammond 1991, p.5). This holistic, integrated approach is even more important for the primary school curriculum in general and for younger children in particular, whose world is not divided into separate curricular categories. Ruane *et al.* advocate a thematic approach, "which allows the teacher to work holistically, infusing an integrated curriculum with justice and global perspectives" (Ruane *et al.* 1999, p.11). However, unless there is a clear commitment from teachers and principals to include development education in whole school planning, opportunities for development education may be lost in several instances. This is equally the case for colleges of education. If development education is to become part of the curriculum for student teachers, it must be evident in the academic plan, course syllabi and an appropriate number of contact times with students. The core programme for B.Ed. students provides insufficient contact time for students to focus on development education. The review of the primary B.Ed programme recommends an extended four-year programme. In this context, opportunities exist for colleges to review their policies in teacher education in general and development education in particular.

POTENTIAL CONTRIBUTION OF DEVELOPMENT EDUCATION TO INITIAL TEACHER EDUCATION PROGRAMMES

The philosophy, methodologies and concerns of development education have much to offer to initial teacher education. According to Shah:

the task of teacher education is to broaden the attitudes of the student teachers so that they understand the meaning and rationale for global citizenship, develop a commitment to a global model of citizenship, have the ability to be reflexive and critical and, at the same time, innovative and adaptable (Shah 1996, p.56).

One of the key aspirations of both development education and initial teacher education is the generation of critical, reflective analysis and action. In *Learning to Teach Reflectively: A Handbook for Student Teachers*, reflective action is described as a process which:

> involves a willingness to engage in constant self-appraisal and development. Among other things it implies flexibility, rigorous analysis and social awareness. A reflective teacher is one who constantly questions his or her own aims and actions, monitors practice and outcomes and considers the short-term and long-term effects upon each child (Horgan and Bonfield 2000, p.3).

Reflection, therefore, can be considered as the reorganisation or reconstruction of experience leading to new understandings of oneself as teacher.

Much of the methodologies advocated by development education seek to inculcate this ability to critically reflect, to question, to challenge and to redefine one's own opinions in the context of new information acquired through the reflective process. However, development education does not have a monopoly over these methodologies, many of which are advocated in the revised curriculum including role play, group work, simulation games etc. Nevertheless, while experiential learning and active learning techniques are very useful in their own right, they will not automatically generate critical global teachers. According to Huckle:

> experiential learning offers a space to contest and re-construct world views and like the new social movements it appeals strongly to the new middle class. Its acknowledgement of the relativity of knowledge and the significance of identify and cultural politics are to be welcomed but without adequate attention to critical theory and emancipatory politics, experiential learning is unlikely to constitute critical pedagogy (Huckle 1996, p.36).

This ability to construct critical pedagogy is particularly important for teacher educators. Nicholson believes that "all students need to be able to deconstruct their own cultural baggage of inherited knowledge, especially student teachers, if they are to help pupils encounter a rapidly changing world" (Nicholson 1996, p.80). However, she believes that there is inadequate time in the timetable for critical thinking and independent reflection. This concern is also articulated in the report of the working group on primary pre-service teacher education. The authors claim that students need more time for reflection. Full timetables, which place excessive pressures on students, are not conducive for reflection. The inclusion of a development education approach in the core curriculum for every student teacher will contribute to the generation of critical global teachers.

All education deals with the preparation of young people for life. In this context, education for citizenship is an area of concern that can also usefully be addressed by development education. In England, citizenship education has been awarded statutory entitlement in the primary and secondary curriculum. The Advisory Group on Citizenship and the Teaching of Democracy in schools published the Crick Report, which sets out a number of recommendations for citizenship education.

The Crick Report identifies three key dimensions: participation in democracy; the responsibilities and rights of citizens; and the value of community action. The report outlines three mutually dependent domains: social and moral responsibility, community involvement and political literacy. Lynch argues that one cannot discuss citizenship without reference to global democracy. He states:

> for educators the challenge of the 1990s is to deliver not just education for citizenship of a pluralist democracy, but education for active global democracy, founded on universal values about the nature of human beings and their social behaviour (Lynch 1992, p.2).

Lynch argues that citizenship education should involve the development of personal consciousness and social participation at local, national and international levels. However, the trend in society today is towards less rather than greater levels of participation. Anecdotal evidence in Ireland suggests that voluntary organisations are finding it increasingly difficult to recruit volunteers. Drawing on a range of data, which reveals Americans' changing behaviour, Robert Putnam argues that we have become increasingly disconnected from each other and that several social structures have in effect broken down.

So the challenges of citizenship education are even greater in a society where young people have fewer opportunities to witness the participation of people in various community and civic duties. The same challenges and dilemmas exist for the action dimension of development education, especially during an education programme where there are so many demands on the students' time. In Mary Immaculate College students have an opportunity to become involved in and organise a range of activities for local and national campaigns, including human rights day, antiracism day, one world week, fair trade initiatives, fund raising initiatives facilitated by Trócaire, Concern etc. These extra-curricular activities provide great opportunities for the students to demonstrate leadership and innovation in a manner that may not have been accessible to them through academic routes. According to Audrey Osler, "development education has an important role to play in contributing to a new broader, more inclusive understanding of active citizenship which acknowledges the global responsibilities of individuals and communities". (Osler 1994, pp. 3-4)

CONCLUSION

This paper has focused on one college's approach to development education in the context of current definitions of development education, the revised curriculum, some international trends and the specific commitment to development education that is exhibited by the college. The paper also highlights the potential benefits of development education for initial teacher education, particularly in areas of reflective teaching and citizenship education. While the scope for development education is limited due to time pressure on the timetable, nevertheless every opportunity is made to introduce students to the benefits of development education in the context of their own personal development and its potential in the classroom. According to John Hammond:

> the ultimate challenge to teachers lies in according development education teaching approaches and the global and justice perspectives *core-curriculum* status in their classroom, in seeing these elements as central to their teaching by consciously and confidently highlighting the perspectives and exploiting the affective value of the teaching approaches in their student's daily learning (Hammond 1991, p.9).

Equally, the same challenge applies to initial teacher education. Mary Immaculate College is continuing to develop its programmes in the context of global and justice perspectives in a response to this challenge.

NOTES

[1] The Development Education Commission was established in September 1996 to review experiences and strategies in Britain and Ireland as well as to identify opportunities for future educational work in support of global citizenship based on social justice.

[2] These opportunities are well documented in Ruane *et al.* (1999) *The World in The Classroom: Development Education in the Primary Curriculum*. Primary School Development Education Project, Curriculum Development Unit, MIC and Trócaire.

REFERENCES

Centre for Research and Curriculum Development, St. Mary's College Belfast (1997) *Sharing our World: Integrating Development Education into the Curriculum*. Belfast: St Mary's College/Trócaire.

Department of Education (1995) *Charting Our Education Future The White*

Paper on Education. Dublin: Government Publication Office.

Development Education Commission (1998) *A Consultative Document on Core Issues.* Birmingham and Bray: DEC Birmingham and 80:20 Ireland.

Development Education Commission (1999) *Essential Learning for Everyone Birmingham and Bray*: DEC Birmingham and 80:20.

DfEE (1998) *Education for Citizenship and the Teaching of Democracy in Schools* (The Crick Report), London: QCA.

Gundara, J. (1997) paper presented at Development Education Association/Institute of Education Conference. London: Institute of Education

Hammond, J. (1991) *A Global Curriculum?: Development Education and the Junior Certificate*, Dublin: CDVEC Curriculum Development Unit /Trócaire.

Horgan, K., (1994) *Team Planet: An Action Pack on Our World and Ourselves* Limerick: Primary School Development Education Project, Mary Immaculate College and Trócaire.

Horgan, K., and Bonfield, T., *(2000) Learning to Teach Reflectively: A Handbook for Student Teachers.* Limerick: Mary Immaculate College.

Huckle, J., (1996) 'Globalisation, Postmodernity and Citizenship' in Steiner, M., (ed.) *Developing The Global Teacher: Theory and Practice in Initial Teacher Education.* London: Trentham Books.

Inman, S., and Wade, R., (1997) *Development Education Within Initial Teacher Education.* London: Oxfam.

Lynch, J., (1992) *Education for Citizenship in a Multicultural Society.* London: Cassell.

Meighan, R and J., and Harber, C (1989) 'Democratic Practice: Missing Item on the Agenda of Teacher Education', in Harber, C. and Meighan, R. (ed) *The Democratic School. Educational Management and the Practice of Democracy*, Ticknall: Education Now Books.

Nicholson, H, H., (1996) 'Crossing Points and Meeting Places: Geography and Global Perspectives in Initial Teacher Education' in Steiner, M., (ed) *Developing the Global Teacher: Theory and Practice in Initial Teacher Education* London: Trentham Books.

Osler, A., (1994) 'Education for Development: Redefining Citizenship in a Pluralist Society' in Osler, A., (ed.) *Development Education: Global Perspectives in the Curriculum.* Council of Europe: Cassell.

Putnam, R., (2000) *Bowling Alone*. New York: Touchstone.

Regan, C., (ed) (1996) *75:25 Ireland in an Increasingly Unequal World*. Dublin: Dóchas.

Remenyi, J., (1999) *An Evolving Agenda: The Role of the Tertiary Sector in Development Education in Ireland.* Dublin: NCDE.

Ruane, B. Horgan, K. and Cremin, P. (1999) *The World in the Classroom: Development Education in the Primary Curriculum*, Primary School Development Education Project, Curriculum Development Unit, Mary Immaculate College, Limerick.

Shah, S., (1996) 'Initial Teacher Education and Global Citizenship: the Context of Permeation' in Steiner, M. (ed.) Developing *The Global Teacher: Theory and Practice in Initial Teacher Education*. London: Trentham Books.

CHAPTER 10

PREPARING TEACHERS TO TEACH SOCIAL JUSTICE:
CONTEXT, CONTENT AND CHALLENGES

Barbara Gill

In relation to teaching social justice at third-level, one sector that can sometimes be overlooked is that of teacher training. However, its importance cannot be underestimated. Incorporating elements of social justice education into teacher-training programmes is strategic and, if carried out effectively, has the potential to affect whole cohorts of children and young people in a positive way.

Teacher-training colleges and Departments of Education recognise that teachers are facing new challenges that place high demands on them professionally and personally. Among the most visible changes in Irish schools and classrooms is the increase in cultural diversity of pupils attending. However, changes are happening on a global scale – changing attitudes to authority and power, changing family structures and value systems, different patterns of consumption as well as increased mobility – and these are creating further challenges for our education system. In light of this changing context, the inclusion of development education and intercultural education modules in teacher-training courses can be heralded as a very timely response by the colleges and universities concerned.

This paper describes a pilot pre-service project initiated by the National Committee for Development Education (NCDE) and carried out in partnership with the Dublin-based Primary teacher–training colleges and 'Grassroots in Development Education in Ireland' (NODE) during 2001/2002. The project, entitled *The World in the Classroom*, was primarily concerned with the design and delivery of development and intercultural education modules in four colleges, and this paper, in addition to outlining the background and context to the project, will describe the types of modules developed and will indicate the content and some approaches used. The paper will also outline the form of assessment used in one college and some insights gained from student review questionnaires will be documented. Concluding remarks will name some of the challenges emerging as the first year of the pilot project comes to an end.

BACKGROUND, CONTEXT AND STRUCTURES

NCDE, in the person of the Education and Resources Officer, had over the past number of years made contact with interested people in a number of different teacher-training colleges and, as a result, had been invited to give once-off presentations to students. These presentations usually involved gaining first hand experience of active learning methodologies (such as the use of photographs) or of the range of resources and education packs available for teaching primary pupils.

In more recent times there had been a notable increase in the number of requests coming to NCDE and the nature of those requests had also changed. For a number of colleges, the proposed introduction of a module entitled Inclusivity Education into their B.Ed. course was the impetus for creating space in the timetable for more than the traditional once-off development education sessions. For all the colleges there seemed to be an increased awareness of the need to respond in some way to the changing context for young teachers, particularly because of the multi-cultural nature of many Irish classrooms.

NCDE was instrumental in getting the project established. However, in keeping with their own tradition, they were keen to work in partnership with an NGO (Non-Governmental Organisation) and with the colleges concerned. Through NCDE's participation on the Primary Group of NODE a natural partnership emerged regarding the management of the pilot project. In March 2001 the decision was made by NCDE to fund the project and over the following few months the necessary structures for its development and implementation were put in place. A part-time Education Officer was appointed in June to work together with the NCDE Resources and Education Officer. A representative of each college and a primary teacher who was also a member of the Anti-racism Education Group were invited to participate on the Project Advisory Group and the Project Management Committee, consisting of representatives of NODE, NODE Primary Group, NCDE and a college lecturer, agreed to continue managing the project.

At the outset, aims and objectives of the project were set down. Since it was intended that the colleges would ultimately have responsibility for the development and intercultural education modules within the teacher-training courses, the overall aim of the pilot project was to 'facilitate capacity building within the Dublin-based teacher-training colleges to integrate a development and intercultural education module into their courses'.

The following were the objectives of the project:
• to develop, design and deliver modules in partnership with colleges
• to design and deliver 'training for trainers' in summer 2002

• to review and evaluate the different modules and produce a report with recommendations for future development

This paper concentrates on the first of these objectives only.

MODULES DEVELOPED

Specifically, the project involved the four Dublin-based teacher-training colleges, namely, St. Patrick's College, Drumcondra, St. Mary's College, Marino Institute of Education, Froebel College of Education, Blackrock, and the Church of Ireland College of Education (CICE), Rathmines. The project made contact with key personnel in the planning stage and timetables were drawn up so that all could be accommodated in a way that suited each college. Figure one shows the different models that emerged during the first year of the pilot project, the number of students involved, the duration of the module and whether it was optional or mandatory. Three models can be identified.

Model A was developed in one college and became the most substantial due to the number of students and the inclusion of an assessment dimension. Model B was developed in two colleges and, although overall numbers are comparable to Model A, important distinctions were that both Third Year and Second Year students were involved, the duration of each module was shorter and there was no assessment. Model C was developed in place of a proposed elective that did not occur due to insufficient numbers, but this evening course proved to be significant from a number of perspectives. A brief summary table of the models developed is given in figure one, followed by a brief description of the main elements of each model in figure two.

Figure One: Models developed

Model type – college	Year/number of students	Duration of module	Mandatory or optional
A. Marino TCD B.Ed.	Second years 93	9 weeks (7 hr 30 mins)	Mandatory + assessed
B. Froebel + **CICE** **TCD B.Ed.**	Third Years 82 54 (Froebel) 28 (CICE) Second years 92 66 (Froebel) 26 (CICE)	5 hours + 5 hours	Mandatory
C. St **Patrick's** **DCU B.Ed.**	15 – 20 (mostly Third years)	9 hours	Optional – evening course

Figure Two: Summary of main elements of models A, B, C

Model A – Long module with Second Years only
Main elements/content:
- theory (definition, appropriate pedagogy, concepts, skills and attitudes)
- identification of curriculum opportunities/links (especially Social, Environmental and Scientific Education + Geography)
- tools to respond to opportunities (methodologies and resources)
- assignment (three lesson plans worked on in groups, assessed individually)
- review by student questionnaire

Model B – Short modules with Second and Third Years
Similar to Model A in content but with the following differences:
- aimed for progression with Third Years so included new topics/themes e.g. human rights, wider issues
- no assignment (in 2001/2002)
- total contact time will spread over two years
- pre-course questionnaire + student review carried out

Model C – Optional evening course
Some features:
- more focus on personal awareness raising
- was a response to an expressed need for anti-racist training by students
- theory had emphasis on racism, culture, etc.
- high level of interest and motivation from students
- no assignment
- certificates of attendance presented by college president

Aim and objectives of modules

The overall aim of the modules was to help student teachers integrate a global and intercultural dimension, based on the promotion of justice and human rights, into their teaching. It was hoped that that this would ultimately lead to developing their capacity to:

- Promote in pupils skills and values conducive to development of active and ethical citizenship and promotion of human rights

- Use an active learning and pupil-centered approach which accommodates a variety of methodologies and teaching strategies, including collaborative learning and teaching

- Help pupils explore links between their lives and experience and those of different parts of the world

- Help pupils develop the knowledge, skills and attitudes conducive to intercultural learning for a multicultural society

- Promote awareness and respect in pupils for their own culture and values, along with an understanding and respect for the diversity of beliefs, values, ethnic origins and cultures of our society and in the wider world

In addition it was hoped that student teachers would be able to access a wide range of development education and intercultural teaching resources relevant to the curriculum in order to achieve the above.

MODULE CONTENT AND APPROACHES

The modules delivered in Model A and B had a number of similar elements. Each module opened with an introduction, an intercultural naming exercise and a presentation of the module outline. This was followed by an introduction to development education theory including definitions, key concepts and the educational approach being advocated. Through a series of interactive group exercises, students were facilitated to come to a greater understanding of the rationale for development education and its relevance to the Primary Curriculum.

Students participated in a range of activities aimed at exploring the idea of 'perspective consciousness'. Their interpretation of, and reaction to, cultural symbols and maps of the world projected in different ways was elicited and students were challenged to think about how their worldview is formed and influenced. The idea of 'eurocentrism' was introduced and its effects on their perception of the developing world.

Students gained first-hand experience of a range of methodologies e.g. brainstorming, ranking and sorting activities, use of photographs etc. using a thematic approach (homes or human rights). A particular focus was given to the strand unit People and Other Lands and students were introduced to a particular enquiry approach using the Development Compass Rose (Birmingham DEC 1995) in order to further develop their capacity to teach about localities, particularly in developing counties.

In all cases, there was a resources session during which students were introduced to a selection of teaching materials and education packs. This session was developed during the pilot phase to allow students to review critically some key resources and make presentations to each other on their overall purpose, content and value. This session was particularly useful for giving students the confidence to develop appropriate lesson plans for use in the classroom. In the case of Model A, which had an assessment component, this session had the explicit purpose of preparing students for the assignment which involved developing three lesson plans for use within their teaching.

Each module ended with students completing a detailed review questionnaire. In the case of Model B, this review questionnaire complemented an initial pre-course questionnaire that had been distributed to students.

As indicated above, Model C differed somewhat from the other modules in that it developed in response to a particular request by students in the college concerned. Following on from an *Anti-racism in the Workplace* initiative, students approached NCDE with a view to running an evening course that would be optional and open to all students. The request was supported by a number of lecturers who had been keen to introduce an elective module for Second Years on development and intercultural education in September 2001 but which had not gone ahead due to insufficient numbers. Three two-hour and one three-hour sessions were organised over a period of four weeks and these included elements similar to those described above for Models A and B. However, an additional emphasis was placed on greater personal awareness raising in relation to the nature of culture, stereotyping and racism, as well as exploring wider issues in the school and education system.

ASSESSMENT

As stated above, an assignment was given to students who participated in Model A. Students were encouraged to work in small groups to research and plan a series of three lessons each of between twenty and forty minutes duration on a development education/intercultural education theme or topic. Generally they worked in self-selected groups of two or three with individual students presenting their work for assessment in the form of a folder. The folder included individual work as well as material worked on by the group. Students were instructed to include certain information in the folder submitted for assessment (see figure three for details)

Figure Three: Details of information to be included in assignment folder

General information
1. The overall aims and objectives of the three lesson plans in terms of pupils' learning
2. An outline of some factors that need to be taken into consideration when planning these lessons e.g. composition of class, room layout etc
3. An indication of the links between the chosen topic and the Primary curriculum in terms of content, concepts and skills

For each lesson
1. State the subject area (i.e. SESE), title of lesson and target class group
2. State the learning objectives (two - three per lesson)
3. List the resources needed for the lesson and reference where appropriate
4. Outline the format which each lesson will take, listing the methodology to be used for each activity and its purpose. Each lesson should include:
   Introduction; Development and Conclusion
5. Include any worksheets used
6. Give the total time anticipated for each lesson and an approximate breakdown of the time allocated to each activity.

There should be clear evidence of progression and development from one lesson to the next.

The following criteria were adopted for correction of the assignments:

• Overall presentation (clarity, logical sequence etc)

• Incorporation of global/justice/intercultural dimension

• Coherence between objectives and lesson content

• Variety and appropriateness (age, purpose) of methodology

• Evidence of progression and development within three lessons

It is expected that the results of the first set of assignments will help evaluate the overall impact of the project on student teacher's ability to integrate a global and intercultural dimension into their teaching.

STUDENT REVIEW QUESTIONNAIRES

As stated earlier, students were asked to complete a detailed end-of-module questionnaire that consisted of a maximum of ten questions. They were asked to complete the questionnaire in as much detail and as honestly as possible so that their comments could contribute to improving future modules.

The initial questions focused on evaluating various aspects of the module, for example, input by facilitators, active participation by students in methodologies, handouts, time and opportunity to ask questions and the overall pace of the course. The students were asked to comment on the approach used by the facilitators (i.e. little emphasis on lecturing, more emphasis on group work, hands on experience of resources etc.) and to say which methods they thought were most effective. In an attempt to discover if the module complemented other courses that were being taken by the students, the questionnaire included a question to elicit opinions on this.

In relation to ascertaining student opinion on where improvements could be made to the modules, students were asked a variety of questions. For example,

• Since it is expected that the module will run again next year what *changes or improvements could you suggest* to the organisers in relation to any aspect of the module (content, approaches etc.)?

• What were some of the *least positive* aspects of the module and why?

• What were some of the *most positive* aspects of the module and why?

In figure four a sample of student suggestions for changes and improvements to the course is given. This sample refers only to students in Model A so some of the comments (e.g. those on the assignment) are specific to this module.

Figure Four: Sample Answers to Review Questionnaire

Assignment
- Clearer description - leave as an individual assignment
- Make clearer distinction re: group/individual
- More time to work on assignments
- More help/ideas on the assignment – clearer instructions/ explain more

Content
- Cover other topics/issues e.g., racism/refugees/fair trade
- More information about other countries, for example middle eastern countries
- More emphasis on culture in Ireland
- Focus on how to deal with racial problems in the classroom and how best to teach children to accept others not just focusing on countries all the time
- Make it more relevant and debatable e.g., deal with social topics
- Outside speakers from different countries and cultures

Approach /method of delivery
- Slightly more emphasis on lecturing
- More involvement in activities
- Allow more time to go through notes in lectures
- Slow down! Don't change topics too quickly. Allow time to take down notes
- Vary methodologies and activities used

Resources
- Allocate extra time for students to review packs thoroughly
- Where and how to get access to resources

Other suggestions:
- Keep a weekly diary
- Sample lesson plans on the topics
- Tell the students exactly what the module is about and why they are doing it, for example, explain the link to SESE/Geography

---

An important dimension to the review was the need to encourage students to name what they considered to be some of the main messages that the module was trying to get across in relation to development and intercultural education. Figure five outlines some of the student responses to this question.

CONCLUSION

At this stage of the project, the future direction is being worked out and plans are under way to continue the project into a second pilot year. This next phase will be guided by some of the emerging challenges that are becoming evident now that certain elements of the project are completed. These challenges can be seen in the form of questions posed in relation to four key areas.

1. Getting the balance between personal awareness raising (attitudes) and training / formation in development / intercultural education approaches and methods (knowledge, skills). Should such a project have the right to address student teachers' attitudes/values in relation to the world we live in or should it concentrate on developing skills and increasing the often-

Figure Five: Sample student response on main messages of the module

- **Respecting difference** - *We should be open to learning about different cultures, societies and the countries those people come from in order to accept their customs, beliefs etc. to learn about their lifestyle comparing it to our own as Ireland is becoming a multi-cultural society.*

- **Awareness of the wider world** - *To make the children aware of the world outside their own.*

- **Challenge stereotypes & prejudice-** *Some people can be very prejudiced and judgmental on foreign countries without knowing the facts. It opened my mind to a lot of things.*

- **Similarities and differences** - *Looking at similarities and differences between cultures within our own society and on a wider world view.*

- **Develop a sense of place** - *Sense of place and importance of your own culture.*

- **Particular educational approach + methodologies advocated** - *I think the module was letting us become aware of the need to allow children to investigate for themselves; develop skills, don't just give information; looking at different methods of teaching.*

Teachers' attitude important - *Be careful not to use biased or negative language in class; give accurate current information.*

---

neglected knowledge base about other cultures and global development?

2. Balancing the global, intercultural, pro-diversity 'agenda' with the global, injustice, inequality 'agenda'. How can the project continue to promote a positive image and understanding of other cultures, particularly those in Third World countries, while at the same time not neglect or under-emphasise the inequalities/injustices that exist and may result in reinforcing negative stereotypical images?

3. Challenge of 'compare and contrast' exercises – what is the 'Third World' used for within curriculum? How can the project best 'unpack' the existing framework that many teachers/student teachers have for understanding the Third World, i.e. using the 'Third World' to illustrate development and doing so through uncritical conceptions of difference; ordering the world into two exact opposites ('developed' and 'developing') defining the Third World by the absence of things which the 'developed' world possesses etc?

4. Addressing the issue of mainstreaming development and intercultural education. How can the project ensure that development education is not just seen as an 'add-on' /marginal activity within teacher education while, at the same time, recognise that there is value in and benefits from bringing in outside 'expertise' in areas such as development and intercultural education? Is this challenge paralleled within schools and education system in general, i.e. what about the issue of mainstreaming these educational approaches in schools?

Questions such as these are vital to the planning process and addressing them should certainly lead to changes, and ultimately improvements, in future pre-service modules in development and intercultural education.

REFERENCES
Birmingham DEC (1995) *Development Compass Rose Consultation Pack* Birmingham: DEC.

CHAPTER 11

SIMULATIONS AND REALITIES – A GLOBAL CONTEXT FOR EXPERIENTIAL LEARNING IN INITIAL TEACHER EDUCATION

Gerry Jeffers and Rose Malone

> Above all, teachers will need to enable pupils to become reflective, analytical and critical and to educate them for citizenship in a global society. To reduce inequality and prejudice, and to facilitate educational equality requires a moral education which will foster a sensitivity to and respect for the needs and rights of others, and an appreciation of the value of diversity (Drudy 2001, p.372).

Teacher education, both pre-service and as part of professional development, is often identified as a significant potential contributor to educational change. Student teachers, as well as developing a repertoire of skills, are expected to act as change agents and to play leadership roles in the re-shaping of various aspects of curriculum. This paper examines some of the implications of this assumption with regard to the area of development education. It is based on a small-scale study of the experience of students who took part in a development education intervention within the Higher Diploma in Education in NUI Maynooth.

This combination of development education and experiential learning arises out of an approach to development consistent with that proposed by the United Nations. This states that development education seeks:

> …to enable people to participate in the development of their community, their nation, and the world as a whole. Such participation implies a critical awareness of local, national and international situations based on an understanding of the social, economic and political processes. (Hammond 1984, p. 12)

The UN approach establishes the content of development education as "…concerned with issues of human rights, dignity, self reliance and social justice in both developed and developing countries"(cited in Hammond 1984, p.6).

This view of development education requires that it be transformational, rather than concerned merely with the transmission of factual knowledge. The process approach to teaching for social justice is acknowledged by a wide diversity of writers. For example Griffin (1997, p.279) asserts that:

Social justice education requires a simultaneous awareness of content and process, as well as an ability to both participate in the process and remain outside of it to assess interactions in the group as a whole and among individuals in the group.

Education for social justice is essentially moral in character and is rooted in the idea of empowering pupils to become citizens in a democracy. Kelly, for example, suggests that education for democracy must be based on process rather than content:

...for education for citizenship cannot at root be based on the transmission of knowledge. It is essentially a matter of developing in pupils a range of capabilities, especially the power of autonomous thinking. And that requires an approach to curriculum planning, a curriculum model, whose central feature is not knowledge to be acquired or facts to be stored or extrinsic objectives to be attained but the processes to be promoted and the procedural principles to be derived from those processes (1995, p.186).

GUIDING ASSUMPTIONS: CONSTRAINING 'REALITIES'

A process approach, based on the empowerment of pupils, on the use of active and experiential learning methodologies and on the teacher's understanding of development issues, makes heavy demands on student teachers. A number of key assumptions about the 'realities' of students' capabilities and attitudes and about the education system at second-level in Ireland informed the design of the workshops.

The subject-centred curriculum at second-level in Ireland

The approach to educational knowledge taken in the second-level curriculum in Ireland fits within the model described by Bernstein (1971, p. 49) as a "collection code", that is, it is characterised by strong *classification* (a high degree of boundary maintenance between subjects) and strong *framing* (very little discretion for teachers or pupils over the selection, pacing, organisation and timing of the knowledge transmitted and received). The special character of development education, referred to above, is not in harmony with this model. The active engagement by pupils with complex issues of social justice and the development of empathy with people experiencing injustice require the integration of several kinds of subject knowledge together with a flexible and creative approach to teaching methodology. Paechter (2000, pp.21-25) refers to the power differential within a subject-centred curriculum between contextualised and de-contextualised knowledge, which greatly favours the latter. Education for social justice is of its nature contextualised and is thus at risk of not being permitted to count as knowledge, or at best, being marginalised.

The subject identity of teachers

Rigid boundaries between subjects and disparities of power between subjects are reflected in disparities of power between the teachers of those subjects. Teachers' status and self-image may be closely bound up with their identity as a teacher of subject x, depending on the perceived status of x in the curriculum. Student teachers who have recently completed a degree in their chosen subjects are perhaps likely to identify with that subject (i.e. to see themselves as geographers rather than as teachers of geography, or indeed, as teachers of young people). Their low status within the school as teachers may make them more likely to emphasise their subject identity rather than their identity as teachers.

The status of student teachers

Student teachers are in an ambiguous position. They are required to enact the roles of authority figures within the classroom, of students while in college and some combination of the two while in the school staffroom. They may have relatively little control of curriculum and are not well placed to be the instigators of innovation, should they meet with resistance in the school setting. They may also be in receipt of quite mixed messages as to what constitutes good teaching.

Time and timetabling

The subject-centred curriculum, referred to above, is associated with a rigid, grid-like approach to time and its management. Hargreaves (1994, pp. 99-114) refers to the actual and symbolic importance of time in school organisation. This has particular implications for the teaching of social justice, with an emphasis on process rather than content. In particular, where the development of empathy is to be encouraged through the use of simulation activities, time is needed for connections to be made and interrogated, for difficult ideas to be voiced and for adequate de-briefing to take place.

Concerns regarding classroom management

Active learning methodologies require classroom management skills over and above those needed for more traditional methods of teaching. Student teachers may have particular anxieties both about their actual capacities to manage classes engaged in these activities and about the perceptions of others regarding these capacities. Noise emanating from classrooms is particularly threatening for student teachers, as Denscombe (1980) has observed, whether or not the pupils are engaged in productive and worthwhile activities.

Assessment

The strong framing of the Irish second-level curriculum can be attributed in large measure to a system of assessment based almost entirely on terminal written examination. The form, significance and subsequent uses of this assessment mode exert effects on what is valued in the curriculum, on the methodologies employed and on perceptions of curricular freedom. The emphasis on examinations tends to reject or undervalue areas which they do not see as being 'important for the exam'.

GUIDING ASSUMPTIONS: POSITIVE 'REALITIES'

On the other hand, not all 'realities' of the education system, or of student teachers are negative.

Student teachers' openness to new ideas

Teacher education courses work on the assumption that student teachers will be prepared to try new approaches and question existing practice. It is a necessary condition for the development of reflective practice that beginning teachers be enabled to engage critically with a variety of methodologies.

Recent curricular policy developments

Some recent curricular innovations, such as Civic, Social and Political Education (CSPE, described below) and Social Studies in Leaving Certificate Applied Programme, provide opportunities for the introduction of teaching for social justice. The invitation to schools to design their own Transition Year Programme also offers extensive opportunities. (Department of Education, 1993).

Encouragement of active learning methodologies

Policy documents from the Department of Education and Science (DES) refer to the importance of active learning. For example, in an evaluation of the Leaving Certificate Applied Programme the DES recommends: "The teaching of Social Education should be improved and consolidated by the use of the recommended active teaching and learning methodologies" (Department of Education and Science 2000, p.53). Similar statements can be found in programme guidelines for CSPE, Leaving Certificate Vocational Programme and Transition Year and to an increasing extent in syllabus guidelines for individual subjects, for example Leaving Certificate English.

Potential 'multiplier' effect

The large numbers of students involved in Higher Diploma in Education courses implies that, potentially at least, some exposure to development education can be provided immediately to pupils in a very large number of schools and to future pupils on an ongoing basis. If practising teachers in some of these schools are also involved as a result of the H. Dip. intervention, then the potential influence is even more significant.

Lifelong learning for teachers

The recognition of Continuing Professional Development as a normal feature in the lives of teachers means that introduction of a 'taster' course during initial-teacher education can lay the foundation for further development of the ideas during a teacher's career.

These 'realities' or assumptions, then, provided a basis for the development of what became known as 'Development Education/Experiential Learning Week' in NUI Maynooth. The content and structure of the week are described below, in the context of the Higher Diploma in Education programme.

THE DEVELOPMENT EDUCATION/EXPERIENTIAL LEARNING WEEK PROGRAMME

The Higher Diploma in Education programme in NUI, Maynooth is a one-year, full time course during which the students are involved in teaching practice for two days every week, as well as engaging in seminars and workshops on pedagogy and curriculum in general, and in teaching/learning seminars on the teaching of specific subjects. They also attend lectures in the foundation disciplines of History, Philosophy, Psychology and Sociology of Education and in Curriculum Studies. Active and experiential teaching methodologies are promoted in all aspects of the course and are particularly encouraged in the teaching/learning seminars. Based on a conviction that teaching for social justice forms part of the moral dimension of education for citizenship and is part of the responsibility of every teacher, the Development Education/Experiential Learning Week is compulsory for all students. The structure and content of the week were designed to articulate with the other areas of the Higher Diploma programme.

The Workshop Structure

Preparation was vital. A workshop co-ordinator drew up a plan, gathered a team of facilitators and accessed particular learning resources. The plan sought to integrate active teaching and learning methodologies with a focus on development education. The day was structured so as to include the following activities:

- Icebreaker activities
- Exploring understandings of development using visual images
- Decision-making activities
- Simulations
- Subject-based planning
- Video

In addition, two other dimensions contributed to making the workshops distinctive.

Firstly, there was a poster display. As part of the Higher Diploma in Education, twenty-seven students follow weekly specific methodology classes in CSPE. The CSPE syllabus includes four units, one of which *Ireland and the World* draws attention to Ireland's relationship with other countries and so has a particular focus on development education. Furthermore, the syllabus is constructed around the central concept of 'citizenship' and the seven related concepts of democracy, rights and responsibilities, human dignity, interdependence, development, law and stewardship (Department of Education 1995). In the month prior to the week, these twenty-seven students approached agencies engaged in development work and sought and obtained posters and other relevant educational material. This made it possible to mount an extensive poster display highlighting agencies and their work during the week being discussed here. The immediacy of the varied images of development and justice issues further heightened awareness. The gathering task was also of practical use to the CSPE methodology students as it clearly established the various agencies as important sources of resources for teaching CSPE and social justice at second-level. It also helped to raise the profile of CSPE among the other students and to ameliorate somewhat the status differential, mentioned above, which tends to operate against this subject.

Secondly, the use of Campaign Tea and Coffee at the morning breaks on the days in question further added to the awareness. This was a conscious effort to emphasise that meaningful education for social justice should lead to action and that our familiar, everyday practices, particularly in relation to economic activity, need to be challenged.

The Team

Rather than see the workshop as a single, disconnected event, the development education week was seen from the outset as an integrated part of the course, articulating coherently with other components of the Higher Diploma in Education. A team of nine facilitators included members of the full-time staff of the Education Department, part-time members of the Department who focus on subject methodologies and experts from outside the Department who had a particular expertise in development education. Facilitators worked in pairs throughout. This co-operative model ensured that the experience was also a developmental one for staff as well as students.

Resources

The photographs used to explore participants' understanding of 'development' were drawn from the packs *Wananchi*, (Ireland Aid, 2001) *Kids Like Us* (ActionAid, Ireland 1995) and *Fair Shares?* (Combat Poverty Agency, 1999). Other resources used included *The Trading Game*, a simulation intended to help players understand more clearly how trade affects the prosperity of a country and to show in a practical way how trade works: who benefits and who loses (Christian Aid 2001). *Food Glorious Food* (in Quigley and Kelly 1998, p. 16) is an activity to illustrate the way food is divided globally and how this inequality impacts on people's rights. A major attraction for teachers at second-level is that the activity can be completed within the restrictions of a typical 40-minute class period. *True or False*, another activity from *The Rights Stuff!* (Quigley and Kelly 1998, p.20) was used to draw attention to some factual information related to development about which people are sometimes unclear.

Having exposed student teachers to a variety of activities and resources the challenge for them was to devise ways in which they could integrate some of this development education/experiential learning perspective into their own classes. As can be seen, for example, in the Trócaire catalogue (Trócaire 2001) or in the NCDE catalogue (NCDE 2002), extensive relevant resources exist and many of these were available to students at the workshop. Furthermore, participants had computer access to web-based resources. Students spent a part of the day discussing in small groups how they would implement the teaching/learning strategies they had experienced in the teaching of their own subjects.

Finally, there was the video. An experienced teacher of development education agreed to have one of her classes videotaped in advance of the workshop. This class, with a group of boys and girls in a fifth year in an urban community school, was based primarily on the activity *Human Rights Auction* (Quigley and Kelly 1998, p. 10) and was shown, uncut, towards the end of the day.

EVALUATION OF THE WORKSHOPS

Students' responses

Over the three days one hundred and fifty two trainee teachers took part in the workshops and each was invited to complete an evaluation form at the end of the session. One hundred and thirty seven evaluations were returned. Sixty per cent rated the workshop as either useful or very useful.

Table 1: How useful was the workshop?

Very Useful	36	26%
Useful	46	34%
Fairly useful	35	25%
Not very useful	16	12%
Not useful	4	3%
Total	137	100%

Table 2: How would you rate your understanding of the rationale for development education in the curriculum?

Very comprehensive	27	20%
Comprehensive	54	39%
Fairly comprehensive	40	29%
Not very comprehensive	11	8%
Not comprehensive	5	4%
Total	137	100%

Analysis of the evaluation sheets (filled in anonymously, but identifying respondents' teaching subjects) indicated some subject-based differentials in the responses. Teachers of subjects such as CSPE, Religious Education, Geography, English and History were generally very positive about the experience and could identify ways in which they would use the ideas. More of the teachers of Mathematics, Science and Business Studies had reservations about the relevance of the workshop for them and for their subjects. Teachers of languages tended to be well disposed to the idea of active learning methodologies but were less sure how they could introduce social justice issues, given the limited language experience of their pupils.

Follow up discussions: Focus groups

Two months after the workshops the experience was revisited by way of focus group discussions. Students were chosen to reflect a range of teaching subjects, taking care to include students of subjects identified as favourable to development education and those with subjects which were less favourable. In the intervening period all students had been in schools for full-time block teaching practice throughout the month of January. A particular interest was to see if the workshop had made an impact on either their methodologies or their incorporation of a development education perspective into their teaching.

Participants engaged very intensely with this reflective process. They talked extensively about a wide range of issues to do with development education, experiential learning and their attempts as student teachers to implement some of what they had learned. We have identified a number of major themes which run fairly consistently through the comments.

Subject specificity

Firstly, there is a very clear strand in the discussion that tends to relate everything to the specific subject being taught. Those teaching subjects such as CSPE saw an immediate relevance to the workshop:

"The next day I used the picture activity to narrow down what action project we would do in CSPE".

Others were conscious that both experiential learning and development education 'belonged' somewhere else:

"You would tend to see it as the responsibility of the CSPE teachers or RE, those kind of subjects".

Occasionally, there is a suggestion that the workshop had quite an impact on such a perspective:

"As an English teacher or a French teacher I wouldn't have seen it as my role to make them aware of the developing world. And I do now".

And yet the move from workshop experience to applying methodologies in the classroom is a big one and not to be underestimated.

"I didn't use them... Didn't know the students well enough, the block wasn't long enough...but I think they gave us great ideas...I teach Irish and French and they're more limited".

An awareness of what students expect in particular subjects is also evident:

"There's a certain degree of resistance from the kids. You are likely to get: 'Why are we doing this stuff, sir, this is meant to be a Maths class'".

Curriculum constraints

Not only do teachers at second-level lay strong emphasis on their subject-specific identities, but some perceive a territoriality about particular subjects:

"From that day I wish I was teaching CSPE. It did appeal to me, this type of subject matter which they should be made aware of. But if you try to bring that into Science or Maths are you going to have another teacher knocking on the door saying, 'What the hell are you doing? This is my baby'. The CSPE teacher or the Geography teacher or whatever... I can imagine if a science teacher went down this road (of social justice) you would be regarded as belonging to the 'loony left', by your peers, by your fellow teachers".

The dark shadow of terminal written examinations is a continual presence in the discussions.

"Of course, we have to be realistic about what is examined".

This student teacher was particularly conscious of school culture and how it can dictate what is, or is not, acceptable.

"Although I am sounding negative, I'm not. I am committed to this kind of teaching. But I think we are being asked to lead from the back".

Separation of content from methodology

Generally, the focus in terms of subject specificity tended to be much more on the active teaching and learning methodologies rather than on development education.

"I'm totally won over on active learning and apply it to Geography and Business Studies".

A number reported that a methodology which appealed had been adapted and put into practice:

"I took that idea of the True-False statements and applied it in Business Studies".

Many were clear that during the workshop they had engaged very much with the specific methodologies and, in some cases, were actively separating out the development education/social justice focus.

"Maybe I haven't brought the exact development issues into the classroom but I have tried to take that concept of the teacher being outside the arena and the kids bringing it along themselves. I have given them enough to get them going and then asking them about it".

'What teaching is' - fluidity of views

One very clear effect of the workshop on some was that it brought into sharp focus the student-teachers' own ongoing clarification of the role of the teacher:

"Why did we become teachers? We became teachers because we were good at what we did and we thought we could impart information clearly to people who were listening to us. I think that's the image most people have. The teacher is someone who is good at their subject, and thinks they are good at explaining to students... You don't come into the H. Dip saying 'Right, when I'm finished this I'm going to be able to set up groups, to let students learn through experience, through the actual doing of something'. That wasn't the image...We had the romantic idea of the whole class working and us on our hunkers explaining to one person. It wasn't setting up an environment in the classroom allowing the students experience something for themselves".

That sense of a shift in their self-understanding is expressed in a variety of ways.

"When you start teaching you can be very cut and dried because you have no experience of the other side of the desk... You get questions that you haven't seen coming from anywhere. You have to start thinking on your feet. My attitude now is completely different from September. I do a lot of discussion. I look for relevant resources. If they have a question about anything – September 11th or whatever – I think you are duty bound to answer it".

What school students expect - impact of examinations

As has been noted, the student teachers were very conscious of the many constraints which inhibit them from bring innovative. These constraints come from a variety of sources: individual school cultures, curriculum constraints, their own understanding of the expectations of a student teacher and the impact of examinations. The following two comments are indicative:

"It's a big jump from doing something in Dev. Ed. Week to trying it with noisy little first years".

"And at the end of the day you feel this bias towards experiential learning is out of step with the emphasis on exams. They may say it's not a real class".

Being a student teacher

Student teachers often describe themselves as living in goldfish bowl like conditions, continually in the public gaze, being observed formally by supervisors and co-operating teachers, and informally by students and an interested staffroom:

"In your H. Dip. year you are very conscious of not losing control of classes and supervisors coming in. You're not exactly relaxed. You're not inclined to take innovative leaps".

This tension is well illustrated by one of the focus group participants who was obviously quite enthused by the Development Education workshop and returned to school keen to implement what she had experienced:

"You have this (workshop) and you are inspired and then you go into school and straight away you are met with 'oh a load of rubbish'. You hear this from your peers. I think it's just a question of having the guts to go in and do it, or not telling them but going in and taking it on for yourself... It's a very nice staff...and it is a human instinct to be like the people around you, to want to fit in, to do the same as everyone around you ... It's a big step between having it on paper and feeling confident to do it in school because of the atmosphere that's in there. But I think we should take the chance.... That Friday I went in full of ideas, photocopied sheets of paper, delighted with myself and I was told 'we don't want any of your fancy Maynooth ideas here'".

Some articulate a sense of deferral about the workshop material.

"Unless you are exposed to it, you are not going to use it. You might not use it this year but next year or the year after, you might".

Deliberation

Some evidence emerged in the discussions that the engagement during the workshop with 'big issues' to do with social justice impacted quite strongly with some of the more reflective participants. For example:

"The simulations...you experience all the emotions...they are not as intense...you might come out of it a bit down...it gives you a perspective that you didn't have before you started the game. You're not there in the actual situation, say, of being excluded but you do experience the emotions and the residue and you get a small taste".

"You are more open to more opinions; you begin to balance out opinions...you become a bit more reflective".

Follow-up

Neither organisers nor participants would wish to overstate the claims for a brief workshop that introduced student teachers to the concept of development education. One of the very striking features to emerge during discussions was an awareness that they would need further follow-up education in order to be comfortable in applying a development education perspective in classrooms. Three comments highlight this:

"It was good to give you a taste".

"We didn't get enough time to work in our subject groups".

"It (experiential learning) is too effective an approach not to seek further training".

It was very clear from all participants in the focus group discussion two months after the actual workshop that it had been an intense and memorable experience. Activities, incidents and comments were recalled with great accuracy. Student teachers' enthusiasm for reflecting on and discussing the many issues thrown up by the workshop underlines the importance of debriefing when teaching about social justice. As has been noted:

> Activities aimed at developing understanding and interpretation ...should involve high degrees of interpersonal action and relationships, and often the confrontation of deeply held personal and cultural beliefs and practices. Examples of such experiences are learning about client or colleague relationships, understanding different viewpoints and developing empathy with other people's circumstances. In all these cases debriefing, which centres upon the sharing of participants' reactions, meanings and understandings, is necessary to achieve the development of interpretative meaning and understanding, (Pearson and Smith 1985, p. 76).

Providing some kind of similar opportunity for all, where they could reflect on the workshop and their subsequent attempts to implement aspects of development education, seems likely to be an effective follow-up to the workshop.

Limitations and reservations

While a majority of participants rated the workshop highly at the time, follow-up work with a selection of them two months later highlighted many of the difficulties faced by student teachers in introducing into their classrooms educational activities perceived to be 'innovative'. While personal convictions, a sense of professional competence and subject relevance are important variables, school culture and the need for in-school support also appear to be critically important. This echoes what previous research has found:

> Teachers indicate a keen awareness of the restrictions on the teaching of contemporary social issues – the pressure of an exam focused curriculum and the need to get 'results', the potential criticism of parents on the relevance of social issues teaching, the sensitivity of some of the issues and the question of appropriate methodologies. (Network of Curriculum Units in Development Education 2000, p. 4)

Debriefing

In terms of learning about teaching for social justice at third-level, the practice of offering student teachers a dedicated workshop on development education towards the end of the first term does seem to be effective, as seen from the evaluations and the later focus-group discussions.

Our own reflections and discussions suggest that a greater integration of the workshop with the rest of the year-long programme would be beneficial. Revisiting key concepts and practices and increasing the time for debriefing appear logical developments.

CONCLUSIONS

Adams (1997, p. 30) identifies five pedagogic dilemmas associated with the teaching of social justice, namely:

- Balancing the emotional and cognitive components of the learning process
- Acknowledging and supporting the personal (the individual student's experience) while illuminating the systemic (the interactions among social groups)
- Attending to social relations within the classroom
- Utilising reflection and experience as tools for student-centred learning; and
- Valuing awareness, personal growth and change as outcomes of the learning process.

The 'realities' identified above delineate the context within which these dilemmas have to be continually resolved, both by teachers and by teacher educators. All of the 'realities' or assumptions which guided this study were found to have some validity. However, they did not always operate in the ways anticipated. The view of student teachers as open to new ideas and to the promotion of change was confirmed. Moreover their conversations about teaching gave evidence of a strong moral sense which placed social justice at the heart of teaching, and of an openness to, and enthusiasm for, the use of active learning methodologies. This idealism was somewhat tempered, however, by the realities of classroom practice and staffroom discourse. Student teachers also felt a need for support in developing their knowledge of social justice issues and their capacity to deal with controversial and sensitive topics.

Subject-based differences were also apparent. The focus groups confirmed the positive attitudes, suggested by the evaluations, held by teachers of CSPE, Religious Education, Geography and English. Teachers of Maths and Science showed more positive attitudes than might have been expected but were unsure of how their subjects could accommodate the content suggested. Based on limited information, there was some indication that teachers of Business Studies, while personally sympathetic to much of the content and methodology of development education, were operating from within a subject culture which found difficulty with critical approaches to economic orthodoxy.

One of the strongest messages coming from the student teachers was the necessity of recognising the limitations imposed by their status within schools. It is unfair to burden beginning teachers with the task of "leading from the back" as one student put it. A whole-school approach requires the development of collegiality and meaningful collaboration, as described by Fullan (1991, p. 131). This requires leadership as well as goodwill. Continuing professional development for existing teachers must go hand in hand with the conscientisation of new teachers.

Finally, it was made very clear that university education departments operate within the same time constraints and dilemmas as do schools. Time is needed for student teachers to develop the necessary concepts and methodological skills needed for teaching justice. They must also be given time for debriefing, as described above, as well as time to interrogate their own practice and to integrate new ideas into existing schemas. It is this challenge which is perhaps most demanding and, at the same time, most necessary for teacher educators who wish to promote the teaching of social justice.

REFERENCES

Action Aid Ireland (1995) *Kids Like Us, Irish and Kenyan Kids Together*. Dublin: Action Aid.

Adams, M. (1997) "Pedagogical Frameworks for Social Justice Education" in Adams M., Bell, L. and Griffin P. (eds.) *Teaching for Diversity and Social Justice*. New York: Routledge.

Bernstein, B. (1971) "On the Classification and Framing of Educational Knowledge" in Young, M.F.D. (ed.) *Knowledge and Control*. London: Macmillan

Christian Aid (2001). *The Trading Game*. London: Christian Aid.

Combat Poverty Agency (1999) *Fair Shares*? Dublin: Combat Poverty Agency.

Denscombe, M. (1980)'Keeping 'em quiet: The significance of noise for the practical activity of teaching' in Woods, P. (ed.) *Teacher Strategies*. London: Croom Helm.

Department of Education (1993) *Transition Year Programme Guidelines for Schools*. Dublin: Stationery Office.

Department of Education (1995) *Civic, Social and Political Education Syllabus for the Junior Certificate*. Dublin: Stationery Office.

Department of Education and Science (2000). *Report on the National Evaluation of the Leaving Certificate Applied.* Dublin: Stationery Office.

Drudy, S.(2001). "The Teaching Profession in Ireland: its Role and Current Challenges" *Studies*, 90, 360, Winter, 2001.

Fullan, M.(1991) *The New Meaning of Educational Change.* New York: Teachers' College Press.

Griffin, P. (1997) "Facilitating Social Justice Education Courses" in Adams, M., Bell, L. and Griffin, P. (eds.) *Teaching for Diversity and Social Justice.* New York: Routledge.

Hammond, J. (1991) *A Global Curriculum?* Dublin: CDVEC Curriculum Development Unit.

Hargreaves A. (1994) *Changing Teachers, Changing Times: Teachers' Work and Culture in the Post-Modern Age.* Toronto: Ontario Institute for Studies in Education.

Ireland Aid (2001) *Wananchi: Education and Action. Together for a better world.* Dublin: Ireland Aid and the National Committee for Development Education

Kelly, A.V. (1995) *Education and Democracy: Principles and Practices.* London: Paul Chapman.

NCDE (2002) *NCDE Development Education Resources Catalogue.* Dublin: NCDE

Network of Curriculum Units in Development Education (2000). *Teaching Contemporary Issues – What Teachers Think* Dublin: CDVEC Curriculum Development Unit.

Paechter, C. (2000) *Changing School Subjects: Power, Gender and Curriculum.* Buckingham: Open University Press

Pearson, M. and Smith, D. (1985) "Debriefing in Experience-based Learning" in Boud, D., Keogh, R. and Walker, D. (eds.) Reflection: *Turning Experience into Learning.* London: Kogan Page.

Quigley, P. and Kelly, K. (1998) *The Rights Stuff!; An Education Resource on the UN Convention on the Rights of the Child* , Dublin: DEFY, Amnesty, Trócaire,.

Trócaire (2001). *Resource Catalogue 2001-2002.* Dublin: Trócaire.

CHAPTER 12

ABROAD AND BACK HOME - HOW CAN FOREIGN LANGUAGE TEACHER EDUCATION HELP DEVELOP INTERCULTURAL COMPETENCE?

Susanne Ehrenreich

Teaching Social Justice? In our increasingly multicultural societies, it is in everyday situations that social justice - a big word - is lived and practised: understanding and misunderstanding, respect for and discrimination of the 'other' occur at a personal level, in situations of bicultural face-to-face communication. If we want to educate our young generation to become active citizens who are competent 'cultural border walkers', we need foreign language teachers in primary and secondary schools who are not only linguistic but also intercultural experts. In this paper, I want to highlight the need for Intercultural Communication as an integral part of foreign language teacher education, with reference to the experiences of Irish and German foreign language learners at home and abroad. The situation is still such that in many educational institutions, schools, universities, and teacher training seminars, we first of all have to identify the needs and neglected potentials for specific intercultural learning activities. 'Institutional awareness' of those needs is a precondition since cultural awareness begins with teacher awareness (Luchtenberg 2001, p. 136f.).

Following a brief outline of the key concepts involved I will take you through the different stages of teacher development and describe the form which intercultural encounters could take in the course of this development. I will start out with an exemplification of the target situation: the foreign language teacher's role in the classroom and beyond. Aims and needs, in terms of professional challenges, will be discussed. Then I will move back, as it were, and turn to the educational setting where future foreign language teachers receive their education, the foreign language course at university. The three different phases which are characteristic of such courses will be analysed and the students' individual needs in their process of developing intercultural competence will be identified (see diagram 1).

Diagram 1: outline of argument - the course of Foreign Language Teacher Education

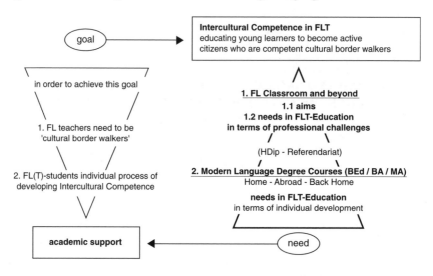

Diagram 2: "Factors in intercultural communication" cf. Byram (1997), p.34

	Skills interpret and relate	
Knowledge of self and other; of interaction: indiv. and societal	Education political education critical cultural awareness	Attitudes relativising self valuing other
	Skills discover and interact	

KEY CONCEPTS

Cultural awareness is a concept which evolved in the 1980s when there was a move away from 'culture' as an objective and static body of knowledge towards a more comprehensive and dynamic concept of culture. Culture was seen as 'a whole way of life' (Williams 1993), as a set of everyday practices which are socially constructed by individuals. According to Risager (2000, p. 159) cultural awareness has an interest in cultural difference and the relationship to 'the Other', and an important dimension of it is the concept of reflexivity, i. e. the idea that an understanding of other cultures is also important for the individuals' cultural understanding of their own identity. The aim of cultural awareness is to replace an ethnocentric viewpoint with the ability to see the world from multiple perspectives.

Intercultural communication describes the negotiation of meaning in an interpersonal interaction under multicultural conditions, conditions which increase the risk of misunderstanding and communication breakdowns due to cultural differences in the use of language. These differences occur in areas such as the lexicon, discourse conventions, communicative styles etc. (Knapp and Knapp-Potthoff 1990, pp. 68ff.). Language, in this wide sense, constitutes and shapes cultural practices and, therefore, teaching a foreign language always implies teaching its culture as well. Apart from this sociolinguistic interpretation of intercultural communication, the term is also used to describe a course type – small units or fully-fledged university degree courses (Roth 1996) – in which the skills of intercultural communication are taught. The teaching also includes an introduction to theoretical concepts of culture, the analysis of 'critical incidents' (Brislin and Yoshida 1994), an investigation of the origin of stereotypes as well as experiential approaches to exploring affective dimensions involved in intercultural communication.

Intercultural competence is a comprehensive concept for which Byram has developed an influential model. The concept of intercultural competence encompasses cognitive knowledge about other cultures, intercultural communication skills and an affective and attitudinal component, i. e. tolerance, solidarity and commitment – a component which is a vital ingredient for successful mediation across cultures in face-to-face situations. Byram's model (1997, p. 34) serves as a useful framework for structuring one's own approach to the teaching and developing of intercultural competence (see diagram 2). If we want our pupils and students to become interculturally competent individuals, we must show them how to expand their knowledge about speaker communities with a different cultural background, how to acquire the necessary skills, how to become affectively involved, how to liberalise their attitudes towards the 'other', and also how to relate these elements back to their own ideas and their own practices.

INTERCULTURAL COMPETENCE AND FOREIGN LANGUAGE TEACHING

After this brief theoretical outline, I will now discuss processes of intercultural learning which occurred both inside and outside the classroom during a school-exchange visit. Drawing on this situation - an intercultural encounter in a school context - several consequences for foreign language teacher education will be highlighted.

Are school exchanges the highlights of intercultural learning? Early intercultural encounters often have a long-lasting effect on individuals and by no means does a school exchange programme result automatically in an increased intercultural competence on the part of the pupils. It therefore seems vital to prepare pupils as well as possible for their first extended stay abroad. It is hoped that young people who realise they can actually leave the secure environment of the foreign language classroom and handle real intercultural face-to-face interactions successfully will develop confidence of a kind that will extend this positive experience to future intercultural contact. A school exchange visit might thus contribute to a general transcultural and transnational communication (Buttjes 1991, p. 8) at home and abroad. To illustrate these considerations I would like to present aspects of a school exchange visit of a German secondary school to a school in Donegal which I co-organised (Ehrenreich 2002). This visit was preceded by a special project in which the pupils were encouraged to go beyond the tourist approach ('Let's see what the teachers have organised') and to become actively and affectively involved in the process.

The idea of this project was to explore several thematic and communication-related areas of German and Irish culture in an autonomous learning environment. The aim was to increase the pupils' cultural awareness of their own and the Irish culture. Departing from the wider concept of culture as 'a whole way of life' and from their own interests, the learners explored the following themes for their group projects: 'Germany/Ireland', 'Donegal and Heidelberg' as the pupils' home towns, 'School in Germany and in Ireland', 'Music and Dance', 'Meals', and 'Sports'. The individual groups' activities included reading information brochures, taking photographs, writing texts and poems, drawing maps, translating recipes, taping cassettes etc. They all designed posters which they then used for their presentations in Ireland. Through this whole process, they become more aware of their own culture and they got a first insight into the target culture. Food for thought and food for talk!

In order to create a general awareness of the complexity of intercultural communication, typical situations were acted out through role plays, situations such as 'Arriving in Ireland', 'Making Plans', or potential conflict areas such as 'Apologising' and 'Requesting'. The major purpose of this activity was to make them feel confident so they would feel free to make the most of their intercultural immersion (a situation which many foreign students would love to have!). Secondly, the importance of active-listening strategies was pointed out and practised, suggestions were given as to how to get involved actively in a conversation and also how to deal with misunderstandings. Through the discussion of the way in which they presented a situation in a role play, they became aware of the role of discourse conventions (small talk etc.) and of different cultural communicative styles (in-/directness, politeness etc.).

What actually happened when we were in Donegal can be summed up as 'a balanced reflexivity in the discoveries with respect to both cultural backgrounds'. The German pupils presented their thematic posters in classes of different age groups, they were taught Irish, they taught Irish pupils how to cook and bake German meals, a Gaelic football match took place and so on. Each group, the German and the Irish pupils, asked questions about the other group's school, sports, music and culture, for example, and each group had to answer questions about their own cultural background. Both groups were 'visitor' and 'host' at the same time, which is a crucial aspect as Byram (1997, p. 32) notes: "The mutual perceptions of the social identities of the interlocutors is a determining factor in the interaction". This ideal situation, of course, only arose when the teacher knew how to integrate the visiting pupils.

One brilliant example was a music class in which I happened to be present: the German girls presented the German music scene with the help of their poster and a demonstration tape with their favourite German music. After that they presented what they knew about Irish music. The Irish girls seemed very surprised and almost honoured when they realised that Irish music (and especially some of the boy groups!) is so popular in distant Germany and when they saw how well the German pupils had researched Irish music with its instruments and its traditional songs. The teacher let the German girls have a go at the uillean pipes and a bodhran. After that, the whole group was taught a tune on the tin whistle – and when finally two of the Irish girls stood up to perform their part of a dance show with which they had been to New York previously, the Germans were thrilled.

This is a small glimpse of successful intercultural moments. The final evaluation of this visit showed that the pupils had developed a balanced and deepened understanding of their own and the foreign culture which did not lack critical observations about both societies either.

CONSEQUENCES FOR FOREIGN LANGUAGE TEACHER EDUCATION

Now, where do the teachers come in? And, moreover, do they receive any training for these kinds of intercultural learning processes? Unfortunately, the situation in most schools and universities has not yet reached the standard as it is optimistically depicted in some recent publications on exchanges and on teacher education (Byram 1999, p. 78ff.; Müller-Hartmann 2000, p. 211; Müller-Jacquier 2000, p. 306). There are at least four aspects of foreign language teaching in schools which need more attention.

Only if foreign language teachers are equipped with intercultural competence, i.e. cognitive and affective understandings of both cultures, ideally paired with personal experience in the target-language country, are they in a position to identify relevant intercultural topics which go beyond the cliché level and know the relevant areas of intercultural communication. They can then initiate learner-centred holistic learning environments in which pupils develop a genuine and informed interest in the host country.

The Irish music teacher mentioned above knew how to adapt her lesson and reacted more than adequately. Unfortunately, school visits for many exchange pupils do not imply anything more than following their partners around, squeezing on some chairs (if there are any at all) at the back of a classroom, with the highlight being a teacher who encourages his or her class to ask questions – an approach which will not take them beyond trivialities and embarrassing silence. It would be a great step forward if teacher education touched upon the issue of how to integrate exchange pupils into classes of different age groups and in different subjects. A better integration of foreign visitors would make the most of the intercultural learning potentials for the whole school community.

In order to organise exchange visits, foreign language teachers need to have an understanding of the cultural differences between the school systems involved. What is the school's profile, what subjects are taught, how are the classes organised, what are the methods used etc.? With an awareness of the foreign institutions it is easier for teachers of different cultural educational backgrounds to support and improve understanding before and during such exchange visits.

Many foreign language education students in Ireland and in other countries at present have to develop a good level of linguistic proficiency and intercultural competence without a residence abroad component being an integral part of their course. Is that still viable? With foreign language learning being integrated in many national primary school curricula all over Europe, primary school teachers play a crucial role in the learners' first contact with a foreign language. Even if travel is not possible, all students have the chance to establish contact with representatives of the target language's culture, i. e. the visiting foreign students, on the campus at home. There is a great potential here for intercultural learning which has so far not been made use of systematically. While the lecturers cannot force the two groups of students to establish relationships, they can provide a learning environment which is more geared towards their integration.

Last year, when I was teaching German in Mary Immaculate College, I asked the students to conduct interviews with German exchange students, a task which encouraged them to seek out contact and which – through the interview structure - provided a secure framework in that they knew which issues they wanted to talk about. The themes which were addressed in these interviews could have been elaborated on much further in an intercultural workshop with both student groups. Approaches of this kind do not have to be confined to language classes. Most subject areas are suited for intercultural projects which will always, as I have shown, provide insight into the foreign as well as into one's own culture. In Education, a contrastive analysis of different national educational systems could be carried out with the help of the foreign experts. Since many of the visiting students are prospective teachers themselves it would also be a great intercultural learning experience if they were asked to prepare a mini-intercultural project together with teacher education students which they would then teach in an Irish primary school. In the light of primary foreign language teaching, this could be a four-dimensional experience from which not only the students but also the teachers and their classes in the school might profit.

In my experience, these examples of how to integrate foreign students into existing classes would also help promote informal integration. The students will have done something together and, through that, gained more insight into each other's social cultures – which, according to the interpretation given before, refers to a shared knowledge of Irish and German 'student culture' with all its possible components, such as university structure, school history, class types, subject areas, types of assessments, work load, jobs, night life, friends and family. With these cultural insights there is more common ground for them to establish relationships. Setting up a tandem learning system or a buddy structure (each visiting student will be in the hands of a native student) are other informal ways of loosening the boundaries between 'our' students and the EFL- (English as a Foreign Language) or *DaF- (Deutsch als Fremdsprache* / German as a Foreign Language) cohort.

We also need to prepare students to travel abroad. The reason we send students abroad seems obvious: "Study abroad is often integrated into degrees in modern languages or other subjects in the belief that extended immersion in a society where the target language is used every day will enhance the learner's proficiency, especially oral-aural SKILLS and less formal registers" (Coleman 2000, p. 582). The year abroad might, then, be the 'meat' in the language course sandwich (Evans 1988, p. 42). Yet, most of us have anecdotal evidence or know from our own personal experience that contrary to the myths of automatic language gain and increased intercultural sensitivity, integration in the host country as the prerequisite of these gains is not always easy.

Among many exchange students and foreign language assistants there is disappointment about not meeting native speakers. Very often we find exchange students resorting to expatriate or international groups, their medium of communication either being their native language or English as a *lingua franca*. Undoubtedly, in the case of the international groups there is a lot of intercultural exchange and often these students return home as 'true Europeans'. If this is what we want, why do we not stop misleading students and call it 'A time of study and touristic explorations in a European country – great chance to meet students from all over Europe (meeting natives may be difficult) and practice English as a *lingua franca*'? In the case of Irish students, the linguistic aspect could even be modified into: 'You will not even have to speak the foreign language'. Coleman, a promoter of year abroad preparation and monitoring, therefore suggests: "Proper preparation at the home institution will include the development of STRATEGIES OF LEARNING appropriate to the extended period of AUTONOMY, and underlining the need to seek out interactive contact with native speakers" (Coleman 2000, p. 583). In the case of English-speaking students, these learning strategies should include some kind of learning agreement which helps them to ask people in German speaking countries to speak German with them, even though they in turn might be happy to practice their English and the conversation might flow more smoothly. What does it help the students if – towards the end of their year they realise: 'I should have been more proactive in that respect'?

Several recent studies (Cormeraie 1995; Coleman 1998; Price 1999) report that "[d]isappointingly, residence abroad seems [...] to have little impact upon the national STEREOTYPES which students hold, and in a minority of cases results in a less positive attitude to speakers of the target language" (Coleman 2000, p. 584). Let me illustrate how challenging intercultural contact can be. A German assistant's car was severely damaged in Birmingham. He was pretty convinced it was because of his German licence plate since the same thing had happened to his German friend's car in the same spot before. When I asked him did this influence his positive attitude towards England and the English he said, with conviction, no. Another German assistant's Irish class decided to welcome her with 'Heil Hitler' and said nothing but that to her for the whole lesson. She did not know what to do. When she reported this to her headmaster he decided to take her out of that class and he punished the group. Although she still loves Ireland, several conflicts of this kind made her decide against a career in teaching. Another German assistant who feels she cannot address problematic issues because she feels uncomfortable expressing herself in the indirect communication style which her English colleagues use. Many English and Irish students, on the other hand, often feel more or less lost when abroad because they do not know enough about the German or Austrian university system. They struggle with the degree of independence which is expected from them and they also miss an organised social student life.

Even though the reported incidents did not result in a negative attitude toward the target language speakers, they highlight the need for more preparation of the year abroad. This should include factual information about the country, the analysis of critical incidents and issues of intercultural communication, such as communication styles, how to repair misunderstandings, and the role of the active listener (Hall 1999, pp. 75ff. and Rampillon 1990). So far, we have assumed that foreign language students pick up these facts and skills for themselves during their period abroad – is this unguided experiential learning with an uncertain outcome or, rather, a guaranteed degree of frustration?

When they return home, students will need to evaluate and appreciate their experience. Is there some kind of recognition of their experience which goes beyond the ECTS (European Credit Transfer System) and informal chats with other returnees and with staff members who happen to be interested? Two observations make me believe that it would be very helpful for the returning students (and rewarding for the lecturers because they can count on a high degree of motivation) if some courses or at least some module topics were co-ordinated with the students' newly acquired linguistic and intercultural knowledge. Most of the former German language assistants interviewed for my current study have expressed their wish to have some kind of forum in which they could share and reflect upon their experiences. Such an opportunity of analysing and systematising their experience within a group of like-minded students might help to balance out positive and disappointing intercultural incidents and observations. In Ireland, in my German classes at Mary Immaculate College, final year students reported on their year abroad with great enthusiasm. These were student-centred classes in which cognitive and affective elements were equally relevant. And would it not be a good idea if final year students with the help of visiting foreign students were in charge of a year abroad preparation workshop for pre-visit students? Workshops in which they provide brief, informative talks about the target language country and in which they conduct role plays and discussions based on theoretical aspects of intercultural communication as well as on their individual experience? Jamieson (1995) describes a project at the University of Hull/England in which fourth year students prepared an interactive multi-media workshop for prospective assistants as an assessed Final Year Option. *The Interculture Project* based at Lancaster University provides a wealth of ideas and information for such workshops on its website of which the searchable databases, in particular, might serve as a good starting point.

Before I move on to my conclusion, I would like to mention the programme *Language Learners as Ethnographers* as an example of outstandingly 'good practice'. It was originally developed by Celia Roberts and Michael Byram and their colleagues at Thames Valley University (Roberts 2001). The programme's aim is to equip language learners with ethnographic skills and knowledge to allow them to carry out some ethnographic research during their residence abroad. It is not only an effective way of encouraging students to get involved and to find out about the cultural practices and values in their host country, it also equips them with methods and concepts which they can use in their later profession as teachers.

CONCLUSION

My aim in this paper was to show that, in view of the foreign language teachers' professional needs and in view of the individual foreign language student's needs - who in most cases is a prospective foreign language teacher - it is necessary to incorporate elements of Intercultural Communication into foreign language teacher education. I have tried to exemplify that there are many different ways of fitting these elements into existing programmes. The first step, however, is teacher awareness. Contrary to prevailing myths, intercultural competence does not develop automatically. To sum up, foreign language students (especially those who go abroad) need guidance in order to develop intercultural competence and it is our duty as university lecturers to give them this kind of support so they can make the most of their intercultural encounters at home and abroad!

REFERENCES

Brislin, R. and Yoshida, T. (1994) *Intercultural Communication Training: An Introduction.* Thousand Oaks: Sage.

Buttjes, D. (1991) 'Interkulturelles Lernen im Englischunterricht'. *Der Fremdsprachliche Unterricht / Englisch.* Vol. 25, No.1, pp. 2-8.

Byram, M. (1997) *Teaching and Assessing Intercultural Communicative Competence.* Clevedon: Multilingual Matters.

Byram, M. (1999) 'Source Disciplines for Language Teacher Education' in Trappes-Lomax, H. and McGrath, I. (eds.) *Theory in Language Teacher Education.* Harlow: Longman.

Coleman, J. (1998) 'Evolving Intercultural Perceptions among University Language Learners in Europe', in Byram, M. and Fleming, M. (eds.) *Language Learning in Intercultural Perspective.* Cambridge: Cambridge University Press.

Coleman, J. (2000) 'Study abroad' in Byram, M. (eds) *The Routledge Encyclopedia of Language Teaching and Learning.* London: Routledge.

Cormeraie, S. (1995) 'Cross-Cultural Training: Perceptions and Personal Growth' in Parker, G. and Rouxeville, A. (eds.) *'The Year Abroad': Preparation, Monitoring, Evaluation.* London: CILT.

Ehrenreich, S. (2002) 'Riverdance und Semmelknödel in irischen Klassenzimmern' *Englisch.* Vol. 37, No.2.

Evans, C. (1988). *Language People: The Experience of Teaching and Learning Modern Languages in British Universities.* Milton Keynes: Open

University Press.

Hall, C. (1999). 'Teaching Intercultural Communication to Modern Languages Students' in Tenberg, R. (ed.) *Intercultural Perspectives. Images of Germany in Education and the Media*. München: iudicium.

Jamieson, D. (1995) 'Preparation for the Assistantship year in France – through the lens of student-led interactive multimedia projects' in Parker, G. and Rouxeville, A. (eds.) *'The Year Abroad': Preparation, Monitoring, Evaluation*. London: CILT.

Knapp, K. and Knapp-Potthoff, A. (1990) 'Interkulturelle Kommunikation'. *Zeitschrift für Fremdsprachenforschung*. Vol. 1, No. 1, pp. 62-93.

Luchtenberg, S. (2001) 'Language(s) and Cultural Awareness: Ein Thema für die Fremdsprachenlehrerausbildung?' *Neusprachliche Mitteilungen*. Vol. 54, No. 3, pp. 130-138.

Müller-Hartmann, A. (2000) 'Exchanges' in Byram, M. (ed.) *The Routledge Encyclopedia of Language Teaching and Learning*. London: Routledge.

Müller-Jacquier, B. (2000) 'Interkulturelle Didaktik' in Byram, M. (ed.) *The Routledge Encyclopedia of Language Teaching and Learning*. London: Routledge.

Price, S. (1999) 'Pride and Prejudice: Evidence for Stereotyping on the Part of British Students of German' in Tenberg, R. (ed.) *Intercultural Perspectives. Images of Germany in Education and the Media*. München: iudicium.

Rampillon, U. (1990) *English Beyond the Classroom. Unterrichtsvorschläge und Materialien zu Förderung der interkulturellen Gesprächsfertigkeit im Englischunterricht*. Bochum: Kamp.

Risager, K. (2000) 'Cultural awareness' in Byram, M. (ed.) *The Routledge Encyclopedia of Language Teaching and Learning*. London: Routledge.

Roberts, C. (2001) *Language Learners as Ethnographers*. Clevedon: Multilingual Matters.

Roth, J. (1996) 'Interkulturelle Kommunikation als universitäres Lehrfach. Zu einem neuen Münchner Studiengang' in Roth, K. (ed.) *Mit der Differenz leben. Europäische Ethnologie und Interkulturelle Kommunikation*. Münster: Waxmann.

The Interculture Project: http://www.lancs.ac.uk/users/interculture (Accessed on

3rd April 2002)

Williams, R. (1993) 'Culture is Ordinary' in Gray, A. and McGuigan, J. (eds.) *Studying Culture: An Introductory Reader*. London: Edward Arnold.

CHAPTER 13

SOCIAL JUSTICE THROUGH ACCESS PROGRAMMES:
PRACTICE, PROBLEMS AND POLICY

Micheál L. Collins and *David McGuire*

Throughout the last five years, the Irish third-level sector has been identified increasingly as an area within which issues of social justice can be addressed. The sector has played a dual role by both encouraging socially disadvantaged students to enrol and integrating these students into the existing third-level environment. Central to both of these processes has been the Access Programme Initiative. In line with European efforts to tackle socio-economic disadvantage, access programmes emphasise the need to support second-chance education through pro-actively adopting measures aimed at reducing the deficit created through unequal access and participation in education. Indeed, the 1995 European Commission White Paper on Education and Training favours a positive discriminatory approach to achieving social equality across Europe.

This paper uses the results of a survey of two hundred and sixty-six access participants to evaluate the benefits of access programmes in addressing issues of social justice at third-level. The survey identifies the background of the access programme participants, their pre-programme education level, the primary influences that encouraged them to avail of the access initiative, and the financial concerns that they face. It also addresses the experiences of participants and the factors central to their retention within the programme.

Following Rawls' (1971) interpretation of social justice as fairness, the paper reviews how current access programmes are attempting to achieve this. Following a review of relevant literature, the paper proceeds to use both quantitative and qualitative data to identify the problems that exist within these programmes and among their participants. Finally, the paper concludes with a policy section, which proposes possible remedies for many of the issues raised.

ACHIEVING SOCIAL JUSTICE THROUGH ACCESS PROGRAMMES

Social justice in education is recognised as a fundamental issue in the creation of an equitable society. In most societies, the education system is the primary institutional mechanism for the distribution of social assets in directing and shaping social change. Rawls' (1971) concept of social justice as fairness maintains that all citizens should have an equal opportunity to develop their skills and abilities. Regardless of social class and wealth, this liberal egalitarian view proposes that the education system should try to compensate for the obstacles preventing the equal participation of all members of society (Baker 1998). The development of access initiatives stands as a response to these ideals.

While the Access Initiative, in one form or another, has existed in Ireland for some years, it has begun to receive considerable funding and academic attention only during the last decade. Internationally, access programmes have evolved to meet some or all of the following demographic and labour market conditions:

- Under-representation of certain socio-economic groups in third-level education
- Shortage of skilled science and technology workers
- The increasing need for flexibility and frequent retraining of the workforce
- A declining youth population
- Rising aspirations among certain social groups

Tomlinson (2000) argues that the middle and aspirant classes are more resistant to notions of social inclusion and access initiatives than other social groupings. She highlights the strong commitment of the middle and aspirant classes to the social and political system which provides them with a "good life", or at least a better life than their parents, and the fierce determination of such groups to see that their children are reproduced in similar spheres. To this end, she suggests that these groups are less concerned with equality of opportunity and are more concerned about the exclusion of those who would interfere with their good credentials. Many commentators point to the central role which education plays in the status attainment process and in the reward structure of society (Clancy 1995; Collins and Kavanagh 1998; Whelan and Hannan 1998). In this regard, research reveals that the selection mechanisms used for third-level entry and access to better positions in the labour market are more discriminating and less favourable to working class achievement in Ireland than in other European countries (Hannan et al. 1996; Muller et al. 1996; Whelan and Hannan 1998).

While there is strong support for access initiatives in the literature, Tight (1996) provides a well-grounded critique of access programmes. He argues that many students, particularly mature students, who undertake access programmes have already gained some qualifications and have a good deal of experience and understanding, yet are required by educational institutions to attend a year-long access programme to demonstrate their ability to cope with higher education. He maintains that other, quicker and more relevant means of enabling access should be made available to these students. While he recognises that access programmes are primarily aimed at the greater involvement of under-represented groups in higher education, he maintains that such programmes may help create and sustain ghettos. He posits that access programme students will be identified and labelled as such throughout their careers in higher education and may be evaluated in such a way by prospective employers. The attitude to encouraging greater representation of socially marginalised groups in third-level education is valuable; however, the subsequent "looking down" on such groups when they enter mainstream higher education is to be discouraged. The inflexibility of many of the educational institutions offering access programmes is also criticised. While many access programmes are flexible and adaptable to the needs of access students, there is limited evidence of how degree/diploma courses have evolved to meet student needs, once they complete the access programme. However, the ACCS (Accumulation of Credits and Certification of Subjects) scheme operating within the Irish Institutes of Technology serves as a noticeable example of positive progress towards resolving this problem.

In Ireland, access programmes have been broadly welcomed as an effort to address the sustained class inequalities existing in the education system (Whelan and Hannan 1998; Callan and Nolan 1992; Breen *et al.* 1990). Numerous reports point to an over-emphasis on academic achievement resulting in an under-participation of particular socio-economic classes in third-level institutions (Lynch 1998; Garavan *et al.* 1995). Despite large-scale educational expansion, there remains remarkable consistency in the relationship between socio-economic background and inequality in educational outcomes (Breen and Whelan 1996; Shavit and Blossfeld 1993; Smyth 1999). Commenting on this, Lynch and O'Riordan (1998) note the widely held perception among disadvantaged communities that the culture of third-level institutions reflects a middle-class ethos which is not receptive to the participation and involvement of the working classes. Similarly, the Euro-Delphi survey (Carey 1995) points to unemployment and social inequalities as the most significant life problems faced by adults in Irish and European society. The survey argues that access programmes have the potential to play an important role in addressing issues of social inequality and in bridging existing class differences in society. Whelan and Hannan (1998) conclude that three factors fuel the persistence of social inequalities in the Irish education system. First, they suggest that the development historically of the Irish education system is linked to local social stratification systems with an over-emphasis on a more academic than technical discourse. Second, these stratification systems influence the choice of second-level schooling for one's offspring. Finally, they posit that the goal of third-level access dominates the culture of most second-level schools and imposes requirements as to the subjects to be taught, to the neglect of the curricular and pedagogical needs of "non-college bound" students. This "back-wash" effect has had the dual consequence of intensifying academic pressure on schools and pupils and erecting further barriers to the achievement of working class pupils in the educational arena.

While access programmes fulfil the task of providing education opportunities for those who would not otherwise achieve them, the literature indicates that they are not the sole solution to educational disadvantage. Tormey and Prendeville (2000) argue that some intervention is required at a much earlier age to counter the effects of poverty which, to a very significant extent, occur before children leave primary school. Though Lynch (1998) welcomes Government initiatives such as Breaking the Cycle, Youthreach and Early Start as constituting an attempt to address the extreme effects of inequality, she argues that they are too small in scale and lacking in scope to address the root causes of much educational inequality. (For a further review of the current literature on access courses see McGuire and Collins (2001).

METHODOLOGY

The data presented in this paper is based on a cross-sectional survey of socio-economically disadvantaged students in four third-level institutions located in the west and mid-west of Ireland. For reasons of confidentiality the four educational institutions shall be referred to as Third Level 1,2,3 and 4. A pilot study was initially undertaken with a group of thirty students selected at random in two educational institutions to ensure the validity of the questionnaire instrument. The questionnaires were then distributed to the students either directly by the Access Officer or by post. Lower response rates were recorded by the third-level institutions where there was an emphasis on the postal approach to distributing the questionnaires. The questionnaire was self-administered and returned anonymously to the authors. The questionnaires were distributed between the months of December 2000 and February 2001. The sample of respondents is of two types:

- Socio-economically disadvantaged students who entered third-level through established access programmes (direct access)
- Socio-economically disadvantaged students who entered third-level via the normal college application route, but who receive financial support from the Access Office

One hundred and ten questionnaires were distributed to each of the third-level institutions. Completed questionnaires were received from a total of two hundred and sixty-six students of the four hundred and forty students contacted, giving a response rate of sixty point five per cent. This response rate compares favourably with a number of benchmark studies conducted in the educational field. The data was analysed using SPSS and an analysis of variance was undertaken using the ANOVA function. The analysis reveals there is sufficient statistical power.

PROFILE OF RESPONDENTS

The two hundred and sixty-six respondents are divided by institution and classified by gender, age and domicile in Table One. The analysis reveals that almost two-thirds of socio-economically disadvantaged students surveyed were female; the twenty-nine plus age group being the dominant grouping to participate. An analysis of respondents by third-level institution reveals that access initiatives are primarily targeted at specific groups within the local area. Male participation in third-level education is significantly lower than female participation for two of the institutions surveyed (Third Level 1 and 2), whereas mature students (twenty-five to twenty-eight, twenty-nine plus) are the focus of access initiatives in two institutions (Third Level 3 and 4).

Research highlights that over sixty per cent of students from disadvantaged backgrounds are from rural areas (Kellaghan *et al.* 1995) and this study shows that rural students are well represented in the four institutions surveyed.

Table One: Demographic Characteristics of Survey Respondents

	Third Level 1	Third Level 2	Third Level 3	Third Level 4	Overall
Gender					
Male	28.6%	35.6%	51.2%	44.7%	37.2%
Female	71.4%	64.4%	48.8%	55.3%	62.8%
Age					
17 – 20	32.1%	30.7%	0%	10.5%	23.3%
21 – 24	16.7%	36.6%	4.7%	7.9%	21.1%
25 – 28	4.8%	12.9%	16.3%	34.2%	13.9%
29+	46.4%	19.8%	79.1%	47.4%	41.7%
Domicile					
Urban	44.4%	45.5%	48.7%	57.9%	47.5%
Rural	55.6%	54.5%	51.3%	42.1%	52.5%

Table Two reveals the educational background of the respondents. Overwhelmingly, they possess a Leaving Certificate qualification, although fifteen per cent have completed only Junior/Intermediate Certificate education, while four point two per cent departed the formal education system on completion of primary school. It is particularly noticeable that the results for Third Level 3, which focused on an older age group, recorded a greater proportion of respondents in the lower education categories. Similarly, it records a large "other" percentage which is principally accounted for by participants with foreign education qualifications.

Table Two: Highest Education achieved by Survey Respondents

	Third Level 1	Third Level 2	Third Level 3	Third Level 4	Overall
Primary	6%	1%	9.8%	2.7%	4.2%
Junior/Inter Cert	21.7%	4%	29.3%	16.2%	15.3%
Leaving Cert	65.1%	89%	41.5%	78.4%	72.4%
Leaving Applied	2.4%	2%	2.4%	0%	1.9%
Other	4.8%	4%	17.1%	2.7%	6.1%
Total	100.0%	100.0%	100.0%	100.0%	100.0%

The students of Third Level 1,3 and 4 display a significant previous commitment to taking education courses. Table Three shows that between two-thirds and three-quarters of these respondents have attended in the past another non-third-level course. Significance may be attached to such previous displays of commitment by these students as it points towards a willingness for self-improvement. Third Level 2 possesses a much younger group of respondents, sixty-seven per cent being under twenty-five years; consequently, a smaller level of previous participation is displayed. Overall, a majority of respondents have participated previously. This finding, when broken down by age, reveals a strong positive correlation across all colleges between age and previous participation.

Table Three: Previous Participation in Education Courses by Survey Respondents

	Third Level 1	Third Level 2	Third Level 3	Third Level 4	Overall
Participated*	66.3%	27.0%	75.6%	73.0%	53.6%
No Participation	33.7%	73.0%	24.4%	27.0%	46.4%

Note: *This category includes those who participated in non-third-level education programmes such as PLC courses, apprenticeships, FAS training courses and CERT courses.

Table Four: Third-Level Courses of Access Students

	Third Level 1	Third Level 2	Third Level 3	Third Level 4	Overall
Arts/Humanities	68.7%	34.3%	16.7%	13.2%	39.8%
Engineering	3.6%	11.1%	5.6%	23.7%	9.8%
Education	7.2%	10.1%	16.7%	0%	8.6%
Science	3.6%	14.1%	2.8%	10.5%	8.6%
Business	14.5%	10.1%	22.2%	15.8%	14.1%
Information Technology	2.4%	17.2%	27.8%	26.3%	15.2%
Other	0%	3.0%	8.3%	10.5%	3.9%
Total	100%	100%	100%	100%	100%

Finally, Table Four displays the course choices respondents have made. Overall, they showed a preference for Arts/Humanities-based courses over other types of course offered by third-level institutions. However, uniformity does not exist across the four third-level institutions. While Arts/Humanities was preferred in Third Level 1 and Third Level 2, more practical courses were favoured in Third Level 3 and 4 in the form of Information Technology courses. Engineering figured strongly in Third Level 4, as did business in Third Level 3. This finding seems likely to reflect the specialities of each institution. An analysis of the course choices by sex reveals that Arts/Humanities is predominantly a female choice (seventy-eight per cent) as is Science, Business and Education. Male students make up the majority of access respondents studying Engineering and Information Technology.

THE ACCESS STUDENT EXPERIENCE: PRACTICE AND PROBLEMS

The following section contains the findings of the primary research data collected. The key factors in the access student experience are first identified and thereafter follows a discussion on the four specific issues of personal aspirations, financial issues, support networks and the location of the third-level institution

Key Factors in the Access Student Experience

Table Five identifies the four key factors in the decision to seek third-level education. These are in order: the personal aspirations of access students, financial considerations (including social welfare assistance), the location of the institution and the existence of support networks (comprising of parents, friends and teachers). Access students attached significant levels of importance to all of these factors included in the study: all of the overall mean scores exceed the mid-point of the scale.

Table Five: Key Factors in the Decision to attend Third-Level

	Third Level 1	Third Level 2	Third Level 3	Third Level 4	Overall Mean Score
Personal Aspirations	3.91	3.84	3.82	3.85	3.86
Financial Considerations	3.22	3.12	3.27	3.04	3.15
Social Welfare Assistance	2.82	2.41	3.23	2.88	2.70
Location of Institution	2.95	2.69	3.55	2.88	2.91
Support of Friends	2.73	2.59	3.00	2.58	2.68
Support of Parents	2.71	2.97	1.91	2.38	2.67
Support of Teachers	2.67	2.48	2.73	2.15	2.52

Note: Scale: 1 (Not at all important) to 4 (Very Important)

In particular, Table Five identifies personal aspirations as the primary factor influencing participation. It records a mean score of three point eight six and is consistently rated as the highest factor across all four educational institutions. Given the socio-economic background of respondents, it is unsurprising that financial considerations and social welfare assistance achieve high levels of importance. The location of the third-level institution is also considered important, attaining a mean score of two point nine one. Overall, respondents regard this factor as more important than support networks.

Personal Aspirations

The high scores attaching to personal aspirations in Table Five reflect a strongly held desire by access students for self-improvement. When taken in conjunction with the modest importance which respondents attach to the support network, it signals that access students are very self-reliant and highly motivated to achieve the standards they set themselves.

Table Six: Break-down of Personal Aspirations for attending Third-Level

	Third Level 1	Third Level 2	Third Level 3	Third Level 4	Overall
Better Job Prospects	22.9%	50.5%	31.3%	45.9%	38.1%
Personal Development	48.2%	44.2%	50.0%	32.4%	44.5%
Enjoys Study	12.0%	2.1%	0%	2.7%	5.3%
Grasps Opportunity	15.7%	3.2%	6.3%	8.1%	8.5%
Other	1.2%	0%	12.5%	10.8%	3.6%
Total	100%	100%	100%	100%	100%

Table Six analyses the composition of personal aspirations by asking respondents to identify qualitatively the principal reason behind their decision to attend third-level education. When the content is analysed, the data highlights the identification of better job prospects and personal development reasons as the primary aspirational factors. Interestingly, in cases where the father is employed, respondents were more likely to attend for personal development. Typical observations received included the following:

> Having left school 20 years ago, it was very daunting going back to education. The access course is the perfect stepping stone to becoming a full-time student.
> (Female Student, Third Level 4)

> I decided to attend third-level to break out of the vicious cycle of my community, i.e. drugs, dropouts, crime etc.
> (Male Student, Third Level 1)

In cases where the father is unemployed, almost sixty per cent of students decided to attend third-level to improve their job prospects. This utilitarian means-end perspective indicates an attempt by these students to improve their standard of living and avoid intergenerational issues of educational disadvantage. It is clear therefore that some respondents are conscious of their role as pathfinders to higher education and of the impact their decision may have on future generations and the people around them.

> The principal reason I decided to go to third-level is that I do not desire to be employed in a non-challenging low-paid job.
> (Male Student, Third Level 4)

> I am a single parent with 4 children (3 teenagers) and my influence of wanting further education influences my children. They also see third-level as a possibility where before it seemed like it was only for the smart and the people with money.
> (Female Student, Third Level 1)

Financial Considerations

It is clear that financial considerations are regarded as highly relevant by respondents, with eighty-three per cent indicating that they were either an important or very important factor in their decision to participate in third-level courses. Furthermore, almost ninety-five per cent of respondents replied that financial considerations play a central role in their continued participation in third-level education. Of this figure, sixty-seven point five per cent regarded them as very important and six point nine per cent as important in ensuring their continued participation. The strength of these results highlights the importance of issues such as funding, borrowing, and part-time employment income to access students.

When respondents were asked if their decision to undertake an access course placed financial strain on themselves or their families, seventy-three point four per cent indicated that it did, while the remaining twenty-six point four replied that it did not. A further analysis, using the economic status of the respondents' fathers as a proxy for social background, indicated that of almost all households where the father is unemployed or engaged in home duties experience financial strain.

Table Seven: Levels of Financial Assistance and Financial Strain experienced by Access Students in Financing Participation in Third Level Education

		Financial Strain		Total
		Yes	No	
Financial Assistance	Yes	64.1%	21.6%	85.7%
	No	9.3%	5.0%	14.3%
Total		73.4%	26.6%	100.0%

Financial assistance, classified as education grants and social welfare payments, were received by almost eighty-six per cent of respondents. Table Seven presents this result and also assesses if these recipients are experiencing financial strain. Within the category of those receiving financial assistance, three-quarters of respondents report feeling under financial strain. This outcome seems to indicate inadequate support for these students. Given the financial pressures, borrowing or part-time employment often emerge as financial necessities. The survey reveals that forty-eight point five per cent of respondents engage in borrowing with almost ninety per cent of these same respondents also receiving financial assistance.

Thirty-seven point seven per cent of respondents indicated that they are engaged in part-time employment, with the average number of hours calculated at 16 hours per week. Of these students engaged in part-time employment, eighty-six per cent also receive financial assistance and seventy-nine point one per cent report feeling under financial strain. Some of the respondents' comments clearly display the significance of these financial considerations.

Having not received a grant yet I have been left in an almost impossible position.

(Male Student, Third Level 4)

Because of my part-time job I experience a lack of sleep during the weekdays. This affects my performance during the morning classes.

(Male Student, Third Level 3)

When I was in VTOS I was on a FAS allowance of around one hundred and fifty two Euro per week, plus travel allowance and meals. Now in third level I only get one hundred and four Euro per week plus my grant. So I am financially a lot worse off trying to further my education.

(Male Student, Third Level 4)

Support Network

The survey also assesses the importance of support from Friends, Parents and Teachers in the respondents' decision to enter third-level. Successive studies reveal that parental encouragement, which operates independently of social class, is an important influence on educational achievement levels (Davies and Kandel 1981; Hannan *et al.* 1996; Heath and Clifford 1990). It is argued that parental educational expectations and attitudes become internalised by children in their early years and this has a significant effect on their subsequent educational motivations and achievements. Research also identifies social context (schooling, learning environment) as an important variable shaping the beliefs, norms and values of students and ultimately influencing their levels of achievement (Hofman *et al.* 2001). Marks (2000) argues that factors such as the absence of a culture of learning and books at home, the "knowledge gap" between parents and children due to changes in the curriculum and the physical restrictions on education created by an inner-city environment can negatively influence attitudes to education. As Table Eight reveals, all three parts of the respondents' support network were broadly supportive of the respondents' decision to attend third-level. Of the three groups, it shows that friends were generally more supportive than parents in the decision to attend third-level. It is important to note that there exists a notable distinction between the data presented in Tables Five and Eight. While Table Five examines how important the support of each group was in the decision to attend third-level, Table Eight measures the actual support given by the parties in the decision by the respondent to attend higher education. Furthermore, the high variation in the figures experienced by respondents of Third Level 3 may be explained by the more mature age profile of access students in that institution.

Table Eight: Support of Respondents' Friends, Parents and Teachers in their Decision to attend Third Level

	Third Level 1	Third Level 2	Third Level 3	Third Level 4	Overall Mean Score
Support of Friends	3.26	3.34	3.22	3.36	3.29
Support of Parents	3.18	3.58	2.36	3.38	3.13
Support of Teachers	3.25	3.03	3.18	2.72	3.05

Note: Scale: 1 (Not at all Supportive) to 4 (Very Supportive)

In relation to parental support, one respondent writes:

I was encouraged by my parents to go to third-level to get a better education than they did...also I am keenly interested in pursuing a career in my chosen course.

(Female Student, Third Level 2)

Location of Third Level Institution

A further key factor in the decision to attend third-level is the location of the institution. Table Five identified that, in terms of an overall rating, respondents saw this factor as important. An assessment of the responses across the four institutions indicates a relationship between the age of the access student respondents and the importance attached to college location. The older respondents of Third Level 3 regard location as very important, giving it a mean score of three point five five, whereas the younger respondents of Third Level 2 do not rate its importance as highly, giving it a mean score of two point six nine.

The survey results also indicate that a number of access students are travelling long distances each day to attend their colleges. While once again this underscores their determination, it also reduces the time available for study and family as well as adding to the cost of the college experience. The following two quotes are indicative of the views expressed:

> Myself and two other women travel over 100 miles to attend each day, five days a week.
> (Female Student, Third Level 1)

> A difficulty for me is the 48 mile round trip every day.
> (Female Student, Third Level 1)

POLICY IMPLICATIONS

It is apparent from our study that personal aspirations play an important role in motivating these socio-economically disadvantaged students to attend third-level education. As such, they view third-level education as an opportunity to develop skills and abilities in order to seek out better employment opportunities. It is also clear that socio-economically disadvantaged students attending third-level education are, as a group, highly autonomous, self-motivated and willing to take responsibility for their own education and development. Their responses identify an appreciation of the opportunity to attend third-level; typical of these observations are:

> Access is a wonderful programme, very helpful indeed, very encouraging.
> (Female Student, Third Level 1)

> The access course has been the reason I turned my life around and I will be forever grateful.
> (Female Student, Third Level 1)

For a significant majority of access students, the funding they receive is inadequate. Engaging in borrowing and/or part-time employment seems to be a necessary response. There is a convincing case for access student funding to be increased. This survey was conducted prior to the publication of the Government's *Report of The Action Group on Access to Third Level Education* (released July 9th 2001), which similarly recommended an increase. Subsequently, the government increased access participants' grants by one thousand five hundred and fifty-six Euro per annum for non-adjacent students and six hundred and twenty-three Euro per annum for access students living within fifteen miles of their college. It is clear from our findings that these increases are necessary, though it seems unlikely that the size of the increase is adequate to reduce the financial strain felt by many access participants. Essentially, over the thirty-six week college year, the grant increases amount to forty-three Euro and twenty-two cent per week for non-adjacent access participants and seventeen Euro thirty cent per week for access participants living within fifteen miles of their college. To address seriously the financial burden felt by access students, we feel that support funding needs to increase further, at the very least by the same amount again.

For many access students, in particular those more mature than the average third-level college student, the challenge of balancing college attendance, study, personal and family life is difficult. A typical response to this experience is a call for greater flexibility at third-level:

> It would be a help to very mature students to have the option of doing less subjects per year and extending the duration of the degree course.

(Female Student, Third Level 1)

As a response, the introduction of course flexibility via modular programmes and longer course duration, is required for many third-level access students. Such reforms, while enhancing the attractiveness of courses to potential access students, will pose difficulties for academics and course administrators, given that they will require reforms to existing course structures. We believe that third-level colleges should be required to reform all programmes so as to enable greater flexibility.

More generally, the next ten to fifteen years will provide policy makers with a once-off opportunity to reduce radically educational disadvantage via structured use of access programmes. The current drop in third-level applicants, and the related drop in numbers sitting the Leaving Certificate, opens up the prospect of advancing social justice at third-level (see Thornhill [2001, p. 17-19] for a brief discussion of these predicted trends). Consequently, spare capacity will emerge at both second- and third-level; however, demographic projections show that it will be short lived. At third-level, both Universities and Institutes of Technology (ITs) will be affected, though the latter will experience the majority of place vacancies, a phenomenon which has already begun. However, it is critical that all third-level colleges are funded to attract educationally disadvantaged locals to participate as access students in their courses.

In essence, this is a low-cost opening for policy makers to address seriously educational disadvantage. The buildings, staff and facilities of third-level colleges are already there and will provide no additional fiscal pressures in addressing the problem. Additional expenditure, such as that signalled in the National Development Plan, will be necessary only to establish flexible methods of participation and to support access students. This is a window of opportunity, one which will close in under fifteen years, and one which - if seriously pursued - can address educational disadvantage and, consequently, create a more egalitarian and inclusive society.

CONCLUSION

The experience of access programmes in addressing issues of social justice can primarily be regarded as positive. Although there are a number of problems to be resolved, most notably increasing levels of participation and addressing funding difficulties, it is clear that these programmes are assisting socio-economically disadvantaged students to achieve their potential and improve their life experiences. In summary, this paper serves two purposes. First, it documents the experience of access students in third-level education and the aspirations, challenges and problems they face. Second, it presents a holistic analysis of the workings of access programmes and sets out a series of policy proposals to address the issues raised. All in all, while access programmes remain only one piece in the social justice jigsaw, their impact should not be understated in creating a fair and more equitable society.

REFERENCES

Baker, J. (1998) 'Equality' in Healy, S. and Reynolds, B. (eds.) *Social Policy in Ireland: Principles, Practices & Problems*. Dublin: Oak Tree Press.

Breen, R. and Whelan, C.T. (1996) *Social Mobility and Social Class in Ireland*. Dublin: Gill and Macmillan.

Breen, R., Hannan, D.F., Rottman, D. and Whelan, C.T. (1990) *Understanding Contemporary Ireland: State, Class & Development in the Republic of Ireland*. London: Macmillan.

Callan, T. and Nolan, B. (1992) 'Income Distribution and Redistribution in the

Republic of Ireland' in Goldthorpe, J., and Whelan, C.T. (eds.) *The Development of Industrial Society in Ireland.* Oxford: Oxford University Press.

Clancy, P. and Wall, J. (2000) *Social Background of Higher Education Entrants.* Dublin: Higher Education Authority (HEA).

Clancy, P. (1995) 'Access Courses as an Aid towards Addressing socio-economic Disparities in participation in higher education' in *Access Courses for Higher Education*, proceedings of the HEA seminar held on 31st January 1995 at Mary Immaculate College, Limerick.

Collins, M. and Kavanagh, C. (1998) 'For Richer, For Poorer: The Changing Distribution of Household Income in Ireland 1973–1994' in Healy, S., and Reynolds, B. (eds.) *Social Policy in Ireland: Principles, Practices & Problems* Dublin: Oak Tree Press.

Collins, M. and McGuire, D. (2002) 'Financial Issues for Third Level Access Programme Participants Identification & Policy Implications', *Administration*, Vol. 50, No. 3, pp. 63-82.

Davies, M. and Kandel, D. (1981) 'Parental and Peer Influences on Adolescent Educational Plans: Some Further Evidence', *American Journal of Sociology*, Vol. 87, No. 2, pp. 363 – 403.

Carey, L. (1995) The *Euro-Delphi Survey: the future goals and policies of adult education in Europe.* Maynooth: St Patrick's College.

Garavan, T.N., Costine, P. and Heraty, N. (1995) *Training & Development in Ireland: Context, Policy & Practice.* Dublin: Oak Tree Press.

Hannan, D.F., Smyth, E., McCullagh, J., O'Leary, R. and McMahon, D. (1996) *Coeducation and Gender Equality: Exam Performance, Stress and Personal Development.* Dublin: Oak Tree Press and ESRI.

Heath, A. and Clifford, P. (1993) 'Class Inequalities in Education in the Twentieth Century', *Education and Training Policies for Economic and Social Development, NESC Report 95.* Dublin: NESC.

Hofman, R.H., Hofman, W.H.A. and Guldemond, H. (2001) 'Social Context Effects on Pupils Perception of School' *Learning and Instruction*, Vol. 11, pp. 171 – 194.

Ireland (2001) *Report of the Action Group on Access to Third-Level Education.* Dublin: Stationery Office.

Ireland (2000) *National Development Plan 2000-2006.* Dublin: Stationery Office.

Kellaghan, T., Weir, S., O hUallachain, S., and Morgan, M (1995) *Educational*

Disadvantage in Ireland. Dublin: Department of Education, Combat Poverty Agency and The Educational Research Centre.

Lynch, K. & O'Riordan, C. (1998) 'Inequalities in Higher Education: A Study of Class Barriers' *British Journal of Sociology of Education* Vol. 19, No. 4, pp. 445 – 478.

Lynch, K. (1998) 'The Status of Children and Young People: Educational & Related Issues' in Healy, S. and Reynolds, B. (eds.) *Social Policy in Ireland: Principles, Practices and Problems.* Dublin: Oak Tree Press.

Marks, A. (2000) 'Lifelong Learning and the "Breadwinner Ideology": Addressing the Problems of Lack of Participation by Adult, Working Class Males in Higher Education on Merseyside', *Educational Studies*, Vol. 26, No. 3, pp. 303 – 319.

McGuire, D. and Collins, M. (2001) 'Tackling Social Exclusion at Third Level: An Analysis of the Participants and Future Direction of the Access Programme Initiative', Paper Presented to the 26th Annual Conference of the Education Studies Association of Ireland, Limerick.

Muller, W., Shavit, Y. and Ucen, P. (1996) 'The Institutional Imbeddedness of the Stratification Process: A Comparative Study of Qualifications and Occupations in 13 Countries', Paper presented at the ESF Network on Transitions in Youth.

Rawls, J. (1971) *A Theory of Justice.* Oxford: Oxford University Press.

Shavit, Y. & Blossfeld, H.P. (1993) *Persistent Inequality: Changing Educational Attainment in 13 Countries.* Boulder: Westview Press.

Smyth, E. (1999): 'Educational Inequalities among School Leavers in Ireland', *Economic & Social Review*, Vol. 30, No. 3, pp. 267 – 285.

Tight, M. (1993) 'Access, not Access Courses: Maintaining a Broad Vision' in Edwards, R., Sieminski, S. and Zeldin, D. (eds.) *Adult Learners, Education and Training.* London: Routledge and Open University Press.

Tomlinson, S. (2000) 'Power and Privilege in Education: The Perpetual Problem of Social Class', *Irish Educational Studies*, Vol. 19, pp. 5 – 15.

Tormey, R. & Prendeville, T. (2000) *Making Sense of the Cacophony: Understanding the Different Voices on Rural Educational Disadvantage.* Limerick: Centre For Educational Disadvantage Research.

Thornhill, D. (2001) 'Challenges for the Millennium: the future shape of third level' in A. Jordan, O'Brien, A., O'Byrne, M., and O'Riordan, J. (eds.) *A Vision of Higher Education Challenges for the Millennium.* NUI Maynooth, MACE.

Whelan, C.T. and Hannan, D.F. (1998) 'Trends in Educational Inequality in the Republic of Ireland: An Analysis of the 1994 Living in Ireland Survey', *Working Paper No. 100*, Dublin: Economic & Social Research Institute.

CHAPTER 14

FEEDING BACK FEEDBACK – TOWARDS A CYCLICAL MODEL FOR LEARNER SUPPORT

Geraldine Brosnan, Anne O'Keeffe and James Binchy

The Learner Support Unit (LSU) at Mary Immaculate College (MIC) was established in 1997 with the aim of providing academic support for students taking a degree at MIC. The centre aims to improve the quality of learning by supporting students in the transition to third-level study. Initially, the unit focused specifically on the needs of mature students. It then emerged that many of these needs were generic to the whole student cohort. Consequently, services were mainstreamed. The unit is also examining the issue of access and is looking at ways of increasing participation rates of a range of socio-economic groups currently under-represented in tertiary education. The work of the LSU divides into three specific strands: services, products and projects. Influenced by development studies and concepts of Participatory Learning and Action (PLA) as outlined by Chambers (1994), participation of the target groups in the development planning process is an important aspect of the work.

This paper will examine a practical application of this methodology by exploring how the quality of student learning can be enhanced at third-level. Based on undergraduate and workshop participant feedback, this paper aims to address:

- Lectures and tutorials as learning environments from a student perspective.

- Student transition academic needs.

- Performance assessment – strategies for optimising learning through feedback.

BACKGROUND

Over the past fifty years, there has been a dramatic shift in the theoretical framework of the methodology used in development education. The modernisation theory, popular in the 1950s and 1960s, emphasised economic growth along the lines of the development of the Western world. This belief was echoed in the traditional didactic pedagogic methodology with its notion of

Western or First World educative philosophical expertise. Despite large-scale financial and personnel investment, progress was small.

The emergence of Freire's Theory of Learning in the 1970s brought a fresh philosophy and novel methodology to the constructs of development education. Freire's theory criticises didactic traditional teaching approaches, believing the inequality in the teacher-student relationship mirrors oppression found in society (Elias 1994, p. 115). Freire summarises this approach by calling it the "banking concept of education wherein teachers make deposits of information into the passive minds of students" (Elias 1994, p. 132).

Freire's approach explores a new dialogical methodology, arguing there is "middle ground between what he sees as total free discovery by individuals and direct impartation of knowledge to individuals", which he considers "domesticating and manipulative" (Elias 1994, p. 133). He believes free dialogue allows learners and educators to participate as equals. This hypothetical construct brings an increased understanding to the active process of learning. Freire's methodology has considerable relevance for all involved in the education process.

Development studies have, in the last five years, focused increasingly on this idea of dialogue. This methodological participation of target groups in the education planning process is now viewed as crucial to the development education model. It stems from the belief that "'much of the best learning is through self-critical commitment to action, to engagement with the world, to learn by doing" (Chambers 1997, p. 100). This approach, which has been induced from effective practice, has become fashionable and is now practised across many disciplines. Within development education theory, it is termed Participation Approaches to Learning or Action (PLA). Mascarenhas *et al.* (1991, cited in Chambers 1997, p. 104) outlines its three foundations:

> The behaviour and attitudes of those, who facilitate, not dominate. The methods which shift balance from closed to open, from individual to group, from verbal to visual and from measuring to comparing. Partnership and sharing of information between insiders and outsiders and between organisations.

Chambers (1997, p. 102) explains how these foundations translate into the application of this model by defining PLA as "a growing family of approaches and methods to enable local people to share, enhance and analyse their knowledge and to act, plan, monitor and evaluate".

METHODOLOGY

Data Collection

Since the aims of the study are to explore (a) lectures and tutorials as learning environments from a student perspective and (b) student transition academic support needs and strategies for optimising learning through feedback, data was collected by administering a questionnaire to two hundred and twenty-five informants randomly selected from a cohort of undergraduate students. Female and male respondents, all aged between seventeen and twenty-three, completed the questionnaire. These data were then analysed and collated under a number of re-occurring themes (see below).

Two facilitated workshops were organised. Participants were self-selected and were either third-level lecturers and/or development workers. These were practical and followed a task-based format. To address our aims, participants reflected in a 'pyramid' fashion, that is, first individually, then in pair groupings, and eventually in plenary. In line with the PLA model, facilitation techniques were used to maximise participants' input and generate discussion.

Survey Results on Lectures

Two hundred and twenty-five undergraduates were asked: *what advice would you give your lecturers about how lectures could be improved?* The broad themes which emerged were: Management, Notes, Delivery and Structure. For each one we provide a more detailed breakdown below.

Management

Almost thirty-nine per cent of the responses under this heading referred to the pace of delivery of lectures. Students felt the pace was too fast. An example of one comment: '*speak clearer, don't rush, give time for students to listen + understand + also to take notes down*'. Related to this, almost twenty-two per cent mentioned that the density of lecture content should be reduced. As one informant puts it: '*don't cover an insane amount in one lecture*'. Other, more minor, concerns were that the lectures begin and end on time and that pre-exam study week should not be used to recoup lost classes or uncovered course topics etc.

Notes

This issue was raised by about thirty percent of respondents. Of these, fifty per cent of respondents advocated the provision of notes to supplement the lecture: as one student states, '*put notes on handout - we can't write and listen at the same time!*'. The remaining fifty percent suggested that all lecturers should make their lectures available on the Local Area Network: '*all lectures should be put on the LAN so that we can listen in class*'.

Delivery

Here one clear theme prevails – that lectures should be supplemented by ample visual aids. Some students suggest using PowerPoint or overheads. A typical response: *'try to use visual aids/overhead/PowerPoint as often as possible - it helps to hold our attention'*. Other students advise lecturers to use these visual aids appropriately. For example: *'do not run too quickly through the PowerPoint, give us time to take them down and listen to what you are saying'*, and, *'use better slides and get colour photographs'*. However, some students would like to see less PowerPoint, or more accurately less cost for printing: *'don't use PowerPoint because it costs me a fortune, downloading them and printing them off'*.

Structure

In this area, around eight per cent of the total cohort recommended that lectures be structured in a more interactive manner. As one informant puts it in concise terms: *'interaction with students needs to improve. More questions directed at us'*. Furthermore, some students point to the structure of the information presented, *'please summarise lecture at the end'*.

Survey Results on Tutorials

The broad themes for informant responses to the question: *'what advice would you give your lecturers as to how tutorials could be improved?'* were, Function, Structure and Workload. These are explained in greater detail below.

Function

All of the responses under this thematic heading (fifty-three per cent of all responses relating to tutorials) refer to the function of tutorials, suggesting that they should relate directly to themes covered in the plenary lectures. An example of a comment in this regard: *'should be more relevant to lectures, help us understand + discuss lectures, not be a totally different topic'*.

Structure

Almost forty-five per cent of responses on the question of tutorials relate to issues of structure. The tutorial sessions *'should be smaller, more personal'*: they should involve more interaction, *'allow students to input more'*, and they should evince more communication between course lecturers and course tutors. One informant deduces that: *'sometimes I get the impression that the tutors and lecturers do not discuss the layout of the material and therefore they don't link up properly'*.

Workload

Nine per cent of responses on this topic advocate that the pre-tutorial workload for the student should be reduced (it is normal in many disciplines that students are required to read, for example, a journal article in advance of a tutorial). The workload includes prior reading but some felt that *'extra readings for tutorials should be shortened'*, and in relation to tutorial assignments, *'too much week-to-week assignments given'* (sic).

Survey Results on Assignments

The broad distribution of responses to the question: *'what advice would you give your lecturers as to how assignments could be improved?'* are clustered under the four headings Management, Communication, Function and Resources.

Management

Eighty per cent of all comments in this area relate to issues of how the assignments are managed. Almost forty-four per cent of these refer to the timing of the assignments whereby students are required to submit up to five essays or assignments around the same week of the semester: *'consult with other lecturers regarding hand-in date'*. Seventeen per cent of these comments refer to the need for clear guidelines for each assignment: *'give more specific directions as to what is required'*. Nine per cent of all comments under this thematic heading say that there should be fewer assignments while nine per cent of comments say that modules should be either exam- or assignment-based as opposed to being a combination of both. Less than five per cent in this area say that there should be more assignments and the same proportion also say that workload involved in the assignment should be reflected more in the marks allotted within the module. Below four per cent said that there should be less group work, but interestingly, all of these responses came from one class cohort, which suggests an issue more at the level of 'class culture or dynamic'.

Communication

Here respondents raised two clear issues: 1) that there should be a feedback mechanism, for example, *'tell you where you went wrong'* and 2) that models or samples should be made available, *'give us some samples'*.

Workshop Results

As described in the methodology section above, workshops were designed so as to bring the student comments back to faculty. This cyclical process aimed to provide a context for professional reflection on the part of lecturers. Each workshop was structured in the following way:

Stage one

Participants were asked individually to identify the salient issues they had with lectures, tutorials and assignments. They were then asked to share these in dyads. In relation to lectures, faculty listed the following:

- Difficulties with definition of a lecture as it was seen to relate to student group size. Some lecturers were teaching to very large groups (more than four hundred) while, for others, thirty was a typical class size.
- Smaller class size would be helpful to all
- Difficult to hold students' attention
- Lack of involvement on the part of the students
- Lack of feedback and interaction for faculty
- Layout/physical space was limiting
- Pace of lectures took no account of individual student needs and no account taken of differing learning styles
- Students were, in the main, receptive and passive
- Providing lecture notes in advance of lectures, whether on the LAN or on handouts runs the risk of students not attending

Faculty listed the following for tutorials:
- Positive learning experience
- Presence should be obligatory
- Tutorial attendance can be irregular if tutorial work is not assessed
- No account of different learning styles
- Physical layout of room can be limiting
- Success depended on the teaching skill and knowledge of tutors
- Success also depended on the relationship between the lecturer and tutor
- Lack of student preparation
- Status of tutorials not considered as important by students and/ or lecturers
- Poor understanding of role of tutorial

The following were identified for assignments:
- Essays are a very good assessment instrument

- Originality of work, specifically with Internet plagiarism, is a rising problem
- Students tend to be result-focused and compete for grades. This can lead to an over-focus on the essay as a product, as opposed to its value as a process
- Correcting is very time-consuming
- No framework for feedback
- Do we support learning process? We have a responsibility to ensure that students can understand the purpose of assignments as a learning tool

Stage two

Participants were asked to imagine what students would say if asked the same set of questions:

In relation to lectures, faculty predicted that students would have the following issues:

- More handouts
- Pace too fast
- Relevance of material
- Course notes should be provided on LAN
- Variation in presentation
- Clarity of content
- Level of interest

With regard to tutorials, staff speculated that students might have the following suggestions:

- More focus on generating discussion
- Raise teaching standards
- Content better co-ordinated between lecturer and tutor
- Tutors more available and approachable

Lecturers predicted the following for assignments:

- Lack of feedback
- Clear guidelines
- Competition for library and other resources
- Unclear relationship of assignments to course
- Fewer assignments required
- Co-ordination of timing

• Group assignments not liked

Stage three

Participants were presented with the jumbled-up results of student survey and asked to predict the ranking.

Stage four

Faculty were presented with a list of areas which students had described as 'issues' for them. They were asked to work in dyads or triads to propose solutions, even if these were sometimes aspirational. Various ideas were proposed and then discussed in plenary.

Discussion

Overall, this process brought to light a number of mismatches between lecturer and student responses. For example, although teaching staff feel that students may find the pace of lecturers too fast at times, they were more concerned about holding students' attention for the duration of the lecture. On the other hand, lecturers had not anticipated students' desire for more visual aids during lecture presentation. Also, lecturers identified a need to accommodate different learning styles. In many of these mismatches, there is a common thread – the need to address how the presentation of information can be provided at 1) a reasonable pace, 2) in an interesting format and 3) in such a way as to accommodate different learning styles. One of the main mismatches was between the students' concern about the clustering of assignment deadlines. Not surprisingly, this was not anticipated by the lecturers, as they are the 'givers' of one assignment rather than the 'receiver' of four or five assignments. Here, there were interesting 'local' solutions proposed at the workshops and most of all attention was raised to the hitherto largely unnoticed cause of student anxiety.

Interestingly, there were also many points of commonality between the two cohorts. This sometimes surprised the lecturers involved in the workshops. For example, many students referred to the need for a more interactive teaching structure and, most of all, there were uniform calls for a need to define the function of tutorials. Lecturers identified the need to clarify this within each course and then to communicate this to the students. Communication was another area of common reference. This included communication of the pedagogic function of tutorials, but also feedback on student performance, especially in terms of assignments. Both lecturers and students identified a need to have frameworks for feedback.

CONCLUSION

This paper reports the findings from a study using a practical application of the methodology of Participatory Learning and Action (PLA) within a university environment. The objective of the survey and workshop was to explore how the quality of undergraduate learning can be enhanced at third-level. Our analysis suggests that this methodological approach can be successful in bringing the views of students to faculty in an unthreatening fashion. Many of the issues raised in this process are for local negotiation of solutions and the main point to be abstracted is that it is both useful and necessary to set up this cyclical process. Faculty found this exercise very helpful as it offered a forum for focused reflection on their immediate work practices, it also allowed for self-evaluation and sharing of personal experience in a supportive environment. In structuring this process care was taken to design workshops so as to be solution- rather than problem-focused. Future research and development in this area could involve using some of the alternative PLA methodologies such as mapping or diagramming.

By way of a final caveat from our informants, which sums up very well the need to make feedback cyclical: *'please do not waste our time with surveys unless you plan to act on them'*.

REFERENCES

Chambers, R. (1997) *Whose Reality Counts? Putting the First Last.* London: Intermediate Technology Publications.

Elias, J.L. (1994) *Paulo Freire: Pedagogy of Liberation.* Florida: Krieger Publishing Company.

Freire, P. (1993) *Pedagogy of the Oppressed.* London: Penguin Group.

McLaren, P., and Leonard, P. (eds.) (1993) *Paulo Freire: A Critical Encounter.* London: Routledge.

CHAPTER 15

THE DISCOURSE OF DEVELOPMENT EDUCATION

Rosalind Duke

One keeps forgetting to go down to the foundations. One doesn't put the
question marks deep enough down. (Wittgenstein 1998, p.71)

I have recently completed research in which I explored the impact of the discourse
of development education on secondary school children. In this research I wanted
to test the hypothesis that development education may, through the use of a
discourse that serves to perpetuate connotations of superiority and inferiority,
reinforce negative stereotyping, and that it may, therefore, work counter to its own
aims of challenging injustice and inequality in the world, building up instead
hierarchical images of Self and Other which undermine notions of equality
(Beattie 2001).

The power of a discourse lies in its hidden assumptions, and depends on its
ability to normalise a particular way of seeing the world. This power is then
"mediated by well-intentioned people acting as agents of oppression, usually
unconsciously, by simply going about their daily lives" (Adams *et al.* 1997, p.11).
That peoples of the South are 'poor' and thus need 'our' help is seen as a natural
state of affairs; the ways in which this framework creates a hierarchy of
superiority/inferiority, and thus of oppression, is obscured by its very normality
and by the good intentions with which it is accepted and reproduced.

RACISM AND 'UNINTENTIONAL INDOCTRINATION'

In carrying such notions about Us and Them, the discourse of development and of
development education may continually reproduce the ideology of superiority
which is the basis of racism. It may not leave space for us to think about people
or countries of the South in terms of equality. A discourse can potentially enmesh
us in 'pre-packed thinking' which might contain implications of which we are not

fully aware[1], undermining our intentions to work against racism. Racism denigrates what is seen as different; it "is rooted in fear: fear of what is different, fear of the other" (Smith and Mutwarasibo 2000, p.32). Rather than being explored and celebrated, diversity and difference are seen as "something to be annihilated or suppressed" (O'Sullivan 1999, p.152). O'Sullivan quotes Lorde:

> we have all been programmed to respond to human differences between us with fear and loathing and to handle that difference in one of three ways: to ignore it, and if that is not possible, to copy it if we think it is dominant, or destroy it if we think it is subordinate. But we have no patterns for relating across our human differences as equals (O'Sullivan 1999, p.152).

Although such responses to difference have been clearly evidenced in Ireland, the existence of racism here is often denied. However, racist attitudes are well documented: Amnesty Ireland reports that "Ireland is facing a serious problem with the growth of racism and xenophobia" (Love 2001, p.3) and Collins (1995, p.8) cites research by McGreil which "found that...approximately twenty per cent of the sample subscribed to the belief in the racial inferiority of Black and Coloured people" and refers to more recent research which suggests that xenophobia is increasing. There are several points where development education needs to be aware of its potential, through its discourse, to further racist thinking, rather than to construct those patterns for relating as equals that Lorde mentions.

Blanco Abellàn of Development Education for Youth (DEFY) (1999, p.21) suggests that "racism operates and is sustained by ignoring the positive contribution of Black people to development and concentrating only on the negative aspects". Certainly, that negative aspects of the countries and people of the South predominate in people's minds is borne out by research, including my own, where interviewees showed that they held overwhelmingly negative images of Africa and of the South generally. Joseph also states that the contribution of Black civilisations to globalisation, though significant, has not always been fully appreciated (2000, p.4). The idea that civilisation is a Western prerogative is very strong; indeed it is often equated with a Western lifestyle. Development education cannot afford to be unaware of the hegemony which feeds on this discounting of the contribution of Black people; it prevents 'us' learning from 'them' and allows the perpetuation of a hierarchical picture of the world.

However, operating at a deeper level than this is what a group of American educators teaching social justice refer to as "the unconscious attitudes and behaviours of a society that presumes an unacknowledged but pervasive white cultural norm", where "racial images embedded in language and cultural practices...are promoted as neutral and inclusive" (Adams et al. 1997, p.7). It is my concern that the discourse of development education may conceal such unconscious attitudes, hiding unacknowledged power relations under the guise of compassion. If we want an education which will challenge rather than reinforce inequality and injustice, whether in North/South relations or between communities at home, then we must examine carefully how we talk about both ourselves – often perceived as generous, compassionate and understanding – and others – seen as poor, helpless, and suffering under many problems.

That we speak of Third World countries as 'undeveloped' and in need of our help implies a patronising attitude which cannot be unconnected with the "negative images of Africans as uneducated, uncivilised and generally dependent on others" which Smith and Mutwarasibo report in their study of Africans in Ireland (2000, p.32) and which my interviews brought to light. How we learn about countries 'out there' affects how we view Black people in our society: and the language we use affects how we think about them.

Development education must, at the very least, be careful not to reinforce the "belief in the inherent superiority of one race over all others and thereby the right to dominance" (Smith and Mutwarasibo 2000, p.149). The ideology of supremacy permeates a whole culture and "every member of that cultural group learns that particular racism" (Carroll 2001, p.12). Many writers point out that, rather than challenging these belief systems, development education can inadvertently reinforce them (Bourn and McCollum 1995; Development Education Support Centre [DESC] 1994; Osler 1994; McCluskey 2001). While we would all castigate such beliefs, it may be that racism and the discourse of development education have more in common than we like to think: true equality cannot emerge from a discourse which considers that others have not yet reached the level we have attained, and may never do so without our help.

Multicultural education has been promoted as a solution to this problem, allowing people to learn about and appreciate cultures other than the dominant one, combating racism by tackling its roots in ignorance and misunderstanding. However, it has been suggested that it is not enough just to inform people about other cultures: "By making them look 'exotic' one might end up by reinforcing the stereotypes that White people hold...To learn about other people's culture is 'not to learn about the racism of one's own'" (Blanco Abellàn 1999, p.22). In fact, Carroll believes that multicultural education rather "confirms established structures, looks for appreciation of culture, dampens down anger and diverts attention from power, inequality and white racism" (2001, p.67). If such education emerges from the context of an ethnocentric curriculum, the reality of power relations is doubly ignored (Osler 1994, p.39; Blackledge 1994, p.251; Blanco Abellàn 1999, p.22).

Ireland is becoming an increasingly multicultural society. While this is something new for Ireland, the connection between Ireland and the countries of the South is long-standing, first through missionary work and later through the work of NGOs; but this has not prevented the emergence of racism. The study mentioned above, 'Africans in Ireland', refers to "the unintentional indoctrination of a nation with a set of negative stereotypes and generalisations about the people of an entire continent". It then draws links between this indoctrination and the "direct negative impact of this process... now being experienced on Ireland's streets" (Smith and Mutwarasibo 2000, p.6). Whether this 'indoctrination' happened because of, or in spite of, Ireland's connections with that continent might be arguable, but even the possibility that development education, through its discourse, might inadvertently reinforce those stereotypes and produce hierarchical images of Self and Other must be considered.

THE DEVELOPMENT EDUCATION DISCOURSE IN IRELAND

In order to escape this trap that discourse lays for us, it is important to locate the source of these ideas about development and civilisation, and the assumptions which have accompanied them and are embedded in our way of thinking of and talking about ourselves and others.

Ireland's contact with the countries of the South had its roots in the missionary endeavour of the nineteenth and twentieth centuries. By the mid-1960s over seven thousand Irish missionaries were working overseas. This high level of missionary activity had its effect in creating links of a very personal nature with those seen to be suffering or in need overseas. Dillon comments (1996, p. 53):

> Thus through direct contact with missionaries as relatives, neighbours and friends, and through missionary magazines which have had a very wide circulation in Ireland in this century, a series of attitudes were constructed and moulded within Irish society.

These attitudes are often summed up as the 'black baby syndrome' and were promulgated by visiting missionaries as well as in magazines whose "stories were often patronising and frequently Eurocentric (and even racist)" (Regan 1997, p. 5). Behind the view of people of the South as in need of charity was the missionary challenge to save the poor benighted heathen: "for the missions to justify themselves the heathen had to be perceived and labelled as degraded creatures sunk deep in darkness who needed to be brought to the light" (Pieterse, quoted by Dillon 1996, p. 53).

We may like to think that we have moved on from attitudes like those, but they lurk beneath the surface, powerful because unacknowledged and therefore neither attended to nor dealt with. My research suggests that the idea that the West has a mission to bring civilisation and salvation to the South is still prevalent. The obligation implicit in this discourse to work for the conversion of the benighted native has been carried through into the discourse of development education. The conversion nowadays might involve good roads and a 'proper' economic understanding of the innate value of efficiency rather than any Christian teaching, but the effect is the same: hierarchical views of civilised/primitive, developed/undeveloped, allowing the attitudes formed by the early missionary teaching to continue to thrive.

DEVELOPMENT AGENCIES AND DEVELOPMENT EDUCATION

The interest in Ireland in the work of the overseas missions meant that Irish people have had a reasonably high level of knowledge about some of the conditions in countries of the South, which has been accompanied by real compassion for the suffering of the poor. Many Irish development agencies have attempted to contribute to the move towards greater public awareness of the complex nature of the problems experienced by countries of the South. Regan, however, referring to the agencies' tactic of sending a 'visiting speaker', especially to schools, considers that "at its crudest, what often passes for 'development education' amounts to nothing more than profile and publicity for individual agencies and their projects" (1997, p. 23). Sinclair similarly is concerned that "such sessions may be a form of indoctrination and/or may make extensive use of negative stereotypes of people from the South" (1994, p. 55).

Trócaire claims that its Lenten Campaign "combines education, fund-raising and information" (1992, p. 13); but this may be a difficult balancing act producing muddled messages about development. Fund-raising depends on arousing compassion which produces images of Self as generous protector and Other as needy and incompetent – far from the equality and justice perspective espoused by development education. Godwin (1997, p. 15) also asserts that, though the "covert (if not overt) aim to awaken compassion in the learner for the problems and plight of people in developing countries and thus, one assumes, lay the foundation for more successful fund-raising activities", has given way to more exploration of issues, development education from non-governmental organisations (NGOs) "still tended to emphasise North/South differences and thus reinforce 'Us vs. Them' attitudes". Where the teaching of social justice intersects with fund-raising, the discourse becomes problematic. Development education has now begun to be mainstreamed into primary and post-primary education but the discourse, which has come to us through the missions and colonialism, has not been sufficiently challenged.

DEVELOPMENT EDUCATION AND DEVELOPMENT THEORY

Another aspect of the problem is that in development education, development is often a given in which the grand designs of the development project of the 'fifties and 'sixties still lie hidden. While we might wish to use the word positively, assuming development to be a good, post-development writers like Esteva consider development to be a 'minefield' which has exploded leaving a trail of suffering, dismembering and destruction (1991, p. 7). Such writers question the very notion of development and force us to consider the hegemony whereby a Western concept is used to judge and categorise people who live by very different standards. Development, they say, is eurocentric and as such can only lead to the further subjugation of the non-West. Indeed, according to Escobar, "the 'Third World' has been produced by the discourses and practices of development" (1995, p. 4). Studies by DEFY and UNICEF show that young people's perceptions of the South are predominantly negative; and that although there is "a sense of injustice about the divisions between the rich and the poor", support for peoples of the South "is all too often seen in terms of 'helping the poor, disadvantaged and helpless'" (Escobar 1995, p.11, 10). Post-development writers would maintain that such patronising and racist attitudes are a direct corollary of the development discourse.

Such writers open up the narrow concept of development to thinking which serves to challenge the stereotypes which too superficial an understanding of development can easily reinforce. If development educators fail to be aware of this thinking, they become subject to the paralysing effect of "the hegemony of a universalist language" of development (Rahnema 1997, p. 400). Development educators need to be aware that there are "other ways of knowing, being and doing" (Sardar 1999, p. 60) so that they can avoid devaluing those peoples whose ways differ from our own. This entails not just 'multicultural' education, but a questioning of our own understanding of development issues with a consequent opening to other systems of thought.

The pupils that I interviewed were puzzled and unhappy at their inability to separate their notions of what 'developed' or 'civilised' meant from overtones of superiority; but the eurocentric concepts of development and civilisation were strongly embedded in their minds. Escobar (1984-5, p. 393) insists that "the discourse of development must be dismantled if Third World countries hope...to overcome poverty, unemployment and inequality". Instead we need "a language that enables us to conceptualise 'developing' social systems in a new manner" (1984-5, p. 393-4). In some of the interviews pupils were attempting to fight the implications of language which suggested that those in the process of 'developing' were 'behind' and so in some way lesser or inferior. Development education had not given them a way to re-conceptualise the development of the world and so become aware of their own assumptions; rather it had tended to reinforce those assumptions.

LANGUAGE AND THOUGHT

The unacknowledged assumptions, which any body of discourse can carry, need to be analysed; and the ways in which our thinking is inadvertently directed by those assumptions need to be brought to light. The relationship between language and thought has long been a matter for debate; Bacon wrote that "Men [sic] imagine that their minds have command of language: but it often happens that language bears rule over their minds". More recently, in the last century, Benjamin Lee Whorf argued that language is "the shaper of ideas, the program and guide for the individual's mental activity" (both quoted in Ullmann 1967, p. 251).

Whether or not we are imprisoned by language quite so totally as Whorf claimed, it is clear that language cannot be considered simply as a system of signs by which we refer to the world, "a transparent medium" (Mills 1995, p. 27). Rather it is an entity with a power of its own to shape our thoughts and impose order on experience. Waldron describes how children learn to fit their experience of the world into the "ready-made index to conceptual categories" (1967, p. 82) which language provides: language learning involves "a gradual adjustment of our own criteria for the use of words in reference so that they agree with those of our fellows" (1967, p. 85). Whitney, another American linguist, saw "the acquisition of language [as] the adoption of certain classifications", which, he thought, gives it value as "a means of training" (in Waldron 1967, p. 77). Conforming to the distinctions and classifications of others is an integral part of learning to use language and of becoming part of a cultural community; and in learning a particular way of seeing the world children absorb the values of that language community.

Language is, then, a social and socialising process, and "language-use which poses itself as natural" is in fact hiding "a system of concepts and images which are a way of seeing and grasping things, and of interpreting what is seen or heard or read" (Trew in Mills 1995, p. 11-12). Language cannot, then, be value-free; ways of thinking are embedded in it and through its use speakers reinforce those ways of thinking. To use a very simple example, to speak of the discovery of America by Christopher Columbus reinforces a eurocentric view of history which denies a history to the population which already lived there. At least one current Irish school Geography textbook does this.

This has profound implications for the way in which we engage in development education. The language we use contains assumptions about the people and situations we talk about. Escobar maintains that it has been through the control of discourse that "the Western developed countries have been able to manage and control and, in many ways, even create the Third World politically, economically, sociologically and culturally" (1984-5, p. 384). This discourse is carried into development education with all its assumptions of knowledge about 'Third World' countries. But this knowledge has been formulated by a Western mindset through which "certain conditions of life [have been] baptised as 'underdevelopment'" (1984-5, p. 389) and normalised into a "regime of truth"(1984-5, p. 387) which then constrains our thinking.

Indeed, many of the children and teachers I interviewed in the course of my research were unable to conceive of the people and countries of the South in any but eurocentric terms, in which poverty dominated their lives and only Western intervention could help them. Senior pupils, when shown photographs of scenes in Tanzania, assumed poverty and helplessness whether the photo justified it or not. So, a surgery where a woman was receiving an injection was assumed to have been the recipient of Western aid; other pupils assumed that the surgery was dirty and that the woman was 'diseased' – in fact she was receiving a routine injection as part of her ante-natal care. The word 'proper' was used negatively in reference to roads, buildings, clothing, while people dressed in Western clothes were described as 'normal'. Buildings constructed in a traditional way were considered 'shabby' or 'dirty', and no glass meant poverty - there was no recognition of differing climatic needs or architectural practice - and the 'boma' (homestead) of a Masai chief was described as 'a depressing and deprived place'.

When asked what images Africa held for them, the majority of the pupils answered negatively, in terms of poverty, famine, war and desert. There was no appreciation that there are millions who are not starving or that there might be people who know how to live in hot, dry regions. When shown photos of happy, smiling people, the first response was often surprise, followed by the idea that their smiles were 'just put on for the camera', or that the fact of there being a camera meant that Western help was close at hand and the people were happy and relieved as a result. Although the pupils were hugely interested in the lives of the people whose photos they saw, they tended also to feel sorry for them, even for those who looked happy.

These assumptions were not limited to the pupils. Teachers very often spoke of development education work in terms of mission, charity and duty. For some, it was about teaching pupils to understand why they should contribute to or take part in charity collections. I do not by any means wish to denigrate these teachers – those I interviewed were all well intentioned, all engaging with issues. But the hidden assumptions of the discourse can trap all of us – one teacher spoke of the richness of the cultures of the South and of how we failed to take cognisance of that, but still felt that 'the ideal thing would be if we could send out, get people there up to the level...where they could do better'.

Pupils were also caught in a language trap. They were aware that the terminology of 'developed' and 'undeveloped' was hierarchical and were very unhappy with the sense of inequality which it implied, but they were unable to escape from the notion of 'development' as natural or of the need to bring underdeveloped countries up to the standard of developed countries. This quandary became very clear when one group debated the meaning of the term 'civilised'. While it was recognised that '[countries of the South] have their own culture' some pupils felt that they also needed 'civilising', but how to define that concept without 'looking down on them' was a puzzle they could not resolve. They thought 'civilised' might mean having 'roads, infrastructure', but they were not satisfied with that answer; they rejected the hierarchy which was implicit in 'civilised/uncivilised' and yet could not totally escape the idea that the West is somehow better.

THE WAY FORWARD

The key to breaking the hegemony of this discourse is to realise, with Foucault, that while "discourse transmits and produces power...it also undermines and exposes it, renders it fragile and makes it possible to thwart it" (in Kelly 1999, p. 45). Freire's notion of 'conscientisation' built on this perception that once one becomes aware of the dominating discourse, one can begin to deconstruct it, thus "mak[ing] visible and vocal the underlying assumptions that produce and reproduce structures of domination" (Adams et al. 1997, p. 11). This critical consciousness is central to the stated aims of development education: the UN definition speaks of 'critical awareness', and the Development Education Commission talks of "pupils who can explore, analyse and evaluate, who are skilled and practised in moral and critical appraisal" (1998, p. 71). Part of the job of development education is to help people to develop this critical faculty, to become aware of the nature of, and assumptions embedded in, the discourse we use to talk about the countries and peoples of the South, and about ourselves in relation to them.

In Ireland we have a situation where, despite long contact with the South, racism is growing. This presents some challenges to development education. First, the most important thing for students at any level to learn is to critique, to analyse, to look for hidden assumptions in all their reading and discussion of social justice. The power of a discourse weakens once it is recognised and the underlying structures of domination are exposed. Secondly, students need to be encouraged to be aware that there are many ways of knowing and being and that the dominant world-view of the West is not the only one, and may not be the best. Thirdly, if development education is to be further mainstreamed, it should be approached with some degree of academic rigour whereby not only the education component, but also the development aspect is addressed, so that teachers of development education have themselves a sufficient grounding in development thinking to allow for critical analysis of the assumptions embedded in the language we use.

Lastly, the students who arrive in third-level education come through first and second level, bringing many learned responses with them; and many return there to teach. So there is a responsibility at third-level, especially in the training of teachers, to ensure that stereotypical thinking is not reinforced. While I was doing my research I was repeatedly told by teachers that they did not feel they were well enough prepared to teach the development education component of their subject. Not only did they not have the knowledge they felt they needed, they also were unfamiliar with the development education methodologies.

Those who teach at any level have a responsibility for which they must be prepared. Teachers cannot tackle the preconceptions which students bring to class unless they have themselves analysed and become aware of the power of the discourse they use. Without such preparation the teaching of social justice may build up those very attitudes which it would wish to dismantle.

NOTES

[1] One definition of 'discourse' sees it as 'a ready-made way of thinking that can rule out alternative ways of thinking and hence preserve a particular distribution of power' (Penguin Dictionary of Sociology).

REFERENCES

Adams, M., Bell, L.A. and Griffin, P. (eds) (1997) *Teaching for Diversity and Social Justice: A Sourcebook* London and New York: Routledge.

Beattie, R. (2001) *Education for Equality? An Analysis of the Impact of the Discourse of Development Education on Irish Secondary School Pupils* Unpublished thesis for M.A. in Development Studies, Dublin: Development Studies Centre, Kimmage Manor.

Blackledge, A. (1994) 'Education for Equality: Countering Racism in the Primary Curriculum' in Osler, A. (ed.) *Development Education: Global Perspectives in the Curriculum* London: Council of Europe and Cassell.

Blanco Abellàn, B. (1999) *Development Education and Anti-Racist Education: a Case Study* Unpublished thesis for M.A. in Development Studies: Development Studies Centre, Kimmage Manor.

Bourn, D. and McCollum, A. (1995) *A World of Difference: Making Global Connections in Youth Work* London: Development Education Association.

Carroll, M. (2001) *Psychology, Racism and Development: Towards Developing Anti-Racism Curricula in Psychology for Development Worker Training* Dublin: Unpublished M.Litt. Thesis: University College

Dublin.

Collins, A. (1995) *all different all equal: Racism and Intolerance in Ireland* Ireland: National Youth Council of Ireland and Council of Europe.

DESC (1994) *Guidelines for Good Practice in Development Education* Dublin: DESC.

Development Education Commission (1998) *Development Education and Human Rights Education in Scotland, Wales, England and Ireland (North and South): A Consultative Document on Core Issues* Birmingham: DEC and Ireland: 80:20 Education for a Better World.

Dillon, E. (1996) *Doing Development: A Discourse Analysis of Irish Development Work* Unpublished M.A. Thesis, University College Cork.

Escobar, A. (1984-5) 'Discourse and Power in Development: Michel Foucault and the Relevance of his Work to the Third World' in *Alternatives,* X Winter 1984-5.

Escobar, A. (1995) *Encountering Development: The Making and Unmaking of the Third World* New Jersey: Princeton University Press.

Esteva, G. (1991) 'Development' in Sachs, (ed) *The Development Dictionary* London and New York: Zed Books Ltd.

Godwin, N. (1997) '"Education for Development": a framework for learning global citizenship' in *The Development Education Journal* Vol. 4 No. 1.

Joseph, J. (2000) 'Why a black perspective on development education?' in T*he Development Education Journal* Vol. 6 No. 3.

Kelly, A.V. (1999) *The Curriculum: Theory and Practice (Fourth Edition)* London: Paul Chapman Publishing Ltd.

Love, S. (2001) 'Director's Desk' in *Amnesty Ireland* Issue 114 September.

McCluskey, A. (2001) 'Anti Racism in Education' in *Focus: Ireland and the Wider World* Issue 64.

Mills, S. (1995) *Feminist Stylistics* London and New York: Routledge.

Osler, A. (1994) (ed.) *Development Education: Global Perspectives in the Curriculum* London: Council of Europe and Cassell.

O'Sullivan, E. (1999) *Transformative Learning: Educational Vision for the Twenty-First Century* London and New York: Zed Books.

Rahnema, M. (1997) 'Towards Post-Development: Searching for Signposts, a New Language and New Paradigms' in Rahnema, M. and Bawtree, V. (eds.) *The Post-Development Reader* London and New Jersey: Zed Books.

Regan, C. (1997) *On Development Education in Ireland Today; Issues in Development Education Series 1* Network of Curriculum Units in Development Education.

Sardar, Z. (1999) 'Development and the Locations of Eurocentrism' in Munck, R. and O'Hearn, D. (eds.) *Critical Development Theory: Contributions to a New Paradigm* London and NewYork: Zed Books.

Sinclair, S. (1994) 'Introducing Development Education to Schools: The Role of Non-Governmental Organisations in the UK' in Osler, A. (1994) *Development Education: Global Perspectives in the Curriculum* London: Council of Europe and Cassell.

Smith, S. and Mutwarasibo, F. (2000) *Africans in Ireland: Developing Communities* Dublin: African Cultural Project.

Trócaire (1992) *Trócaire and Development Education: A Policy Statement* Dublin.

Ullmann, S. (1967) *Semantics: An Introduction to the Science of Meaning* Oxford: Basil Blackwell.

Waldron, R.A. (1967) *Sense and Sense Development* London: Andre Deutsch.

Wittgenstein, L. (1998) *Culture and Value* Oxford: Blackwell Publishers.

CHAPTER 16

DEVELOPMENT EDUCATION AND CRITICAL THINKING

Roland Tormey

WHAT DOES CRITICAL THINKING MEAN?

This chapter explores two different meanings of the term 'critical thinking'. It will be useful to begin with the following exercise. Answer question one before looking at question two or three.

Quotation A:

...in many cases the policies promoted in the name of globalisation have not addressed human development problems...The end result is a process of globalisation that is redistributing wealth and opportunity in the wrong direction, from the poor to the rich. This is morally indefensible, economically inefficient, and socially unsustainable.

Quotation B:

Globalisation generally reduces poverty because more integrated economies tend to grow faster and this growth is usually more widely diffused. As low-income countries break into the global market for manufactures and services, poor people can move from the vulnerability of grinding rural poverty to better jobs, often in towns and cities.

1. These two quotations present very different views of the relationship between globalisation and poverty. Which of them do you think a critical thinking person would accept as true? Why?

2. The first quotation comes from Oxfam. The second comes from the World Bank. In light of this new information, which of them do you think a critical thinking person would accept as true? Did the extra information change your mind or make you more secure in your opinion? If so, why?

3. Think back over your answers to the previous questions. What do they tell you about your own view of what constitutes critical thinking?

What does 'critical thinking' mean? When we engage in development education, is it to discover the 'truth' about development and underdevelopment? How should development education thinking and learning relate to taking action? How do the answers to these questions affect the ways in which we teach/learn when we engage in development education? These are some of the issues that this paper seeks to address.

Critical thinking and acting are two elements that are commonly cited as components of development education. In this chapter, I explore the way in which these two components of development education fit together, through an exploration of how the Brazilian writer Paulo Freire – one of the key influences on the development of development education (Osler, 1994; Regan and Robinson, 1996) – grappled with these issues from the 1960s to the 1990s. I would suggest that, although they arrive at similar destinations, the French writer Michel Foucault offers a more coherent account of how to make sense of the problems which lie at the core of development education than Freire's own work does.

For many writers, critical education, such as development education, is seen to be necessary because many people are unaware of the 'truth' in relation to aspects of their lives, including development and underdevelopment. Through a critical education process, it is believed that learners will develop a critical consciousness – an awareness of the truth – that will, in turn, spur them to act for development. Development education is, in this understanding, a process of uncovering the truth for previously misled or partially informed people, and spurring them to act on the basis of that truth. It is believed that when development education's learners find out the truth about the evils of the current terms of trade, the World Bank, globalisation or GMOs, they will act against these forces of underdevelopment and, in doing so, act for development.

Some writers (commonly called postmodern writers) would suggest a need to re-evaluate the relationship between 'critical thinking', 'truth' and 'action'. The French philosopher/historian Michel Foucault argued that critical thinking is never about discovering 'truth'. It is, instead, about exploring the different ways in which people claim to have identified the 'truth'. For him, critical thinking means looking at the different claims that exist, exploring the basis on which each claim is made, and ensuring that a variety of different claims are heard. Our job is not to teach the truth but to engage in a process of unpacking the bases for a range of different truth claims and to ensure that a range of truth claims is heard. Yet, modernist writers contend, in a world without truth, what basis can there be for action? If we cannot say definitively that the problem is a specific way of dealing with trade, debt, globalisation or GMOs, what basis do we have for acting to change these things? If we can never know for sure, why not just sit at home or go shopping? Without a 'truth' basis for acting for development, is there any such thing as development education?

CRITICAL THINKING AND ACTING IN DEVELOPMENT EDUCATION

There is no shortage of formal definitions and discussions as to what development education is about: examples include the definition offered by the Joint United Nations Information Committee (1975 quoted in Sterling, *et al.* 1995, p. 32), as well as ones used by the National Committee for Development Education (1996, p. 11) and the Development Education Commission (1999, p. 13). Despite their different emphases, these definitions share a number of characteristics. All identify an 'action' component to development education (they use phrases such as "participate in the development of their community"; "effective and long-term responses"; "'writing' the world and the dynamics of change") and most contain the term "critical", either as part of the term "critical thinking" or in "critical consciousness/critical awareness". While it is possible to find definitions of development education (such as the National Committee for Development Education's definition) that do not explicitly use the word "critical", nonetheless, references to "analysis" and "reflection" act as synonyms.

Osler (1994, p. 2) identifies that the linking of the development of ideas to an action orientation in development education definitions betrays something of the roots of development education thinking in the work of educators of the Third World such as Paulo Freire. Freire argued that radical education was about producing a critical consciousness, through a process of engaged, problem-based, democratic education. Such an approach to education would enable people to move beyond accepting what they are told is true and to see the real truth. It would enable people to see through the myths, veils and lies of ideology to the truth of their situation in the world. This, in turn, would give people a basis for acting to change their world. For Freire, these three things fitted together: *critical thinking* gives rise to seeing the *truth*, which encourages people to *act*. In *Pedagogy of the Oppressed*, for example, he cites a former factory worker who says, "When I began this course I was *naïve*, and when I found out how naïve I was, I started to get *critical*" (emphasis in original, 1970, p. 15). An almost identical phrase appears almost thirty years later in *Pedagogy of Hope* (1999, p. 45).

This conceptualisation of the term 'critical' has a long history in Marxist and neo-Marxist scholarship. When faced with the question as to why the poor were not rising up and overthrowing their oppressors, Marx identified that they were the victims of ideology; that their exploitation had been veiled by illusions cast by those in power (for Marx this meant those who owned and controlled companies and their allies in governments and in the churches) (1967, p. 82). Overcoming ideology meant engaging in a "relentless *criticism* of all existing conditions" (emphasis added, Marx, quoted in Carr and Kemmis 1986, p. 138) that would enable people to overcome the veil of ideology and see clearly the reality of their situation. This meaning of the term 'critical' is central to a European philosophical tradition called *critical theory*, and is found in the work of writers like Jurgen

Habermas:

> Critical theory is not 'critical' in the sense of voicing disapproval of contemporary social arrangements, but in the sense that it attempts to distil the historical processes which have caused subjective meanings to become systematically distorted...[It] is particularly focused on the ways of thinking which support such subjugation...[such as] in the dominance of a way of thinking which makes such oppression seem unproblematic, inevitable, incidental or even justified (Carr and Kemmis 1986, p. 138)

In this respect, Freire seems broadly in agreement with Marx and with critical theorists like Habermas, both of whom would be described as being 'modernist' thinkers. For him, arriving at a critical consciousness means seeing things that one has not previously seen, "learning to perceive social, political, and economic contradictions, and to take action against the oppressive elements of reality" (1970, p. 15). For Freire and his followers, critical education such as development education, is part of a process of anti-ideological action in which anti-oppressive forces sought to challenge the justifications for oppression and the learned-lethargy that allows oppression to continue. Although his broad conceptualisation later seemed to change, Freire continued to defend this basic position right up to the 1990s. In *Pedagogy of Hope*, for example, he continues to identify that the function of critical education is to uncover the 'truth', and indeed, uses the same image that Marx uses in *The Communist Manifesto* – that of ideology as a veil which hides the truth: he writes, "...the educational practice of a progressive option will never be anything but an adventure in unveiling. It will always be an experiment in bringing out the truth" (1999, p. 7).

CRITIQUING 'CRITICAL THEORY': TAKING A POSTMODERN TURN

Although Freire's imagery, language and conceptualisation of ideology locate him alongside modernist thinkers like Marx or Habermas, Freire actually described himself as a postmodern thinker: "Let us be postmodern: radical and utopian", he writes (1999, p. 10). The term 'postmodern' is perhaps a difficult one to make sense of. While some tend to see all postmodernists as sharing a basic idea, this is really not an accurate description. Postmodern writers like Dreyfus and Rabinow (1986), for example, work very hard to distance themselves from other postmodern writers (such as Derrida) whom they call 'anti-thinkers'. Kumar argues that it is only the rejection of the key concerns of modernity – a belief in the inevitability of progress, a belief in science and a humanistic or romantic conception of the individual - that unites what is otherwise a "hopelessly diffuse and dispersed series of propositions" (1997, p. 104). It would be as wrong, therefore, to think that all postmodernists hold the same views, as it would be to think that all modernists hold the same views.

For Freire, the difficulty with modernist writers lies in their rigid conception of truth and falsity, which he sees as being arrogant (1999, p. 79) and which he describes as being sectarian (1999, p. 50). In this, he draws on the postmodern critique of the modernist conception of truth. In the modernist worldview, there is a truth that can be known. Consequently, someone can be right and those who disagree with this person are wrong. Marxists, critical theorists and development educators who believe they know the truth about oppression, trade, debt, or GMOs imply that the those who do not share their views actually do not properly understand what is going on and are victims of ideology. They believe that by engaging people in a process of critical education, people will come to see the same truth as they. But what if, having engaged in a process of critical thinking, the learner arrives at a different conclusion about oppression, trade, debt, or GMOs to the teacher? From a modernist perspective, this outcome is not possible. For modernist critical educators, 'critical' thinking is defined in terms of the coherence between its outcomes and its processes. In this context, a failure to agree with the educator at the end of the process constitutes a failure to properly engage in the process: a failure to be critical. 'Since I am critical, and I am right, if you disagree with me it is because you are not critical', the modernist says. Despite all of the discussion of democratic educational practices, because of the modernist's faith in their own knowledge of the truth there is effectively no basis for the learner to come to a different conclusion than the teacher.

This is one of the forms of what Benton calls the paradox of emancipation (1981, p. 162) – one can be freed from the ideas of dominant groups only by accepting the ideas of other groups. While the World Bank, the IMF and various other bodies tell us they want to make our lives better, and while anti-ideological campaigners say they want to make us free, is it not also fair to suggest that what they all really want is for us to accept their view of our lives instead of our own? For postmodern writers, the decision to believe one group rather than another is based more on faith than on logic:

> Are conditions of religious conviction or liberal political participation or communist party membership guaranteed to lift scales from eyes and reveal interests as they are? Only if one happens to believe in the authenticity of the post-conversion state, be it due to the correct reading of the new testament, John Stuart Mill or Karl Marx (Clegg 1989, p. 97).

For Freire, the guardians of the one true truth, whether they are from the right or the left, share a common authoritarian attitude:

> Manipulation and authoritarianism are practiced by many educators who, as they style themselves progressives, are actually taken for such...To criticise the arrogance, the authoritarianism of intellectuals of Left or Right, who are both basically reactionary in an identical way – who judge themselves the proprietors of knowledge, the former, of revolutionary knowledge, the latter, of conservative knowledge ...– this I have always done (1999, p. 79).

At the same time, as we have seen, Freire, apparently contradictorily, continues to use the language of 'truth' to describe his own position. Freire seeks to inoculate himself against arrogance in at least two ways. First, he identifies that a mutual attitude of tolerance for other people's 'truths' must rise above the differences in positions adopted (1999, p. 13). Second, the 'truth' of the educator is of secondary importance when compared to the development of creative capacity and the investigative and judgemental skills of the learner (1999, p. 79). For Freire, the truly important content is in the skills and attitudinal focus of the learning, rather than in the knowledge base.

Freire shares his discomfort with the idea of 'one true truth' with Michel Foucault. For Foucault, each 'truth' has, hidden beneath it, a range of assumptions and ways of thinking that have given rise to it. None can ever be the indisputable truth. Consequently, he argues that the concept of ideology is not a useful one, precisely because it implies someone is right and someone is wrong (1980, p. 118). While critical theorists see truth as something that frees us from the ideological effects of power, for Foucault all claims to truth, no matter who makes them, are an articulation of power:

> The important thing here, I believe, is that truth is not outside power, or lacking in power...[Truth] isn't the reward of free spirits, the child of protracted solitude, nor the privilege of those who have succeeded in liberating themselves. Truth is a thing of this world. (1980, p. 131).

The tying of power and truth together like this should be read in two ways. The right to name something as true, and the mechanisms through which something is deemed to be true, and the context within which that happens, are the subject of dispute and negotiation in which each participant tries to use whatever power they can to influence the outcome. Put differently, to identify who has power, look for people or groups who are believed to know the truth and the context in which they are believed. Those people or groups are using power in the context within which they are believed. If the IMF is believed to know the truth at inter-governmental conferences, then they are articulating power in that context. Those who are believed to have a good analysis within the Socialist Workers Party or the Latin America Solidarity Group are using power in those contexts. Those who are believed in broader public discourse are using power in that context. Of course, in the next argument or discussion, someone else may come to be believed. For this reason, Foucault is not terribly interested in who is using power at any one time. He is more interested in how they came to articulate power, that is, the rules of the game or the taken for granted assumptions about the nature of 'proof' in a given context (and the different assumptions about proof that apply in different contexts) that enables someone to articulate power.

Secondly, by naming something as 'true' it is given a power over people.

Because medical knowledge is true, doctors have the right to confine us in hospitals and sanitoria, because what the World Bank says is true, trade is liberalised and because what Oxfam says is true people donate money and buy fair trade coffee, and so on. Because of its power, truth has the capacity to be dangerous for those who live under it. Foucault looks at 'good' and 'bad' in the same way as he looks at 'true' and 'false' – as representing positions rather than universal values. When faced with an apparently self-evidently good thing like 'justice', Foucault identifies how this term has been used to imprison and punish people (Foucault 1977; Rabinow 1991, p. 6). Because all power and, therefore, all claims to truth have the capacity to affect people, all such claims need to be questioned and challenged.

For Foucault, the problem is not to distinguish between truth and falsity, but instead, to explore different ways in which truth claims (and 'good' claims) come to be accepted and to examine the effects of different claims to truth (Rabinow, 1991, p. 4). For Foucault, there is no problem with making claims to 'truth' but they must be understood as taking a position, not a lifting of the veil:

> The essential political problem...is not to criticise the ideological contents [of people's thought], but that of ascertaining the possibilities of a new politics of truth. It's not a matter of emancipating truth from every system of power (which would be chimera since truth is already power) but of detaching the power of truth from the forms of hegemony, social, economic and cultural, within which it operates at the present time (Foucault 1980, p.133).

Clearly, this means examining the basis of the claims of dominant groups like the World Bank or the IMF. However it also means examining the claims of other groups, (the 'good guys') such as Oxfam, Greenpeace or anti-globalisation activists. For Foucault, "critical rationality consists in the unflinching examination of our most cherished and comforting assumptions" (Dreyfus and Rabinow 1986, p. 110). Having used our scalpel to dissect the views that we comfortably identify as ideological, we need to turn the scalpel on ourselves: "The practitioner of interpretative analytics realises that he himself is produced by what he is studying [i.e. Power]; consequently he can never get outside it" (Dreyfus and Rabinow 1986, p. 115). For Foucault, our position is just that: a position. Like all other positions, ours must be open to examination, analysis and critique.

Although they share a common critique of modernist notions of truth, Foucault goes further than Freire. Foucault identifies a problem not only with the term 'truth' but also with the term 'good'. There is little in Freire to suggest that he would be comfortable about following his own logic to this extent. Indeed, while he identifies his 'truth' as a position, Freire continues to use the language of 'truth' rather than the language of 'positions', and shows little inclination to turn the scalpel of analysis on his own basic position over a twenty-five year period. While Foucault insists that self-reflective analysis and critique are necessary and that what is needed is an analysis of the basis on which positions are taken, Freire seems content to fight for his own position, within the context of tolerating the positions of others. In all these ways, Freire seems less consistent in his own analysis than Foucault.

Yet the similarities are also clear. Like Foucault, Freire seeks to be free from the demands of being correct. Like Foucault, he seeks to be able to listen to other people and positions more openly precisely because we recognise our own position as being just that: a position. By letting go of their own claims to eternal truth both seek to remain open to debate, discuss and explore the positions of others.

WHAT BASIS FOR ACTION IN A WORLD WITHOUT TRUTH?

The postmodern rejection of truth has not gone uncontested by modernist thinkers. Jurgen Habermas, asks of Foucault "...why fight at all?" (1994, p. 96). If we do not believe wholeheartedly in the rightness of our cause (including the factual correctness of its arguments) do we not become relativists who are willing to live with anything no matter what its effects upon people are simply because all things are justifiable from some position. Postmodernism, writes Agnes Heller:

> ...has a simple enough message: anything goes. This is not a slogan of rebellion, nor is postmodernism in fact rebellious... 'Anything goes' can be read as follows: *you* may rebel against anything you want to rebel against but let *me* rebel against the particular thing I want to rebel against. Or, alternatively speaking, let me not rebel against anything because I feel completely at ease (quoted in Bewes, 1997, p. 25-26).

Seen in this way, postmodernism is a decadent, self-indulgent nihilism that leads to an embrace of consumer culture in the cause of dressing up irony as struggle. And yet, both Freire and Foucault found time to get away from their shopping and engage in political action. Freire's work in Brazil is well known, while Foucault was one of the founders of the Information Group on Prisons, which was set up to "create conditions that permit prisoners themselves to speak" (Foucault quoted in Smart 1985, p. 17). How does one explain such political action if their position should condemn them to a cynical individualism?

Freire seems not to offer much by way of an answer to this question. He does what he does because it is his position. While he insists on the need to tolerate alternative positions, he does not adequately identify the relevance of that tolerance for his own position – he does not turn the scalpel back upon himself – and therefore can comfortably engage in or move people to action without seeing clearly the problem that would undermine the action. Foucault, by being more rigorous in his analysis, makes the problematic nature of his own activism clearer.

For Habermas, Foucault's decision to be an activist was an example of his own contradictions (1986, p. 108). Foucault sees things differently. For him, one does not need an eternal truth or good to want to play a role in changing the world.

> Foucault insists that saying there is no social existence without power relations does not entail that particular, oppressive power relations are necessary. The field of possibilities that give rise to such current injustices...also contained ...alternatives that were not acted upon. (Hoy 1986, p. 144-145)

Every social formation has the potential to be oppressive, including, incidentally, those that are not currently oppressive:

> My point is not that everything is bad but that everything is dangerous, which is not exactly the same as bad. If everything is dangerous, then we always have something to do. So my position leads not to apathy but to hyper- and pessimistic activism (Foucault 1997, p. 256).

What form was this hyper-activism to take? Foucault suggests that one form of appropriate action was to create a space in which the voice of the subject of power relations was to be heard. His aim was to support 'local criticism' of the experience of power in particular instances (Smart 1986, p. 167). Indeed, one can interpret Foucault's writings as a political act: an engaged and self-critical exploration of the uses and construction of notions of sickness/wellness, justice, and the self in society.

What this self-critical hyper- and pessimistic activism means in practice can be seen in relation to Foucault's use of the language of Human Rights. Foucault does state formally his practical support for the concept of 'human rights' in relation to his political work (1980, p. 108). However, even if we accept the concept of rights, we are expected to think about them. We need to concretely support human rights while questioning their foundations: "we need to remain sceptical at one and the same time precisely of those rights that we support (and perhaps campaign for), if only to avoid the kind of self-subjugation...which stifles critical judgement" (Knights and Vurdubakis 1994, p. 191). As such, the concept of rights, which is supported in concrete ways, must at the same time be viewed "in terms of methods of subjugation that it instigates" (Foucault, cited in Keenan, 1987, p. 24). Since the use of the conception of rights as a tool of resistance is always itself an articulation of power, Foucault remains uncomfortable with terms like 'rights' (as he is with comparable terms like 'justice'), while at the same time being willing to use them. He is willing to work against what he sees as oppressive, but not to suggest that he knows the ultimate alternative since any conception of utopia is likely to give rise to its own problems. Therefore, he does not promote an alternative utopia, nor does he want everyone to do things his way. Instead, he want to question what it is that he, and others, do:

> ...the real political task in a society such as ours is to criticise the working of institutions which appear to be both neutral and independent; to criticise them in such a manner that the political violence which has always exercised itself

obscurely through them will be unmasked, so that we can fight them (Foucault, quoted in Rabinow, 1991, p. 6).

This applies as much to 'neutral and independent' institutions that are commonly thought of as the good guys as it does to institutions that are commonly portrayed as soulless or uncaring.

CONCLUSION

Both "critical thinking" and "acting" or "transforming the world" are central to how development education defines itself. Yet the relationship between these two components is made problematic by the various understandings of what "critical thinking" means. While Freire's writings in the late 1960s and early 1970s seem to suggest that critical thinking means unveiling the lies, the half-truths and the naïveté that veils the truth and, by seeing the truth, being motivated to change the world, his later work re-interprets this position less dogmatically. He later identifies that he was always opposed to the manipulation of learners by educators who are thought of as progressive (1999, p. 79).

Although there is much of value in Freire's work, he stops short of applying his ideas consistently in relation to his own thinking. For such a consistent application of these ideas, I have turned to Foucault, who sees 'criticism' as constituting an exploration of the standards of proof and the mechanisms of truth that apply in different contexts. Such an analysis is not simply critical of the things we do not like, but must, in turn, be critical of the very ideas we hold most dear. For writers like Habermas the approach of both Freire and Foucault leads logically to an inability to act to change the world, since all competing truths are open to being accepted and there is no consequent reason for action. Yet for both, action in the world was a key part of their lives. For Foucault, saying that everything is potentially dangerous does not mean everything is bad. Consequently he argues for action that is constantly self-critical. This, I suggest, is a far more coherent basis for building tolerance and democratic debate than either the traditional modernist conception of critical education, or Freire's more limited analysis.

REFERENCES

Benton, T. (1981) '"Objective" Interests and the Sociology of Power' *Sociology* Vol.15, No. 2, pp. 161-184

Bewes, T. (1997) *Cynicism and Postmodernity*. London: Verso

Carr, W. and Kemmis, S. (1986) *Becoming Critical, Education, Knowledge and Action Research*. London: Falmer Press

Clegg, S. (1989) *Frameworks of Power*. London: Sage

Development Education Commission (1999) *Essential Learning for Everyone* Birmingham and Bray: DEC Birmingham and 80:20.

Dreyfus, H.L. and Rabinow, P. (1986) 'What is Maturity? Habermas and Foucault on 'What is Enlightenment?'' in Hoy, D.C. (ed.) *Foucault: A Critical Reader*. Oxford: Basil Blackwell

Foucault, M. (1977) *Discipline and Punish; The Birth of the Prison.* Harmondsworth: Penguin

Foucault, M. (1980) *Power/Knowledge; Selected Interviews and Other Writings 1972-1977* London: Prentice Hall

Foucault, M. (1997) *Ethics; Essential Works of Foucault 1954 – 1984.* Harmondsworth: Penguin

Freire, P. (1970) *Pedagogy of the Oppressed*. Harmondsworth: Penguin.

Freire, P. (1999) *Pedagogy of Hope: Reliving Pedagogy of the Oppressed.* New York: Continuum Books

Habermas, J. (1986) 'Taking Aim at the Heart of the Present' in Hoy, D.C. (ed.) *Foucault: A Critical Reader*. Oxford: Basil Blackwell

Habermas, J. (1994) 'Some Questions Concerning the Theory of Power: Foucault Again' in Kelly, M (ed.) *Critique and Power; Recasting the Foucault Habermas Debate*. Cambridge, Massachusetts: MIT Press

Hoy, D.C. (1986) 'Power, Repression, Progress: Foucault, Lukes and the Frankfurt School' in Hoy, D.C. (ed.) *Foucault: A Critical Reader.* Oxford: Basil Blackwell

Keenan, J. (1987) 'Power/Knowledge: Reading Foucault on Bias' *Political Theory*, Vol. 15 pp. 5-37.

Knights, D. and Vurdubakis, T. (1994) 'Foucault, Power, Resistance and All That' in Jermier, J. M., Knights, D. and Nord, W.R. (eds.) *Resistance and power in organizations*. London: Routledge

Kumar, K. (1997) 'The Post-Modern Condition' in Halsey, A.H., Lauder, H., Brown, P., and Wells, A.S. (eds.) *Education Culture Economy Society*. Oxford: Oxford University Press

Marx, K. and Engels, F. (1967) *The Communist Manifesto*. Harmondsworth: Penguin

National Committee for Development Education (1996) *1994-1996 Annual*

Report. Dublin: NCDE.

Osler, A. (1994) 'Introduction: The Challenges of Development Education' in Osler, A. (ed.) *Development Education, Global Perspectives in the Curriculum*. London: Cassell

Rabinow, P. (ed.) (1991) *The Foucault Reader; An Introduction to Foucault's Thought*. Harmondsworth: Penguin.

Regan, C. and Robinson, R. (1996) 'Putting You in the Picture' in Regan, C. (ed.) *75:25 Ireland in an Increasingly Unequal World*. Dublin: Dóchas

Smart, B. (1985) *Michel Foucault*. London: Routledge.

Sterling, S. Bobbett, P. and Norris, A. (1995) *Preparatory Study Module Notes – MSc/Pg Dip Environmental and Development Education*. London: South Bank University

CHAPTER 17

DEVELOPMENT STUDIES AND DEVELOPMENT EDUCATION: SOME QUESTIONS IN THE LIGHT OF POST-DEVELOPMENT THEORY

Eilish Dillon

This paper presents some questions for development studies and development education in the light of post-development theory.

Addressing development constructions, I outline the assumptions which underlie development studies. I argue that despite the eclecticism in development studies, it can reinforce some of the representations of mainstream development thinking.[1] I address the links between development studies and development education and ask whether the incorporation of development education concepts, principles and practice into development studies offers a useful alternative to 'mainstream development constructions', or whether the idea of teaching for and about social justice is too nebulous for the task.

I argue that the post-development critique opens the way for critical reflection on what both development education and development studies are trying to achieve. While it offers no easy solutions for either development studies or development education, post-development questions about power and knowledge in development discourses are worthy of consideration.

I'd like to begin by looking at development studies and development education and the connections between them. I will then introduce post-development theory before concluding by addressing some of the questions of post-development to development studies and development education.

DEVELOPMENT STUDIES AND DEVELOPMENT EDUCATION

What is development studies?

The origin of development studies (which I'm defining as the institutionalisation of knowledge production about development, associated with different institutional and epistemological practices) can be associated with the project of development in the post-World War 2 era (Edwards 2000). Webster points out that:

the growth of detailed research on less-developed countries, begun during the early 1960s, was prompted in part by the political events that accompanied the end of the old Western empires. Third World countries struggled for national independence and did so often under the banner of national socialism. To a large degree, the rapid expansion of work on specific Third World societies can be attributed to the West's concern over its loss of influence in the old colonial areas (Webster 1988, p. 3).

As such, specialist research and teaching institutions were established, especially in North America and Europe, to promote information gathering about so-called 'developing countries'[2]. These, in conjunction with departments of economics, anthropology, geography, politics and sociology, among others, produced research on measurements of development, intervention strategies and cultures etc., and they served as training institutions for development practitioners.

In the 1970s and 1980s, development studies became established as part of the development landscape in Ireland. It coincided with, and in the case of courses in development studies at Kimmage Manor, preceded, the establishment of a bilateral aid programme in Ireland and the expansion of NGO (non-governmental organisation) development activity. One of the first areas of support under official development aid was the funding of overseas students. Jennings (1977, p. 51) points out that: "In 1963/64 a grant was paid for the first time to the Overseas Club. This Club (and the Irish Council for Overseas Students to which a grant was later paid) catered for students from developing countries who were resident in Ireland". This was associated with training and the apparent need for expertise and 'skills' in different fields, including development. This establishment of development studies courses and institutions contributed to an increasing professionalisation of development work in Ireland. NGOs began to expect that staff not only had experience of working in development 'overseas', but increasingly that they should have a 'development qualification'. Different post-graduate diplomas and master's programmes were offered and research funding and publications were put in place by NGOs, the NCDE (National Committee for Development Education) and academic institutions.

While there were different emphases in different geographical locations around the world, it was through development studies, that much of what we call development theory was produced, with its temporal preoccupations, its orthodoxies and its differing fashions. Pieterse (2001, p.9) points out that "development thinking and policy, then, is a terrain of hegemony and counter hegemony. In this contest of interests there are many stakeholders and multiple centres of power and influence". Development studies, therefore, is not just about the production of theory, but it also relates to the institutional and strategic practices of development, as well as to the professionalisation of development. Its production of knowledge about development and consideration of development debates is not neutral. It has aimed at times to promote development policies, to reform development practice and, sometimes, to employ its transformative potential. It establishes the epistemological and institutional boundaries for consideration of development in particular ways, through legitimising and emphasising certain ways of thinking about and doing development.

There have been significant changes in the direction of development studies internationally since the 1960s in terms of different theories, practices, institutional approaches, research agendas and epistemologies of development related to development discourses. Without wishing to proffer a linear reading of development studies or development theory here, I am referring to the approaches of modernisation, dependency and world systems, neo-liberalism, alternative developments and post-development, as explored in depth by Rist (1997), Preston (1999) and Pieterse (2001). In 1989, Michael Edwards argued the 'irrelevance' of development studies. He pointed out that:

> we need consciously to adopt a position of humility with respect to our own limitations and the limitations of our kind of education and training. We must learn to appreciate the value of indigenous knowledge and the importance of popular participation in showing us what is relevant and what is not. In this way, we will begin to move from practice based on the philosophy of knowledge, to practice based on the philosophy of wisdom, to a form of enquiry in which what we do and what we are matter more than what we know (Edwards 1994, p. 134).

One of the features of development studies is its eclecticism, i.e. there is no agreed approach to it. It can reflect a neo-liberal economics approach, a political economy perspective, an emphasis on development tools, planning and project management (Wallace, 1997) or the search for alternatives and post-development critique. Despite what Munck (1999) describes as the search for paradigmatic certainty espoused by the impasse theorists in the 1980s, he argues for example, that though:

> Development studies was nearly always interdisciplinary... a deep-rooted Western tradition has always cast its dominant shadow over development studies. It counterpoises its civilised to the barbarian of the Other, its rational to the Other's irrational, the West to the non-west: It is a worldview that pervades the very notion of development, which holds that the European model is the benchmark for all other types or modes of development (1999, pp. 197 – 198).

Critics advocating alternative developments and alternatives to development or 'post-development' often level this critique at mainstream development.

Alternative conceptions of development have been articulated since the 1970s in many forms: 'people-centred development' (Rahman, 1993), 'human scale development' (Max Neef, 1991), an 'actor-oriented approach' (Long, 1992), PAR

(Fals Borda and Rahma, 1991), 'self-reliance' and 'putting the last first' (Chambers, 1983). Other approaches to development such as sustainable development, gender and development, endogenous development, participation, human needs and empowerment have all served to identify what development other than mainstream development might mean and how it might be achieved. Pieterse points out that:

> Presently the development field is bifurcating into a managerial stream – managing development as part of development bureaucracies – and an interpretative stream whose major concern is to deconstruct development, to unpack its claims and discourses, and once that is done, to deconstruct the deconstruction, for deconstruction is a never-ending task (2001, p. 163).

In the light of post-development (which is also reflected in some approaches to development studies) and which I will return to later, there are some important questions that need to be asked of development studies. When addressing these questions to development studies, we need to be aware that we are not addressing them to a homogeneous field.

Development Education

According to some definitions, development education is challenging. As outlined by the NCDE in 1999, it:

> seeks to engage people in analysis, reflection and action for local and global citizenship and solidarity...[and it]...develops the appropriate skills and attitudes which promote action for global solidarity, social justice and sustainable development for all people (NCDE 1999).

As in the case of development studies, Starkey and Osler (1996) show that development education has not remained static. In terms of content, it tends to focus on global and local social, economic and political processes. It can be about human rights, about the way the world works and about social justice. Their discussion of development education highlights the uncertainty about what development education is. This uncertainty influences understandings of how development education relates to development studies. Anecdotal evidence would suggest that many see the difference between development studies and development education as being that development studies is about development whereas development education is education for development. There may be a sense in which development studies takes a didactic approach in education methodologies whereas development education is participatory and that development studies is concerned with 'objective' information and analysis whereas development education is concerned with the political goals of transforming society. I think these simple dichotomies are not very useful because they fail to take into account the eclecticism of development studies or indeed different approaches to development education or the significant links and overlaps between development studies (or rather particular approaches to development studies) and development education.

Though elastic and apparently nebulous, development education has been influenced by a number of strands in development studies, namely dependency and world systems theories as well as alternative development approaches. There are also particular educational approaches or philosophies, which underpin development education. These are influenced in part by Freirian notions of conscientisation and praxis, experiential learning and democratic approaches to education and are in part influenced by people-centred research techniques such as participatory rural appraisal (PRA). Osler points out that:

> Development Education encourages the linking of ideas with action for change and a radical approach to the issues we all face working 'for a new international social and economic order'. Indeed, it is educators from the South, such as Freire and Nyerere, who stressing the importance of education processes, community participation and a forging of theory with practice, have inspired much of the learning methodology in development education (1994, p.2).

Building on the analysis of Osler (1994), I am arguing that some of the central assumptions in development education are that:

- There is global injustice and inequality. This is experienced in terms of a North/South divide, but also between communities and peoples in the North. The causes of injustice need to be identified, so that they can be overcome.
- Development is possible and desirable; in fact it is increasingly recognised to be a right. Here development is often defined in terms of concepts such as human development, sustainable development and empowerment.
- There are ways in which development can be achieved. These include participation of people in development and sharing different knowledges. People are the key to development and they are agents of change in challenging structures of domination and injustice.

Many of these are the assumptions of alternative development approaches in development studies, which are also concerned with social transformation, the values of justice and empowerment and communities mobilising. In promoting a complex understanding of social, economic, political and cultural factors which cause global poverty and injustice, such approaches aim to empower people to search for creative solutions to the problems facing people at local, national and global levels.

What can post-development offer this discussion that I have not considered so far? In order to illuminate some of the questions for development studies and development education in the light of post-development theory, I'd like to introduce key arguments in post-development theory before outlining what I think it has to offer.

What is post-development theory?

The term 'post-development' is now commonly used to refer to the work of theorists such as Sachs (1993), Escobar, (1984/85 and 1995), Ferguson (1990), Crush (1995) and Rahnema and Bawtree (1997). The term which may suggest a time or condition after 'development' is more often used to identify a critique of development that takes its influence from post-structuralism, postcolonialism and related critiques in postmodernism.

Post-development theory is about deconstructing our notions of development. Though there is no one post-development approach *per se*, post-development theorists are united in their scathing critique of development. Much of this criticism is directed at mainstream constructions of development, defined in terms of modernisation, neo-liberalism and project management approaches, which are regarded as hegemonic. Some, including Latouche (1993) concentrate on attacking the naiveté of those who claim to be able to reform development in the form of alternative development constructions (alternative developments and development education). Such critiques are complicated by the fact that many who are placed within the 'post-development' camp share many of the assumptions of alternative theorists, e.g. in terms of a critique of modernisation assumptions and looking to communities, indigenous knowledges and social movements for alternatives.

Some post-development theorists, especially Escobar (1984/5 and 1995), adapt Foucault's treatment of discourse for a deconstruction of development and an exploration of the knowledge/power relationships in development. He argues that he is trying to expose the Eurocentric assumptions in development discourse, to show the "disciplinary and normalising mechanisms" of development (Escobar, 1984/85, p. 377) and to show how alternative conceptions of development have been co-opted within a dominant discourse and mainstream development theories. As such, post-development critique explores the 'taken for grantedness' of development. The notion of 'underdevelopment' is contested and deconstructed, as are notions such as 'traditional', 'modern', 'evolutionary change' and 'economic growth'. This is a call to question what concepts such as 'development' and 'underdevelopment' mean, how these terms are used and the effects of their use. According to post-development theorists, development is essentially a 'western' construction, which reinforces a superiority/inferiority relationship between the 'North' and the 'South'. In development, they argue, 'we' in the 'North' are 'developed' and 'they' in the 'South' are 'underdeveloped' or 'developing'. 'If they follow our lead they will catch up, become like us and all will be well'. Even in its alternative incarnations, many of these assumptions are seen to prevail in the sense of 'modernisation plus' approach, e.g. economic growth and participation, technology and capacity building.

Post-development theory addresses power relations in development. Post-development theorists are interested in how the discourse of development is employed through knowledge practices and development institutions or what Ferguson (1990) calls the "development apparatus". Escobar tries to identify "those mechanisms through which a politics of truth is created and maintained, through which certain forms of knowledge are given the status of truth" (1995, p. 45). Here he suggests that "this is accomplished through a set of techniques, strategies, and disciplinary practices that organise the generation, validation, and diffusion of development knowledge including the academic disciplines, methods of research and teaching, criteria of expertise" (1995, p. 45). The central point here is that discourses have effects. How reality is framed and versions of the truth are constructed has an impact on relationships and structures. If development education explores the causes of underdevelopment, for example, without exploring what is meant by underdevelopment, it can reinforce the notion that there is a particular way of viewing development and that those who are represented as underdeveloped are somehow 'less' than those represented as 'developed'.

Post-development promotes the validation of different types of knowledge as alternatives to development. Post-development theorists are critical of meta-narratives that offer a 'reading of the truth' in relation to development. They suggest that a focus on development as discourse is a powerful tool of critique, sometimes focused on the concepts associated with development (Sachs, 1993), and on the texts and language of development (Crush, 1995). They argue that discourse critique opens the space for other ways of knowing and resisting hegemonic socio-cultural, economic and political forces encapsulated in development. Storey argues that "it is the methodological orientation of the post-development school – especially its seemingly 'negative' predilection for deconstruction and critical discourse analysis – that has, I believe, most to offer, rather than its problematic attempt to formulate a more 'positive' model for social change" (2000, p.45). The critique of knowledge constructions in the World Bank is a useful example here. Rather than taking statistics as quoted in development policy reports, for granted, it is useful to address how knowledge about different parts of the world is named and framed, measured, categorised by development institutions and acted upon.

In post-development theory, how peoples, problems and solutions (among other things) are represented by mainstream development is challenged. Representations of the peoples of the 'North' and 'South' are challenged as homogenising and Eurocentric. 'They' are 'the poor', 'victims', 'traditional', 'needy' whereas 'we' 'have the answers', 'are experts', 'are in control' and 'know what's best'. The privileging of western notions of scientific knowledge and technological advancement that are rooted in enlightenment thinking are problematised. Post-development advocates the interrogation of the use of development images and how the stories about development construct particular notions of the world. How these representations approximate or not to the 'real' is not usually the question for post-development thinkers. Development is seen as a hegemonic discourse, one that excludes other conceptions of reality. Concepts such as 'human needs', 'human rights', 'justice', 'participation' and 'empowerment' are explored and found wanting in terms of their application. They are regarded as being idealistic and open to 'co-option' by mainstream constructions of development, rendering what appeared to be radical, meaningless in terms of the construction of meaningful alternatives. If alternatives are required, they should be sought outside development.

Questions from post-development

One of the strengths of post-development has been its challenge to development thinking and practice in terms of the assumptions therein. At the same time, it has been criticised for homogenising development and for being strong on critique but weak on alternatives. Pieterse also points out that "it may divert attention away from relations 'on the ground'" (2001, p. 14). While development education may be strong on advocating alternatives and on addressing structures of inequality, it has been weak on interrogating the assumptions about development that it often employs. This can also be said of much of development studies. Though there are contradictions and difficulties with post-development, it has provided us with a number of useful questions for consideration for both development studies and development education.

I take from post-development the importance of deconstructing development discourses and their related practices in terms of knowledge construction, organisational structures and strategic practices. Here we might ask:
- What are the assumptions of development in development studies and development education?
- How do they represent the peoples, problems and solutions of development?
- Do these representations help to reinforce or challenge relationships and structures of inequality?

I agree with Escobar (2000) that critical inquiry does not have to set up alternatives and with Storey (2000) that one of the greatest contributions of post-development has been in the area of critique. Here we could ask:
- Does development studies provide the necessary critique of development processes that create inequality?

- Is critique of development discourse enough?
- Does development education represent a viable alternative, especially in the light of post-development challenges to the assumptions that often underline alternative constructions of development?

I argue with Tucker (1999), that development cannot be regarded as one overarching discourse that subsumes everything related to it. There are many discourses of development and many different practices associated with them (Dillon 1996). At the same time, we need to consider the construction of meta-languages of development (Mawdsley *et al.* 2001). With alternative development theories, we need to move away from a simplistic under-valuing of the role of actors in development or a reading of the dominance of mainstream development discourse that views people as passive recipients or victims. The complex interrelationship between discourses and actors needs to be explored. How discourses and practices relate to each other needs to be mapped out, as do the context-specific structures, which allow for discursive hegemony. We do not have to underestimate the importance of how language constructs reality in order to recognise the validity of social, economic, political and cultural factors in creating space for particular discourses, strategies and organisational practices of development. Here we could ask:

- How have different development institutions contributed to hegemonic ways of conceptualising and practising development?
- How can and do different development academics, educators and activists challenge hegemonic ways of viewing and organising the world?

Post-development suspicions about the co-option of 'alternatives' into mainstream development discourses are important to consider, especially in the light of the importance development education gives to concepts such as 'participatory' processes, 'empowerment' and 'action for change'. Post-development warns us that these concepts are often too nebulous or elastic to guide transformative processes and that they have often become diluted by mainstream development. If development education is to apply such concepts as the goals of development, it needs to do so in a way that articulates their limitations, contextualises them and recognises that there are no easy answers in development. Here we could ask:

- Do notions of social justice espoused by development education offer a useful way forward in the face of post-development critiques?
- Is the concept of social justice too nebulous for the task?
- Can development be re-imagined or transformed and if so, what is the role of development studies and development education in this?

CONCLUSION

Finally, I think there are a number of questions that development education and other alternative approaches to development have to ask of post-development. Can we say that though development carries modernist and often neo-colonial connotations and effects that it is always essentially bad? As Storey (2000) points out, we need to ask if alternative conceptions of development can entail relationships of non-domination. Does post-development's concentration on critique, though important, make political action difficult? This relates to the paralysis that many feel in the light of an understanding of postmodern relativism reflected in the concentration by post-development theorists on critique rather than the articulation of alternatives. Can development education take on the post-development challenge while allowing for critical challenge of global structures of inequality? As Edwards (2001) points out, we need to consider how development studies, "social science, and our institutions of learning [can nurture] active citizenship and global democracy...active participation in shaping a collective destiny, in all aspects of life – social, economic and political".

It is to this last point that I would like to finally turn. In commenting on sustainable development, Mary Robinson has pointed out that:

> One of the tasks we need to undertake is a rigorous examination of the words we use, and the way we lock realities into those words, and influence approaches to the problem through relatively poor definitions of it. Until our definitions are made in a collaborative way by those who have a day-to-day knowledge of the reality and suffering, those definitions will be wanting (in Kirby 1997, p. 11).

This points us to the importance of what Pieterse calls 'reflexive development'. "Reflexivity is enabling if it is taken as the achievement of a new level of awareness, awareness of the meanings of trying as well as of failure" (2001, p. 164). I think that post-development is an important enabler of such considerations in relation to development studies and development education. Post-development is particularly useful for exploring development assumptions, development representations and their effects. While it offers no easy solutions for either development studies or development education, its questions about power and knowledge in development discourses are worthy of consideration.

NOTES

[1] The term 'mainstream development' generally refers to "a single, homogeneous thrust towards modernisation" (Pieterse 2001, p. 77). This term is not unproblematic as it tends to hide the complexity of power relations in determining development agendas and different development discourses. I use it here, while acknowledging the lack of coherence within this position (Pieterse, 2001).

[2] I am using terms such as 'developing countries', 'North' and 'South' with caution, because of their tendency to homogenise geographical locations and because of the connotations associated with them.

REFERENCES

Booth, D. (1992) 'Social Development Research: An Agenda for the 1990s.' *The European Journal of Development Research*. Vol. 4, No. 1 pp. 1 – 39.

Chambers, R. (1983) *Rural Development: Putting the last first*. Harlow: Longman.

Crush, J. (1995) 'Imagining Development' in: *Power of Development*. London and New York: Routledge.

Dillon, E. (1996) *Doing Development: A Discourse Analysis of Irish Development Work* University College Cork: Unpublished Masters Thesis.

Edwards, M. (1994) 'Rethinking Social Development: The Search for "Relevance"' in Booth, D. (ed.) *Rethinking Social Development: Theory, Research and Practice*. Harlow: Longman Scientific and Technical.

Edwards, M. (2000) *Future Positive: International Co-operation in the 21st Century*. London: Earthscan.

Edwards, M. (2001) 'Is there a 'Future Positive' for Development Studies? Confessions of a Manchester City Fan'. Development Studies Association Conference. (Web site: www.bham.ac.uk/DSA/) (Accessed on 9th Feb. 2002)

Escobar, A. (1984/85) 'Discourse and Power in Development: Michel Foucault and the Relevance of his work to the Third World'. *Alternatives*. Vol. X pp. 377 – 400.

Escobar, A. (1995) *Encountering Development: The Making and Unmaking of the*

Third World New Jersey: Princeton University Press.

Escobar, A. (2000) 'Beyond the Search for a Paradigm? Post-Development and Beyond' *Development* Vol. 43, No. 4, pp. 11-15.

Fals Borda, O. Rahman, A. (eds.) (1991) *Action and Knowledge: Breaking the Monopoly with Participatory Action-Research* London: Intermediate Technology Publications.

Ferguson, J. (1990) *The Anti-Politics Machine: 'Development', Depoliticization and Bureaucratic Power in Lesotho.* Minneapolis: University of Minnesota Press.

Hulme, D. (1994) 'Social Development Research and the third sector: NGOs as users and subjects of social inquiry' In Booth, D. (ed.) *Rethinking Social Development. Theory, Research and Practice.* Harlow: Longman Scientific and Technical.

Jennings, M. (1977) *Irish Government Aid to the Third World: Review and Assessment.* Dublin: Trocaire and the Irish Commission for Justice and Peace.

Kiely, R. (1999) 'The Last Refuge of the Noble Savage? A Critical Assessment of Post-Development Theory'. *The European Journal of Development Research.* Vol. 11, No. 1 pp. 30 – 55.

Kirby, P. (1997) *Poverty Amid Plenty: World and Irish Development Reconsidered. Dublin: Trócaire and Gill and MacMillan.*

Latouche, S. (1993) *In the Wake of the Affluent Society: An Exploration in Post-Development.* London: Zed.

Long, N. (1992) *Battlefields of Knowledge: The Interlocking of Theory and Practice in Social Research and Development.* London and New Jersey: Zed Books.

Max Neef, M. (1989) 'Development and Human Needs - Reflections on a new Perspective'. *Development Dialogue.* Vol. 1 pp. 17 – 46.

Mawdsley, E., Porter, G. and Townsend, J. (2001) 'The role of the transnational community of NGDOs'. Development Studies Association Annual Conference. (Web site: www.bham.ac.uk/DSA/) (Accessed on 9th Feb. 2002)

Munck, R. (1999) 'Deconstructing Development Discourses: of Impasses, Alternatives and Politics'. In: Munck, R. & O'Hearn, D. (eds.) *Critical Development Theory: Contributions to a new paradigm.* London: Zed Books.

National Committee for Development Education (1999) *Funding Guidelines.* Dublin: NCDE

Osler, A. (1994) *Development Education; Global Perspectives in the Curriculum.* London: Cassell.

Osler, A. and Starkey, H. (1996) *Teacher Education and Human Rights.* London: David Fulton.

Pieterse, J.N. (1996) 'My Paradigm or Yours? Alternative Development Post-Development and Reflexive Development'. *Development and Change.* Vol. 29 pp. 343 – 373.

Preston, P. W. (1999) 'Development Theory: Learning the Lessons and Moving On'. *The European Journal of Development Research.* Vol. 11, No. 1 pp. 1 – 29.

Rahman, A. (1993) *People's Self-Development* London: Zed.

Rahnema, M. & Bawtree, V. (eds.) (1997) *The Post-Development Reader* London: Zed Books.

Rist, G. (1997) *The History of Development: from Western Origins to Global Faith* London and New York: Zed Books.

Sachs, W. (1993) *The Development Dictionary* London and New Jersey: Zed Books.

Schumacher, E. F. (1974) *Small is Beautiful.* London: Sphere.

Schuurman, F. (1993) *Beyond the Impasse: New Directions in Development Theory* London and New Jersey: Zed Books.

Storey, A. (2000) 'Post-Development Theory: Romanticism and Pontius Pilate politics'. *Development.* Vol. 43, No. 4 pp. 40-46.

Tucker, V. (1999) 'The Myth of Development' in Munck, R. & O'Hearn, D. (eds.) *Critical Development Theory: Contributions to a new paradigm.* London and New York: Zed Books.

Wallace, T. (1997) 'New Development Agendas: Changes in UK NGO Policies and Procedures'. *Review of African Political Economy.* Vol. 71, pp. 35 – 55.

Webster, A. (1988) *Introduction to the Sociology of Development.* London: Macmillan.

LIST OF CONTRIBUTORS

James Binchy is employed as Research Officer with Learner Support Unit, Mary Immaculate College.

Geraldine Brosnan works as Learner Support Unit (LSU) Adult Learner Support Counsellor in Mary Immaculate College, Limerick.

Micheál L. Collins is Research Fellow of the Urban Institute, Economics Department, Trinity College, Dublin.

Eilish Dillon is currently teaching the Sociology of Development on a part-time basis in the Development Studies Centre, Kimmage Manor.

Anne Dolan is a Lecturer in Social Environmental and Scientific Education at Mary Immaculate College, Limerick.

Nora P. Donnelly works as an educator, critic and artist. She is now lecturing in the Education Department at Mary Immaculate College.

Rosalind Duke has a background in secondary teaching in Scotland and Ireland.

Sabine Egger is a Lecturer in German at Mary Immaculate College, Limerick.

Susanne Ehrenreich is *Wissenschaftliche Mitarbeiterin* (Assistant Lecturer) at the University of Munich, where she teaches ELT methodology.

Paddy Fulham is a Lecturer in Social Environmental and Scientific Education at Mary Immaculate College, Limerick.

Barbara Gill is the education consultant on the jointly managed NCDE/ Compass pilot pre-service project in development and intercultural education. She is a qualified second-level teacher.

Neil Haran is an independent educational consultant, specialising in education and social justice issues.

Jones Irwin is a Lecturer in Philosophy of Education in St. Patrick's College, Drumcondra.

Gerry Jeffers works in the Education Department, NUI Maynooth as a Lecturer.

Aisling Leavy is a Lecturer in Mathematics Education, Mary Immaculate College, Limerick.

Rose Malone is a Lecturer in the Education Department in NUI Maynooth.

David McGuire is Government of Ireland Scholar, Human Resource Management Research Group, University of Limerick.

Eugene O'Brien is Head of the English Department in Mary Immaculate College, Limerick.

Neil Ó Conaill is a Lecturer in Social Environmental and Scientific Education at Mary Immaculate College, Limerick.

Anne O'Keeffe lectures in TEFL and Academic Writing at Mary Immaculate College. She is also Co-ordinator of the Learner Support Unit (LSU).

Roland Tormey is a Lecturer in Sociology of Education in Mary Immaculate College, Limerick. He is Co-ordinator of the Centre for Educational Disadvantage Research (CEDR), and Chairperson of the development education charity *80:20 Educating and Acting for a Better World*.

Ken Wiwa is the author of *In the Shadow of a Saint*. He is an activist campaigning on behalf of the Ogoni of the delta region in Nigeria, a journalist with the *Toronto Globe and Mail* and Senior Resident Writer at Massey College in the University of Toronto.

CONTENTS

THE AMAZING ADVENTURES OF THE DC SUPER-PETS!™

The Ice Cream Caper

by **Steve Korté**

illustrated by **Art Baltazar**

Batman created by Bob Kane
with Bill Finger

raintree 🦋

a Capstone company — publishers for children

Raintree is an imprint of Capstone Global Library Limited, a company incorporated
in England and Wales having its registered office at 264 Banbury Road, Oxford,
OX2 7DY – Registered company number: 6695582
www.raintree.co.uk
myorders@raintree.co.uk

978 1 3982 0620 5

British Library Cataloguing in Publication Data
A full catalogue record for this book is available from the British Library.

Designed by Ted Williams
Design Elements by Shutterstock/SilverCircle

Printed and bound in the United Kingdom

He is Batman's
loyal friend.
He is a super-smart
crime-fighting canine.
He is known as the World's
Greatest Dog Detective.
These are . . .

THE AMAZING
ADVENTURES OF

Ace the
Bat-Hound!

CHAPTER 1

A zoo mystery

Batman zooms through the streets of

Gotham City in the Batmobile.

His loyal dog, Ace the Bat-Hound, sits next to him.

There was a robbery at the Gotham City Zoo. Batman and Ace are on their way to help.

"Someone stole all the penguins!" the zookeeper says.

"I wonder if the evil criminal, the Penguin, was here," says Batman. "Let's look for clues."

Ace sniffs a snowy area at the edge of the penguins' area.

He barks to get Batman's attention.

Batman joins Ace. Together, they study the wet ground. They see footprints from a man's shoe. There are pointy holes by some of the footprints.

"These holes look like they were made by the tip of an umbrella," says Batman. "The Penguin carries an umbrella. Excellent detective work, Ace!"

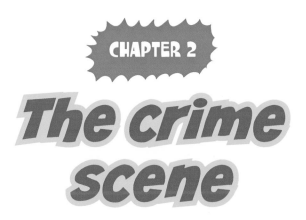

CHAPTER 2

The crime scene

Batman and Ace drive to a wide river.
A narrow bridge stretches across the
water. The Penguin's sinister hideout is
on the other side of the river. It looks
dark and scary.

"This bridge looks flimsy. It will never support the Batmobile," says Batman. "Ace, you stay here while I get out and look around."

Batman quietly enters the hideout.

Suddenly, he is ambushed! Two of the

Penguin's helpers to tie up Batman.

Batman struggles to free himself.

The ropes are too tight.

The baddies leave the hideout. They run across the bridge. They make it safely to the other side. Then they cut the ropes.

The bridge tumbles into the water. Laughing, the bad guys disappear into the woods.

Ace jumps out of the Batmobile. He runs to the edge of the river. The distance across is too far to jump.

The quick-thinking dog sees an old, tall tree nearby. The tree looks dry and dead.

Ace backs up and then takes a

running jump.

Ace's weight is enough to snap the

dead tree. It falls. Its trunk stretches

across the river.

Ace uses the tree like a bridge to
cross the river. Then he crashes into the
hideout.

Ace chews on the ropes around
Batman. Soon the Caped Crusader
is free!

CHAPTER 3

The ice cream trail

The Bat-Hound sniffs the floor of the
hideout. He finds some spilt ice cream.
There are black feathers stuck in the
ice cream. Ace runs out of the building.
Batman follows him.

The trail leads to the Sweet Treats Ice Cream factory.

Inside the building, Ace and Batman find the Penguin. He has all the penguins from the zoo!

"The zoo exhibit was too warm," the villain explains. "I brought the penguins to a chilly place where they would be safe."

"You should not have stolen the penguins," says Batman. "But you did the right thing bringing them to a cold location."

The Caped Crusader thinks.

"Because you were looking out for the safety of the penguins, I'm going to ask the judge to give you a lighter punishment," Batman says.

In a courtroom two days later, the judge agrees with Batman. The Penguin is ordered to pay a large fine. The money will allow the zoo to build a better penguin enclosure. The Penguin must also spend time volunteering at the zoo.

Batman reaches down to pat his loyal friend's head.

"Ace, it was your quick thinking that solved this case!" says Batman.

"Woof!" says the World's Greatest Dog Detective. He happily wags his tail.

AUTHOR!

Steve Korté is the author of many books for children and young adults. He worked at DC Comics for many years, editing more than 600 books about Superman, Batman, Wonder Woman and the other heroes and villains in the DC Universe. He lives in New York City, USA, with his husband, Bill, and their super-cat, Duke.

ILLUSTRATOR!

Famous cartoonist Art Baltazar is the creative force behind *The New York Times* bestselling, Eisner Award-winning DC Comics' Tiny Titans; co-writer for Billy Batson and the Magic of Shazam, Young Justice, Green Lantern Animated (Comic); and artist/co-writer for the awesome Tiny Titans/Little Archie crossover, Superman Family Adventures, Super Powers, and Itty Bitty Hellboy! Art is one of the founders of Aw Yeah Comics comic shop and the ongoing comic series! Aw yeah, living the dream! He stays home and draws comics and never has to leave the house! He lives with his lovely wife, Rose, sons Sonny and Gordon, and daughter Audrey! AW YEAH MAN! Visit him at www.artbaltazar.com

"Word power"

ambush a surprise attack

detective a person who investigates crimes or collects information for people

enclosure an area closed in by a fence or wall

exhibit a display that usually includes objects and information to show and tell people about a certain subject

fine money a person must pay for breaking a law

flimsy weak or easily broken

hideout a secret place for hiding

sinister looking evil or harmful

support to help something

WRITING PROMPTS

1. Reread the story. Make a list of all the clues Ace used to find the Penguin.

2. Draw a Wanted poster featuring the Penguin. What words would you use to describe him?

3. Make a timeline of the events in the story. Place events that happen in a shorter period of time close together. Leave more space between events that happen further apart in time.

DISCUSSION QUESTIONS

1. The Penguin was trying to help the penguins stay cool by taking them to the ice cream factory. What other locations would have worked? Explain your reasoning.

2. What do you think would have happened to Batman if Ace hadn't been along?

3. Batman and Ace think the Penguin's hideout looks sinister. Do you think the Penguin would agree? Draw the hideout from the Penguin's point of view.

THE AMAZING ADVENTURES OF THE

DC SUPER-PETS!™

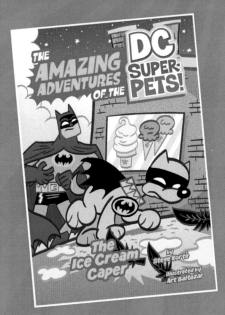

Collect them all!